Sexuality in Europe

M000283337

This original book brings a fascinating and accessible new account of the tumultuous history of sexuality in Europe from the waning of Victorianism to the collapse of communism and the rise of European Islam. Although the twentieth century is often called "the century of sex" and seen as an era of increasing liberalization, Dagmar Herzog instead emphasizes the complexities and contradictions in sexual desires and behaviors, the ambivalences surrounding sexual freedom, and the difficulties encountered in securing sexual rights. Incorporating the most recent scholarship on a broad range of conceptual problems and national contexts, the book investigates the shifting fortunes of marriage and prostitution, contraception and abortion, queer and straight existence. It analyzes sexual violence in war and peace, the promotion of sexual satisfaction in fascist and democratic societies, the role of eugenics and disability, the politicization and commercialization of sex, and processes of secularization and religious renewal.

DAGMAR HERZOG is Professor of History and Daniel Rose Faculty Scholar at the Graduate Center, City University of New York. Her previous publications include *Sex after Fascism: Memory and Morality in Twentieth-Century Germany* (2005) and *Brutality and Desire: War and Sexuality in Europe's Twentieth Century* (as editor, 2009).

NEW APPROACHES TO EUROPEAN HISTORY

Series editors
WILLIAM BEIK *Emory University*
T. C. W. BLANNING *Sidney Sussex College, Cambridge*
BRENDAN SIMMS *Peterhouse, Cambridge*

New Approaches to European History is an important textbook series, which provides concise but authoritative surveys of major themes and problems in European history since the Renaissance. Written at a level and length accessible to advanced school students and undergraduates, each book in the series addresses topics or themes that students of European history encounter daily: the series embraces both some of the more 'traditional' subjects of study and those cultural and social issues to which increasing numbers of school and college courses are devoted. A particular effort is made to consider the wider international implications of the subject under scrutiny.

To aid the student reader, scholarly apparatus and annotation is light, but each work has full supplementary bibliographies and notes for further reading: where appropriate, chronologies, maps, diagrams, and other illustrative material are also provided.

For a complete list of titles published in the series, please see:
www.cambridge.org/newapproaches

Sexuality in Europe

A Twentieth-Century History

Dagmar Herzog

CAMBRIDGE
UNIVERSITY PRESS

CAMBRIDGE UNIVERSITY PRESS
Cambridge, New York, Melbourne, Madrid, Cape Town,
Singapore, São Paulo, Delhi, Tokyo, Mexico City

Cambridge University Press
The Edinburgh Building, Cambridge CB2 8RU, UK

Published in the United States of America by Cambridge University Press,
New York

www.cambridge.org
Information on this title: www.cambridge.org/9780521691437

First published 2011

Printed in the United Kingdom at the University Press, Cambridge

A catalogue record for this publication is available from the British Library

Library of Congress Cataloguing in Publication data
Herzog, Dagmar, 1961–
Sexuality in Europe : a twentieth-century history / Dagmar Herzog.
p.   cm. – (New approaches to European history ; 45)
Includes bibliographical references and index.
ISBN 978-0-521-87096-2 (hardback) – ISBN 978-0-521-69143-7 (pbk.)
1. Sex – Europe – History – 20th century.   I. Title.   II. Series.
HQ18.E8.H47   2011
306.7094′0904 – dc22   2011013516

ISBN 978-0-521-87096-2 Hardback
ISBN 978-0-521-69143-7 Paperback

Contents

Illustrations

Introduction

The twentieth century is often called "the century of sex" and it is frequently understood as a time of increasing liberalization of sexual mores and attitudes. It is understandable that many retrospective observers look at the twentieth century in this way, and for a variety of reasons. These include: the growing perfectibility and availability of contraceptives; the advancement of homosexual rights; the greater acceptance of premarital sex as well as burgeoning importance ascribed to sex in marriage; and the more generally growing celebration of sexual pleasure – along with the ever more pervasive stimulation of desire in advertising and pornography as well as the exploding profusion of advice for intensifying partnered sex. Further evidence could be found in the relaxation of church teachings on sex, especially from the 1930s to the 1960s (and certainly in the increasing popular disregard for church teachings over the course of the entire century), or in the growing sensitivity to the need to combat sexual violence and coercion and greater appreciation for female sexual self-determination advanced by the women's movements of the 1970s to 1990s.

However, to tell only a narrative of gradual progress would be to misunderstand how profoundly complicated the sexual politics of the twentieth century in Europe actually were. Three issues are especially important to consider in detail. The first has to do with the recurrent *backlashes* against liberalization. It turned out to be remarkably difficult to achieve and to maintain liberalizing gains, and indeed some of the most important aspects of sexual rights, including access to contraception, or freedom from persecution for homosexual sex, were for extended periods extraordinarily fragile. The backlashes were sometimes coordinated at the state level – this is especially evident when we look at National Socialism in Germany and Austria, fascism in Italy, Spain, or Portugal, or Stalinism in the Soviet Union. Sometimes the backlashes were fostered by the churches. But they were also often carried by popular movements from below. What makes sexual conservatism appealing is thus a crucial subject that requires more study. The renewed ascent of various forms of sexual conservatism and neofundamentalism within European Christianity, Judaism, and Islam in the early twenty-first century suggests how timely and necessary such an investigation can be.

A second matter is just as essential, and that has to do with the *problems* often embedded also within what were thought to be liberalizing efforts – together with the very difficulty we at times have in defining what a truly sexually free society would be. In some cases, we can look back and see what contemporaries could not, or did not care to, see – for example, the horrifically disdainful racism against the disabled and against people of color in many lands that was used for much of the twentieth century to justify the promotion of contraceptives. In other cases, we ourselves today remain challenged to make sense of such matters as the increasing commercialization of sexuality in the course of the twentieth century. Is the sexing of sales and the selling of sex liberating? Here there are as many answers as there are people, and more differentiated and thoughtful responses are needed in order to respect the diversity of human desires while also acknowledging the changes that commercialization has wrought in sexual relations and in people's ability to pursue (and, hopefully, find) whatever happiness means to them. And in yet other cases – whether over prostitution, for instance, or more broadly over the connections (or lack thereof) between sex and love – the disputes over how best to organize sexual politics remain ongoing and will undoubtedly persist into the future. Here the reconstruction of past conflicts over sexuality can be enormously helpful in reinvigorating our imaginations while also making us more modest in our assumptions about what is "natural" or "best."

And third, there is the related matter of *ambivalences*. Sex does not always make people happy. Quite apart from the recurring dark sides of sexuality in the form of rape, abuse, exploitation, hurt, and harassment – which also have their important histories, both with regard to what human beings have done to each other but also with respect to the campaigns fought against such pain and against the conditions that facilitate it – also consensual sex, after all, can be a site of many conflicting feelings.

In the course of the twentieth century, moreover, sex became burdened with enormous significance. Sex became perceived of as ever more central to individual identity. The growing interest – and success – in controlling fertility changed heterosexual experiences, albeit in often contradictory ways (as newly heightened expectations of pleasure, especially for women, and the hopes of separating sex from reproduction, collided with the challenges and sometimes unpleasantness of contraceptive strategies). At the same time, the growing professionalization of research into sex – in dialectical interaction with the self-representations of sexual minorities – intensified preoccupation with questions of sexual orientation. Ordinary people increasingly understood and represented themselves not only as beings with sexual identities, but also as beings with sexual rights – whether to privacy or to public attention, to "normal" functioning or to the transgression of norms perceived as illegitimate, to intensity of experience or to safety from sexual harm.

Throughout the twentieth century, sexual matters also acquired growing political salience. Sexuality became a key element in processes of secularization and religious renewal, a main motor of economic development, and a locus of increasing government–citizen negotiation (whether in courtrooms, classrooms, military brothels, government-funded maternal welfare and marital guidance clinics, or street demonstrations). In a constantly reconfigured combination of stimulus and regulation, prohibition and exposure, norm-expounding and obsessed detailing of deviance, liberalizing and repressive impulses together worked to make conflicts over sexual matters consequential for politics writ large.

This amplified political significance of sexuality has to do – and this is difficult to express but crucial for our comprehension – with yet another intrinsic complexity of sexual matters: their ever-spreading intersections with almost all other domains of existence. One need only think of the vital role of sexual scandal in making newspaper reading a mass and not just an elite phenomenon in the 1900s–1920s. (Is voyeurism itself a sexual act?) Or we can consider the saturation of anti-Jewish rhetoric with sexual innuendo and the role of this sexualized rhetoric in making persecution of Jews seem morally acceptable in the 1930s–1940s. (Is there a libidinal element in cruelty?) Or we might reflect on the inseparability of antiwar protest from efforts at sexual liberation in the 1960s–1970s. (How can we make sense of this moment when so many human beings sincerely believed that making more love could also profoundly change the world for the better?) In these and other instances, we can recognize the poverty and inadequacy of the theoretical language and conceptual frameworks available to us. Yet, for all the diffuseness and elusiveness of the terms, looking back on the twentieth century as a whole from the vantage point of the twenty-first, we can also recognize that over the course of that century something like a semi-coherent entity – a complex of physiological and emotional impulses and sensations, acts and ideals – took shape and was designated as "sexuality" in the collective imaginary.

This book will use the subject of sexuality as a focus for thinking through broader challenges facing historians. Among other things, it will emphasize the epistemological problems raised by the topic: What exactly are the relationships between ideologies, social conditions, bodies, and emotions, and how might these relationships have changed over time?

How might we use the tools of comparative history and the similarities and differences across boundaries of nations (and transnational regions) but also the differences within nations (rural versus urban, middle class versus working class, diversities of religious adherence and subcultures) to find more compelling answers to difficult questions of causation, periodization, and interpretation? How are our assumptions about the history of sexuality in Europe challenged when we understand its inextricability from the histories of European colonialism and decolonization? How might we more effectively analyze transnational flows of people and ideas?

After all, what drives historical change in this realm that is at once so intimate and so publicly scrutinized? Is it primarily (as many have presumed) market forces and technological advances? Or is it something as seemingly mundane as the party-political balance of power within national governments? Do shifting popular values lead to pressure for legal change, or is it the opposite? How important are individual activists for sparking society-wide transformations? How important are social movements? What is the role of religious teachings, of generational changes, of wars and military occupations?

What we know about the history of sexuality in Europe in the twentieth century certainly remains incomplete. Scholars of sexuality have been enormously inventive in seeking out sources and developing innovative strategies for reading them. They have pored over police and court and military records, medical texts and Sunday sermons, popular magazines and legislative debates, activist manifestos and meeting minutes, private correspondence and diaries, epidemiological and demographic statistics and sociological surveys, fiction and music and film. They have also produced data of their own through oral history interviews and participant-observer ethnography. Yet some countries have received far more coverage than others (England, France, Germany, Denmark, Sweden, the Netherlands, and Switzerland, for instance, have been researched more thoroughly than Italy, Austria, Ireland, or the Soviet Union, and we know more about those countries than we do about Scotland, Norway, Belgium, Portugal, Spain, Greece, Romania, Poland, Czechoslovakia, Hungary, or Yugoslavia). Some themes have also been studied far more than others. However ironically, we have often learned more about homosexuality than heterosexuality, more about abortion than contraceptive strategies or noncoital practices, more about prostitution than pornography, more about rape in wartime than in peacetime. And in the meantime, much of the scholarship has been organized conceptually around the puzzle of how individuals and groups made progress, or failed to make progress, in overcoming obstacles (the obstacle in question could be the technological inadequacy of mechanical or chemical means of preventing pregnancy, the illegality of abortion or homosexuality, or the stubborn resistance to treatment of a particular disease).

It is not least precisely as a result of reliance on a framework which assumes increasing progress toward liberalization over the course of the twentieth century that we have been left with too little capacity for thinking effectively about the tangled texture of emotions that human beings have brought to sex over the last century. Sex meant many different things to people. For some it was indeed a site of cruelty and violation. But also sex that was mutually willed could be experienced in extraordinarily varied ways: as a site of explosive, transformative ecstasy, delight, and excitement; of serene security, satisfaction, status confirmation, the pleasures of conformity to norms; of anguished longing, vulnerability, conflictedness, insecurity, jealousy; or of habit, duty, boredom – even repulsion. It is not least because sex is complicated that human beings are so politically and socially manipulable in this area – although historians have too rarely reflected openly on this complicatedness when trying to explain how sexual cultures change.

A task of this book, then, will be to try to reconstruct the ways people in the past *imagined* sex and what kinds of assumptions and emotions they brought to it. Not only what was considered appropriate or normal or good (in the eyes of God, or of the neighbors, or of those self-appointed experts, the doctors), but also what was considered anxiety-producing and – not least – what was considered sexually thrilling and satisfying has clearly varied considerably across time and place. Another task, however, will be to analyze how activists of all ideological stripes sought to change laws, attitudes, and practices. In other words, the aim is to explore how Europeans battled over the *ethics* of sex – and what the outcomes of those battles were.

1   Reconceiving sexuality 1900–1914

At the turn from the nineteenth to the twentieth century, a number of factors came together to make sex a highly public topic. One factor was growing media attention to the issue of prostitution. This attention was intensified by military and government authorities' worry about the perceived spread of venereal diseases, and by public fascination with titillating stories of sex trafficking. The rise of a women's movement also spiked concern with prostitution. The movement challenged the entirety of the entrenched double standard of sexual morality, and above all expressed anger at the nonchalance with which authorities and the male public alike appeared to accept prostitution as simply a natural supplement to the institution of marriage. A second crucial factor was the growing desire for fertility control. Across European nations, couples sought to limit family size using a variety of measures and, despite the fact that contraceptive strategies often clashed with longings for pleasure, birthrates in all nations and all classes of society began dropping. Medical doctors and government authorities alike paid close attention to this phenomenon. Intersecting with these two developments was a third: an increasing voyeuristic public interest in scandals surrounding same-sex activities – many of them involving high-ranking military officials, members of the aristocratic elites, and celebrities. What once had been a rather unremarkable feature of some individuals' sexual habits became fodder for mass gossip. Same-sex scandals also fueled speculation about human sexual predilections more generally – as, at the same time, increased efforts at policing and repression of same-sex activities were met with newly organized resistance from individuals who came to think of their preferences as an important part of their identities.

At the beginning of the twentieth century, in short, and in a multitude of ways, sex became political. The explosion of discussion, in turn, inescapably also influenced how sex was practiced. People's expectations – about love and physical sensations, about the purposes of sex and preferences while having it – all were profoundly affected. No less deeply affected were people's experiences.

Prostitution, venereal disease, and the double standard

For a long time, prostitution had been the "open secret" supplement to marriage. It had been quietly tolerated as a necessary evil or even a basic good. It was considered the normal way of things – both the accepted site for young men's initiation into sex and a recurrent side opportunity for men also after they were married. But around 1900, prostitution emerged as a focus for loud and vitriolic controversy. This was due in no small part to the perceived (in some cases quite real but often hysterically exaggerated) spread of venereal disease, especially syphilis, but also gonorrhea and soft chancre. And it was above all this fear of disease that initially prompted medical doctors to urge governments to be more active in sex education (or rather, *anti*-sex education) addressed both to adolescents in schools and to soldiers in the various nations' militaries.

Public health experts expressed special concern about the need to combat venereal disease in European nations' overseas possessions: in northern and western Africa (in the cases of Italy and France), the East Indies (in the case of the Netherlands), Africa as well as India, Hong Kong, or Singapore (in the case of Great Britain), and yet other parts of Africa (in the cases of Portugal, Belgium, and Germany). Very frequently, colonized men of color were represented as unable to control their sexual impulses and thus more of a danger to efforts to stem the spread of infections. Notably, the elaboration of these distinctions really served to deny the prevalence of promiscuity among white European men. It was a transparent attempt to use racism to flatter those white men into restraining themselves and desisting from extramarital sex.

Also the growth of urban centers within Europe, with their increasingly large working-class populations, pushed the issues of working-class women's participation in prostitution as an additional (or, more rarely, sole) source of income and working-class men's own resort to prostitutes (middle-class men were not the only customers) into public awareness. Much discussion focused on the visible public "nuisance" of streetwalking and/or on the scandal of trafficking (in which innocent rural girls were imagined as lured to the big city and/or across national boundaries with promises of work but then were confined against their will in brothels).

Yet although stories about trafficking garnered avid attention in the sensationalist press, they were usually at best only partially true. They served as a kind of journalistic pornography under the fig-leaf of moral outrage – even as they could have very real legislative consequences. (For instance in Britain in 1885, based on an early set of these stories, legislation was passed in which the age of consent for girls was raised, brothelkeepers were more readily prosecuted, and – through a complex conjunction of circumstances – an amendment was tacked on which criminalized male homosexual acts for more than eight decades.)

Particularly in Poland and Austria-Hungary in the first decade of the twentieth century, stories about trafficking (a profession frequently ascribed to Jews) served more as occasions for lurid anti-Semitic invective. The reality of extensive acceptance of prostitution among gentiles (Polish and Austro-Hungarian police and medical reports made clear how much and how unapologetically gentile men indulged), the economic calculation and initiative taken by women entering the sex trade, and the frequent connivance of their families were blatantly erased as the specter of the Jewish pimp and trafficker captured the frenzied popular imagination. In addition, in some countries – for instance again in Austria-Hungary (especially in Budapest, which was considered a hotbed of vice, as well as in Vienna), but also in Russia, Germany, and France – homosexual male prostitution, while sometimes considered a less likely source for the spread of venereal disease than female prostitution, also garnered increasing (variously alarmed or titillated) public attention.

In the early twentieth century, the strong involvement of medical men in public debates, in scholarly journals, or in negotiations with the military authorities or municipal or federal governments was ironic not least due to their inability to provide a cure for syphilis. Mercury treatments were recommended – and gruesomely painful – but ineffective (although the disease's tendency to go into phases of remission misled the experts for quite some time). It would not be until the discovery of the arsenic derivative Salvarsan in 1909 that syphilis was thought to become more effectively treatable. But although Salvarsan and its variants were more widely used in World War I and its aftermath, it too could be highly toxic, and recent researches have cast doubt on its efficacy as well. In any event, in the colonies the use of the cheaper and definitively ineffectual mercury continued well into the twentieth century. It would not be until the 1940s that penicillin became broadly accessible.

Some doctors at the turn of the century – for instance in Germany, which tended toward a more pragmatic public health approach – did urge distribution to soldiers of condoms (made at this time either from sheep's intestines or from rubber) as well as prophylactic injections of antiseptic liquids into the penis before or after intercourse with prostitutes. But many men resisted the use of condoms because they inhibited sensation, opting to rely on the idea that prostitutes' health had been regularly checked. Some medical doctors bluntly acknowledged that subjecting prostitutes to recurrent medical examinations only functioned to provide that sector of men who liked to visit them both "a maximum of convenience and an – unfounded – sense of security."[1] But other medical and military authorities (for instance in Britain) pretended ignorance of the prevalence of visits to prostitutes among soldiers and preferred to urge officers to counsel premarital abstinence and marital fidelity instead. And many physicians remained in studied denial of the fact that the married clients of prostitutes frequently also infected their wives – with some doctors explicitly deliberating on how to keep wives ignorant of their condition. The main strategy remained the effort to keep prostitutes under police surveillance, inspect them regularly, and take them out of "circulation" if they showed signs of disease.

A second major reason for the preoccupation with prostitution at the turn of the century was the rise of an – increasingly transnationally networked – women's rights movement which challenged the so obviously pervasive sexual double standard. The women's movement joined a rising "moral purity," anti-vice activist movement which involved both men and women. Purity activists declared that men should be able to control their lusts and they also used fear of disease to encourage greater continence. Feminists and purity activists of the era made a variety of (at times overlapping, at times mutually conflicting) arguments both about how governments should handle prostitution and about the nature of human sexuality. Increasing success of these activists in acquiring public notice in the press and in petitioning national parliaments to shut down brothels (as of 1895, for instance, abolitionists proudly announced they had succeeded in convincing governments to close all brothels in Norway and many in Denmark and the Netherlands) in turn prompted defenders of prostitution – or at least those who accepted prostitution as an inevitable part of life – to develop counter-strategies of their own.

The escalating debate – and the spotlight it shone on proletarian habits – had unexpected consequences for the women who made occasional money by selling their bodies. Among the urban working classes, there had often been a rather blurry line between prostitution and casual sex – and between both of these and longer-term premarital and extramarital relationships. Generally, those working-class women who pursued prostitution had done so only seasonally and for a few years, as just one additional source of income along with laundering, waitressing, seamstressing, sales, domestic service, or factory or agricultural work.

---

[1] Albert Eulenberg, a doctor in Berlin, quoted in *Zur Geschichte einer Petition gegen die Errichtung öffentlicher Häuser in Wien: Protokoll der Frauenversammlung vom 20. Februar 1897 im alten Wiener Rathause* (Vienna: Allgemeiner Österreichischer Frauenverein, 1897), 27.

It was an unfortunate irony that precisely the intensified attention given to the phenomenon due to the battles between abolitionists and pro-regulationists caused working-class women to have more difficulty both with balancing occasional prostitution with other kinds of work and with leaving prostitution for marriage and/or respectable jobs.

For and against regulation

Most European states at this time did not officially criminalize prostitution. Rather they insisted that it be state-regulated, with prostitutes limited to certain areas of towns and subjected to the recurrent medical examinations. There was considerable variety in the details. Some states permitted only brothels (tellingly they were often called "houses of tolerance") but prosecuted streetwalkers. Other states permitted street-walking as long as prostitutes registered with the police and submitted to regular health checks. Yet others technically maintained the criminalization of prostitution but did not prosecute women who submitted to medical controls. In all cases unregistered prostitutes – of which there were thousands, in some cases tens of thousands, in larger cities – were perpetually liable to police harassment and criminal prosecution. Police across European cities frequently treated any working-class woman as potentially suspect and had no qualms about hauling women into custody and forcing them to be subjected by doctors to brutal vaginal checks with speculums (instruments that often enough had not been sterilized and thus themselves could spread disease), subsequently also often sending them to jail or hospital. This was the so-called "regulationist" system, modeled on the one first developed by Napoleon during his wars of conquest in the early nineteenth century.

Arguments about the costs and benefits of this system criss-crossed peculiarly on the ideological spectrum. Some activists called for even more stringent penalties for prostitution and especially for those (madams, pimps, traffickers) who profited from it; pro-regulationists defended the system as the sensible middle ground; and an increasing number, called "abolitionists," wanted to do away entirely with this system of state-run, police-supervised regulation of prostitution – but their motives varied. Some professed sympathy for prostitutes as among the most impoverished and exploited of working-class women. But many saw in regulated prostitution an affront to morality – a system which failed to stem the spread of disease but simply permitted men to feel encouraged in their persistent infidelities, with the government functioning as a kind of enabler – and they hoped with their activism to abolish prostitution itself, and not just government regulation of it. Yet even when abolitionists succeeded in shutting down brothels, prostitution persisted – and thus in some places the streetwalking sector only grew larger while prostitutes became more vulnerable to and dependent on pimps.

Many feminists of the era saw the near-ubiquitous official toleration of the sexual double standard as part of a broader climate of disrespect for and hostility to women. But they differed in their views of both male and female sexuality. Some believed – and this was a view shared by many anti-feminists – that women did not have especially strong sexual desires and the sex drive was largely the preserve of men, but that men should most definitely be encouraged in self-restraint. The British suffragist Christabel Pankhurst, for instance, famously called for "Votes for Women and Chastity for Men." And many abolitionists argued – as one Swiss moral purity activist writing under the pen-name "Mentor" did – that dissolute, prostitute-craving men would learn to regret their lack of self-control (and the lack of self-valuing he asserted that it demonstrated), not only because they would find that they had become incapable of a true, pure, and lasting love but also because they would waste away from the diseases they were likely to acquire. Among the opponents of prostitution, as among its proponents, there were some who thought that prostitutes happened to be women with stronger (and more diverse and deviant) sexual desires than respectable women – and either that this had drawn them into prostitution in the first place or that their first seducer had brought this out in them. Others assumed that prostitutes did not much enjoy their job and simply endured. Many commentators of the era speculated that if women had a drive, it was for motherhood, not for sexual pleasure per se.

Yet there was also, already in the early twentieth century, a minority of (both female and male) feminists who believed that all women were – or could be – sexual beings. Of these, many hoped prostitution would eventually wither away if marriage itself could be reformed into a more egalitarian and more mutually erotic institution. For this purpose they also called for wider use of contraceptive products within marriage. Pro-sex feminists also proposed that rather than (like the Catholic church) justifying sex primarily through the possibility of procreation, sex should be justified on the basis of love – and precisely not on calculations about economic security. (In this way they also pointed out that marriage was too often like prostitution, since in marriage as well women exchanged sexual services for financial security and gain.) Some pointed out that men slept with prostitutes rather than non-prostitute unmarried women above all to avoid "unpleasant" consequences (like child support payments). And yet others highlighted the utter incoherence and cruelty of a system that facilitated men's access to prostitutes but could not keep them from infecting their own wives.

Under pressure from abolitionists, moral purity groups, and feminists, defenders of regulation reiterated old arguments and found new ones. At international conferences about prostitution and venereal disease – two major ones were held in Brussels in 1899 and 1902 – pro-regulationists faced off against abolitionists; the majority of medical doctors present advocated for regulation. Like their opponents, pro-regulationists also organized across national lines and translated and disseminated each other's ideas. Often, they simply counseled realist acceptance of many men's recourse to prostitution and advised that since men would inevitably continue to visit prostitutes, it would be best to supply them with condoms and prophylactic potions and above all to check the women regularly for signs of disease. "Closed houses" (as in the French system) kept the spectacle of vice from public view, ensured that prostitutes were kept under proper control, and guaranteed that customers could trust that the women's health was under surveillance. Sometimes there was the additional point that police regulation protected prostitutes from exploitation by pimps and traffickers. Pro-regulationists envisioned a hygienic future in which medicine would become ever more exacting and effective, and regulation would be reformed to turn prostitutes over entirely from the vice squad to the medical professionals. They assembled statistics from many lands, which they claimed demonstrated that their system had succeeded in bringing down rates of infection (while supposedly in the few places where abolitionists had succeeded in closing brothels, infection rates were once again climbing).

Abolitionists realized how futile their own struggle for moral reform might be and openly admitted that their own hopes for eradicating regulated prostitution, especially in countries like France and Germany where the practice was widespread, were most likely utopian. There was, moreover, considerable evidence that purity activists were hardly reaching the masses. While it has been suggested that purity activists' fomenting of the fear of disease was a tactic used quite instrumentally as it was becoming apparent in the early twentieth century that religion was in decline as a source of moral authority in sexual matters, it was also apparent that, for many young men, neither the fear of God nor the fear of syphilis was making much of an impact. One Italian priest told a story about how after hearing a doctor lecture about venereal diseases, students at the Catholic University of the Sacred Heart would walk out of the room and

Fig. 1.1 Prostitutes in a French brothel, 1900.

persuade friends to accompany them to a nearby brothel to "examine whether the fruits of sexual life were indeed so bitter."[2]

Pro-regulationists in many countries also contended that, while monogamous marriage might be necessary for civilization, the male sex drive was too strong to be contained by marriage, and therefore prostitution was the only sensible compromise solution – a kind of safety valve. Or, as one Belgian doctor put it in 1890, prostitution was a "*necessary evil* which derives directly from human nature, its physiological needs and passions." He went on: "If one were, imprudently, to suppress prostitution, there would be a proliferation of cases of venereal and syphilitic illnesses . . . and subsequently one would see a sequence of strange, unhealthy and criminal passions; a frighteningly exponential accumulation of seductions of poor victimized girls, illegitimate births, adulteries, rapes."[3]

Fascinatingly, some prostitution enthusiasts went so far as to argue that prostitution *protected* the institution of the family. An Austro-Hungarian specialist writing in 1907 noted that in garrison towns, with their large populations of soldiers in their early twenties, providing brothels was the best means for keeping young men away from the wives and daughters of both the bourgeoisie and the workers – as well as from sex with each other. Meanwhile, the Italian anthropologist and politician Paolo Mantegazza went so far as to contend that "paid sensual pleasure is one hundred times better than infidelity in the home, than adultery integrated into our moral customs, than marriage becoming a business transaction and a mirror image of polygamy; in short, it is one hundred times better to have sensual pleasure brutally detached from love than to betray friendship and to sully love within the sanctuary of the family."[4] What he meant was that husbands should be able to "brutally detach" sex from love by visiting prostitutes, but wives should never be permitted to have extramarital romances themselves – especially not ones that actually involved loving feelings – for *that* would mean that adultery had been "integrated into our moral customs" and/or that a husband's friend had betrayed his trust by becoming lovers with his wife. For many women – as Mantegazza himself noted at a different point – marriage was a business transaction: "If anyone who sells the pleasure of her body is a prostitute, then those girls who marry rich old men for their money or a place in the world

[2] Father Gemelli quoted in Bruno P. F. Wanrooij, "Sexualities: The Theory, Praxis and Representation of Sex in Fascist Italy," paper presented at the conference "Fascism, Nazism and Sexuality," Brown University, February 23, 2008.

[3] Prof. Thiry of Brussels, "De la prostitution," *La Presse Médicale Belge* 42 (August 31, 1890), 553–4.

[4] Paolo Mantegazza quoted in Thiry, "De la prostitution," 554.

are surely to be inscribed as members of this sorry legion, as are wives who put a price upon their kisses in order to obtain a bit of money or a carriage."[5] Untroubled by his own incoherence, Mantegazza was happy to mystify the sanctity of wifely devotion while defending men's rights to emotionless sex on the side – all the while utilizing the racist gesture to the "polygamy" of non-Europeans as a way to disavow the "mirror image" similarities between it and European men's infidelities.

The defense of the double standard of sexual morality, in short, was in full swing. So too was the division of women into good women and bad. Prostitutes put themselves into compromising situations, and so had forfeited their right to be treated with the esteem that respectable women expected. Abolitionists were outraged that women were subjected to medical inspections in order to provide men with (purportedly) disease-free indulgence; pro-regulationists scoffed at the purity activists' clamor, pointing out that "honest women" would not be inspected. "In truth, have not those who are so passionately being defended themselves abdicated all sense of shame and dignity" by choosing of their own accord "voluntarily to ply their hideous trade?"[6] Yet other commentators gloried in the boost to masculinity that the experience of visiting prostitutes – and even acquiring diseases – could bring. Emilio Settimelli, one of the Italian Futurists, phrased the point this way:

Gonorrhoea – I can't deny it – is annoying, it hurts and it's slightly embarrassing. Yet – due to the funny mechanisms of morality – it also is what makes a man really a man ... To be forced to treat our most delicate parts roughly, to clean yourself like a rusty rifle, the frankness of touching yourself like a surgeon, all this gives a new aplomb to a man, and eliminates forever the down of boyhood.[7]

Theorizing desire

All through these discussions, it was apparent that there was quite a variety of both directly expressed theories and unreflected, mostly inchoate assumptions about what exactly human beings sought in sex. Some commentators contended that men simply sought "release" of sexual tension, and that the object into which they released it did not matter to them at all. Others opined about men's desires for sexual variety and refinement of technique, speculating condescendingly that while simple rural

---

[5] Paolo Mantegazza, *The Sexual Relations of Mankind*, trans. Samuel Putnam (New York: Eugenics Publishing, 1935, 1938), 256. The book was first published in Italian in 1885.
[6] Thiry, "De la prostitution," 556.
[7] Emilio Settimelli quoted in Wanrooij, "Sexualities," 7.

folk might be perfectly satisfied with reliably regular sex with a lifelong spouse, city people sought novelty and spice. Yet other men, themselves customers, boasted at the pleasures which they had provided *to* a particular prostitute. (Thus for instance the German playwright Frank Wedekind described his visit to a Parisian prostitute that he had visited before: "When she finally lies by my side, I first arouse her with my hand to the point of madness, before I show her mercy. But then she also enjoys it like a wild animal.")[8] And yet others, also theorizing about city sophisticates, did believe there could be such a thing as passionate attachment to a particular lover (though often this was precisely not the wife).

Also in non-transactional sex, the lack of equality between the sexes was notable. Literature, memoirs and court cases occasionally reveal that also married women of the middle classes sometimes did have extramarital affairs – although female adultery was in many countries, for instance in both France and Britain, punished far more harshly than male, and in all countries the risks of loss of social status if the affair were exposed could be enormous. And also with respect to non-remunerated premarital sex between middle-class individuals, the double standard was intensely in force. Bourgeois men who had any number of premarital affairs with women of their own class nonetheless refused to marry any of those women, repulsed at the idea that other men had known them intimately. More frequently, working-class women succeeded in sustaining longer-term affairs with middle-class young men before moving on to marry working-class men. The danger, as always, in addition to disease, was the possibility of illegitimate pregnancy. In some countries, this did not necessarily harm a working-class woman's chances at marriage; in others, it was catastrophic. In some cases, in fact, women were pushed into prostitution specifically because they had been domestic servants who had been made pregnant by a master or his son.

In the meantime, among the more conservative – and, strikingly, often remarkably defensive – authors, some asserted that sexual moderation within marriage (understood as the happy medium between abstinence and licentiousness) was beneficial not only to overall physical health but also to mental focus and career success. Others were anxious to refute the pragmatists' assumptions that seeking sexual outlet was either simply inevitable or actually necessary to health and instead declared that, for the unmarried, abstinence could be both possible and non-damaging. Some were dismissive of the kind of men who went to prostitutes, describing

[8] Frank Wedekind, *Die Tagebücher: Ein erotisches Leben*, quoted in Manfred Schneider, "Erotische Buchhaltung im Fin de siècle: Über Walters 'Viktorianische Ausschweifungen' und Frank Wedekinds 'Tagebücher,'" *Merkur* 41 (May 1987), 435.

them – as one official who had worked in Prague put it in 1907 – as "notorious libertines, those with hereditary diseases, old men, and immature boys."[9] Or as an abolitionist professor from Zurich opined a few years later, a man who "threw himself away" by visiting prostitutes "will have difficulty finding himself again; whoever throws himself away constantly, will lose himself entirely." "Vice enslaves," he argued; it "robs the individual of strength," and "something within the person is desacralized."[10] Some commentators did praise the joys of a pure and lasting marital love, sincerely and rapturously extolling durable marital romances.

Surveying the range, however, what becomes most noticeable is just how few commentators believed that most married men were genuinely aroused by their wives. Middle-class men were in many cases prepared from birth – breast-fed and toilet-trained as they were by working-class women, experimenting with the domestic servant girls long before they started to court women of their own class – most strongly to desire women who were socially "beneath" them. And while many working-class marriages initially may have been based on mutual sexual attraction, the daunting damages done to working-class women's bodies through hard physical labor and multiple births and abortions, the lack of privacy in working-class dwellings, the frequent abuse of alcohol as a coping strategy especially for the men, and the many internalized taboos and inhibitions into which both men and women were socialized made enduring eroticism within marriage an elusive goal at best – if it could even be imagined at all.

What is thus crucial to understand about the situation around 1900 is the – highly paradoxical – fact that quite a lot of the increasingly loud and public discussion of sexual matters was prompted not only by feminists hostile to the longstanding climate of discreet tolerance for prostitution but also by sexual *conservatives*. And no less counterintuitive but essential to comprehend is that those who worked to defend sex against conservative efforts to control it and restrict it to marriage tended – with the exception of only a tiny handful of daring pro-sex feminists – to be unapologetic misogynists. The defense of women's rights to sexual pleasure and, simultaneously, to respect and love was very much a minority venture.

One of the great dramas of the early twentieth century, then, would be the effort to eroticize marriage itself and the related effort to make women's sexual agency and experience be understood as a positive good,

---

[9] Mayor of Cilli, quoted in Nancy Wingfield, "Echoes of the Riehl Trial in Fin-de-Siècle Cisleithania," *Austrian History Yearbook* 38 (2007), 45.
[10] Leonhard Ragaz, *Die Prostitution: Ein soziales Krebsübel* (Zurich: Grütliverein, 1912), 7.

rather than as a source of shame and dishonor. This meant openly defending premarital sexual experience also for women, as well as arguing for a sexual ethics that was based on the moral value of mutual consent rather than marital status. This also meant – and this was perhaps even more difficult – learning to think about sexual desire and love as potentially connected rather than at odds. And what becomes evident in tracing those avid activist efforts to encourage men to see women as both sexual *and* respected was how typical it had once been for many men to disdain the women with whom they had sex – how profoundly physical desire had been compatible with, indeed even saturated with, contempt.

Separating sex from reproduction: contraception and abortion

There was, in short, an important link between the effort to re-envision marriage as a site for lasting mutual eroticism and the effort to shift cultural mores away from an acceptance of prostitution as the inescapable accompaniment to marriage to a notion of premarital sexual experience as perfectly appropriate, even beneficial, also for women. European nations only gradually – and never without struggle – switched from what we might call the prostitution paradigm to the premarital paradigm. Moreover, the shift from a prostitution paradigm to a premarital paradigm for organizing heterosexual relations was inseparable from the campaigns to improve access to information and products to control fertility (products which at that time included spermicides and cervical caps and diaphragms as well as condoms). Already before World War I, Germany was making this switch from one system of values to the other. Some national cultures were slower to change. For England, for instance, studies have shown that the often quite desperate desire among working-class couples to control fertility was frequently not accompanied by efforts to use contraceptives, nor mutually pleasurable non-coital practices. Instead in many cases the major strategies used were sexual abstinence *within* marriage and husbands' recourse to prostitutes. Similar evidence exists for other nations as well. The Polish poet, physician, and sex rights activist Tadeusz Boy-Żeleński in his *Pieklo Kobiet* (Women's Hell), first published in 1930, remarked that "The specter of pregnancy is something so oppressive that it destroys all happiness in life, paralyzes marital relations, turns love into disaster; often a loving husband's wife drives him – with her consent – to prostitutes."[11]

---

[11] Tadeusz Boy-Żeleński, *Pieklo Kobiet: Jak skonczyc z pieklem kobiet* (Warsaw: Państwowy Instytut Wydawniczy, 1958).

By 1900, the French had already been restricting fertility for close to seventy years. Other nations in Europe followed suit by the end of the nineteenth century. Especially as populations were booming due to reductions in infant mortality and longer life-spans, and as industrialization as well as compulsory schooling served to make children more of an economic burden than an asset, interest in fertility control strategies grew throughout Europe. Over the course of the twentieth century, although at varying rates, all national birthrates declined as marital contraception became standard practice even as more people married, and married at younger ages.

Already at the beginning of the twentieth century, contemporaries – medical doctors and government officials especially – started to notice the change in population statistics and to debate openly what might be done. They noted that although national populations had grown dramatically – often as much as doubling – over the course of the nineteenth century, the birthrate in many European lands had unmistakably begun to decline. Abruptly, governments which had not paid much notice to the prevalence of contraceptive tips in popular household medical advice texts started to consider possible responses. (The very explicit "Bilz," for instance, a German natural health guidebook for home use authored by a Dr. Friedrich Bilz and which gave detailed instructions not only on non-reproductive sexual practices but also on pessaries and condoms – including mail-order addresses for the products – as well as abortion techniques, had sold 1 million copies by 1902 and an additional 2 million more by the 1920s, plus 875,000 in French translation.) The French were the first to feel the problem (by 1870 the French had the lowest birthrate in Europe and their defeat in the Franco-Prussian war triggered massive demographic alarmism). They were also the first to set up commissions to study the issue, and by 1909 the French parliament had begun earnestly to consider not only tax reform (proposing tax breaks as incentives to families with multiple children) but also to move toward the criminalization of birth control products. Other countries rapidly followed suit. As of 1914, when a German doctor included a transnational survey of government policies in his book on declining birthrates, Belgium too was just taking steps to suppress contraceptives, the Dutch had included the criminalization of the public display and advertising of contraceptives in an omnibus bill passed in 1911 enforcing a whole range of anti-vice efforts, the British were considering similar legislation, and in the Austrian capital of Vienna, all the rubber pessaries had been confiscated by the government. Nonetheless, and ironically in view of this flurry of legislation and intervention, the very mechanical and chemical means of contraception whose advertisement and sale were being outlawed were not the primary means utilized at the time by European couples.

In the first two decades of the twentieth century, and despite most working-class couples' increasingly strong preference to limit the number of births, it was actually rather difficult for the handful of sex reform activists who sought to promote the barrier methods of contraception to get their message across. This was in part due to the spate of new laws restricting the advertising and sale of contraceptives, and in part also to the Christian (especially the Catholic) churches' vehement opposition to any kind of object or practice which might make sex less risky. Condoms, for instance, did not only protect both men and women from diseases, but also prevented pregnancy, and that is precisely why the churches, and moral purity organizations, relentlessly opposed making access to condoms easier. Sex, these conservative constituencies felt, *should* be filled with risk.

Yet the difficulties encountered by contraception advocates were no less due to the inhibitions and inner conflictedness of the very same ordinary people who so urgently hoped to restrict their own fertility. In the early twentieth century, and in some nations for many decades thereafter, the main means used to control fertility (aside from marital abstinence and prostitution), especially in the working classes which made up the great majority of the population, were twofold: coitus interruptus (withdrawal) and abortion. And the vast majority of abortions were sought by married women who were already mothers.

Abortion was popularly considered far *less* immoral than mechanical or chemical contraception. There were a number of reasons for this. Contraception required planning ahead, mentally deciding not to risk pregnancy. Abortions, by contrast, could be interpreted as the simple restoration of a woman's health by "bringing back the monthlies." After all, in a time of widespread poverty and inadequate food and hard labor, there were multiple explanations possible for why a woman might miss her period – or have an unplanned miscarriage. Abortifacients were seen as remedies to restore not only menstrual regularity but also overall well-being – especially in situations in which "going in reverse gear" or "getting off early" or "eating the fish without sauce" (typical euphemisms for withdrawal in Italy, Scotland, and France, respectively, while Hungarian peasants said they would rather "wash bed linen than babies' diapers") had not worked. Women tried an enormous variety of abortifacients and practices: poisonous drinks or pills containing quinine, pennyroyal, yew, juniper, bitter aloes, lemon balm, or castor bean oil, or mustard baths, or hot lye soap injected or pointed objects like knitting needles or slippery elm bark stuck into the cervix. One Polish source from 1911 describes hair pins inserted into the uterine canal and spun around twice-monthly as a pregnancy prevention method – "a brutal action which circumvents the law" – as well as long balloon droppers filled with poison liquid.[12] However cruel an incongruity this was, it is also telling about both cultural moods and individual psychologies that the very fact that self-, quack-, midwife-, or doctor-induced abortions sometimes did not succeed in their aims and led either to a pregnancy carried to term or to permanent injury (or even death) for the woman, actually alleviated guilt. Feeling that these matters were not within one's own control and that outcomes were always uncertain was in some ways emotionally easier than rationally planning to prevent pregnancy.

And the means used were culturally acceptable; abortion was illegal but most people did not consider it criminal. As one report to the French senate remarked, abortion had become "practically a social habit."[13] In Britain, slippery elm was sold by many ordinary chemists, as were a variety of abortifacient "salts" and pills (marketed as remedies for menstrual irregularity). Many women took the pills as a preventive measure *before* the period was due; others inserted rubber syringes or catheters of various types into the cervix on a monthly basis as a kind of precautionary measure. One of the biggest fears women had about abortion concerned the potential damage to their own health. This was a very real possibility as some lead-based potions blinded women and quinine could lead to droning in the ears, cloudy vision, and cardiac failure, or as self-induced abortions with objects like knitting needles frequently led to perforations of the uterus and, in this pre-antibiotic era, to life-threatening and often lethal infections. (In the 1920s–1930s it was found that 15 percent of maternal deaths in Britain were due to self-induced abortions.) Another great fear was the possibility that the pills, rather than succeeding in preventing pregnancy, might damage the fetus and hence lead to the birth of a handicapped child. One midwife commented, on a questionnaire prepared for a British government commission, that "the reason women so frequently asked if the baby was 'all right' at birth was because they had so often taken abortifacient drugs."[14]

---

[12] W. Falgowski, "Niezwykłe spostrzeżenia z dziedziny poronień zbrodnichzych," *Gazeta Lekarska* 31, no. 40 (1911), 1083–7.

[13] Quoted in Max Hirsch, *Fruchtabtreibung und Präventivverkehr im Zusammenhang mit dem Geburtenrückgang: Eine medizinische, juristische und sozialpolitische Betrachtung* (Wurzburg: Curt Kabitzsch, 1914), 7.

[14] Summarized in Malcolm Potts, Peter Diggory, and John Peel, *Abortion* (Cambridge University Press, 1977), 258.

Fig. 1.2 "A Boon to Womankind: Dr. Patterson's Famous Female Pills." Abortifacient pills advertised in a "hygienic stores" catalogue, Britain, early 1900s.

There was as well a considerable amount of abortion "tourism" – and not only to Paris, where many Englishwomen were said to go and where by the early twentieth century there were hospitals that routinely performed abortions. Also cities like Geneva in Switzerland, Naples in Italy, and Constantinople in the Ottoman Empire were destinations for women seeking abortions. In Geneva there was an entire underground industry, largely tolerated by the police, which saw to it that women who arrived daily from elsewhere in Switzerland and from other countries were met at the train station and led to various midwives and other abortion providers. In the early twentieth century, estimates were that approximately fifty dilation and curettage procedures – much safer for a woman's overall health and future fertility than other methods – were undertaken in Geneva every day, and that 80 percent of the city's midwives provided abortions in addition to their other services (often with the help of doctors, who performed the curettage). It was also estimated that close to 90 percent of miscarriages were provoked abortions. So renowned was Geneva for this infrastructure that the handful of women who ended up being arrested there stated in court that they firmly believed that abortion was permitted within the city.

After withdrawal and abortion, condoms were the next most likely strategy. But many couples that tried condoms at one point or another tended to revert to the more traditional methods. Among other problems, condoms (known – perhaps indicatively – as "French letters" in England and "Pariser" in Switzerland) had a strong association with illicit (not married) sex. And they cost more money than many working-class couples could afford to spend on a regular basis – although sex reform activists in Germany for instance did, already in the first decade of the twentieth century, work to advertise the news that there were condoms (one of the first was the "Coekal-Condus") which could be washed and dried for repeated use.

In England and Wales, while abortion was feared but accepted, there was in the early twentieth century surrounding the topics both of sex and of birth control a widespread atmosphere of awkwardness and unease. This was due not only to a perpetual juggling of risks but also to a sense of never knowing for sure, of being utterly confused about what or who to trust, and of a constant struggle to decipher and make sense of the scraps of contradictory information as well as the extraordinary amount of *mis*information floating about. Rival mail-order companies and quack salesmen for rubber supplies and potions, for instance, routinely denigrated each other's products as frighteningly dangerous (as causing, for instance, infertility or cancer) while they also praised their own products in the most glowing terms and invoked the supposedly most up-to-date and "modern" scientific authorities as endorsers for their own offerings. And meanwhile, also within a couple, communication was not always clear or direct. Frustration, circumlocution, guesswork about the other's desires, fear of doing something morally wrong or physically damaging: all of these factors frequently made sex fraught for men and women both. For many women, remaining ignorant about contraceptive details was part of their sense of female respectability.

In this triple context of widespread individual confusion and conflictedness, a swirling abundance of misinformation jostling with potentially useful information, and increasingly loud political conflict as well as media discussion about matters of both sex and reproduction, a small handful of activists struggled to continue to make contraceptive knowledge and products more broadly available and acceptable. Some promoted contraceptives by advancing the ideal of couple sex as a site of reciprocity and joy for both partners. Others emphasized the benefits also for children of being wanted and planned for. (In many cultures – England, Germany, and Spain are just three examples – fertility control was thus referred to by its advocates as "conscious" or "voluntary" motherhood and fatherhood.) And some argued for contraceptives on the grounds that their use would reduce the incidence of abortions and the damage that both multiple pregnancies and multiple abortions could do to women's bodies. As one doctor in Berlin phrased it, "Whoever wants to reduce the incidence of abortion while forbidding contraceptives does the same as someone who wants to stop the spread of a plague but prohibits disinfectants."[15] The prohibition of contraceptives, he declared, would lead to a yet further exponential rise in the number of abortions. Yet others lobbied for decriminalization of abortion as well, stressing the point that self-induced or illegal abortions were so often dangerous to women's health and – as they also often emphasized – dangerous to a woman's future fertility. The Swiss abortion rights activist Henri Gächter, for instance, who fought for decriminalization of abortion in the first trimester (arguing especially that legalization would put an end to the extreme profits abortion providers made off women's desperation, and reduce the number of abortions undertaken later in a pregnancy), also provided sex counseling and promoted condom and diaphragm use. He was prosecuted several times for "contraceptive propaganda."

Eugenics

Often, the promotion of contraception became inextricably bound together with eugenic ideas. Eugenics was the attempt to improve the

[15] Hirsch, *Fruchtabtreibung und Präventivverkehr*, 131–2.

"quality" and not just the quantity of a population and it was racist from its inception: in its vigorous disparagement of the physically handicapped and especially the "feeble-minded"; in its concern that the less educated and the poor (and therefore also often less healthy) tended to "outbreed" the middle and upper classes; and in its inextricability from issues of empire – and the anxiety that so-called civilized white people of Europe were limiting their births while "yellow" and "black" people in other parts of the world, including in Europe's colonies, were continuing to have many children. The problems inherent in a eugenic worldview were, however, not particularly evident to its defenders, nor even its detractors, at the time.

Eugenics was the almost entirely unquestioned "progressive" cultural common sense of the first decades of the twentieth century, perceived to be *the* modern way to solve social problems. Its appeal extended far beyond the reaches of the overtly racist Right and the unapologetically imperialist middle to incorporate also wide swaths of the Left, including socialists, anarchists, liberals, and feminists. Catholics were almost its only critics, because they believed that there should never be interferences with fertility – although there were Catholic eugenicists as well.

Generally, scholars make distinctions between "positive eugenics" (financial and propagandistic incentives to encourage those deemed to be of "higher value" to have more children – an approach that could also include the denigration and criminalization of contraception) and "negative eugenics" (strategies, including promotion of contraception, sterilization, coerced abortions, and even murder, to discourage the reproduction of those deemed to be of "lesser value" – whether due to disability, class, or color). The eugenic framework was so widely unquestioned that both critics *and* advocates of contraceptive technologies worked within its terms. The trick in this context became for advocates of contraception to make their case without being accused of discouraging births among the "fit."

So intertwined was the desire to separate sex from the inevitability of reproduction, and thereby also to improve women's experience of sex, with both the idea of white superiority and an uninterrogated disdain for the disabled that contraception advocates did not think twice about promoting their products and agendas in eugenic terms. Eugenic ideals seemed to offer to contraception advocates a way to defend family planning as a *moral* project. Thus, for instance, Marie Stopes, the most prominent early twentieth-century birth control advocate in England, both celebrated the beneficent delights of mutually pleasurable married sex and did not hesitate to market the cervical caps and other products she promoted under the brand name "Pro-Race." Similarly, a German advocate for contraception insisted that the growing desire among the western European middle classes to limit births responsibly was in fact a welcome sign of heightened civilization (rather than of the degeneracy or downfall of European cultures). Meanwhile, he dismissed fears that the comparatively still quite high Slav birthrates meant that Russia was a threat (since Russia had just been trounced militarily by the much smaller Japan) *and* pointed out that reducing illegitimacy by encouraging contraceptive use among poor and unmarried women was good because such women in any event tended to produce "less valuable" offspring. The Swiss physician Auguste Forel was blunter: "The sick, the incapable, the mentally deficient, the bad ones, the inferior races must be systematically educated to birth control. The robust, good, healthy and mentally higher standing ones, however, must be, as I have repeatedly argued here, encouraged to multiply strongly."[16]

While contraception was controversial and contested, in short, racial condescension and fear and hostility to the disabled were not. These attitudes constituted the foundational framework and ideological consensus of the era. Yet while in retrospect (and especially in the aftermath of the hideous experiment in eugenics and vast mass murder that was Nazism) the problematic aspects of such arguments are more obvious to us, it is also important to understand how plausible and even how especially sensitive to the sufferings of the poor eugenic approaches to contraception could appear at the time. Specifically because concerned doctors and activists saw how debilitated particularly poor women's bodies became due to multiple pregnancies, arguing that contraception could improve their lives seemed not only compatible with but absolutely central to a social justice agenda. Thus, for instance, the inventor of the diaphragm (in 1882), the German gynecologist Wilhelm Mensinga of Flensburg, son of a pastor and himself a believing Christian, refused a patent because he was more concerned with widening the availability of the product than with his own gain; he also was completely unabashed about recommending abortifacient strategies within three or four days of a missed period if the diaphragm should occasionally fail. Mensinga's express motivation was to preserve the health of exhausted working-class women specifically so they could take better care of the children they already had. And it is thus as well no surprise that precisely some of the strongest social-democratic, socialist, communist, and anarchist critics of capitalist exploitation of the working masses were also the ones who dared to challenge the new anti-contraception laws and to work to make contraceptive information and products accessible. The Dutch contraception activist Aletta Jacobs, for instance, the first female doctor in the

---

[16] Auguste Forel, *Die sexuelle Frage* (Munich: E. Reinhardt, 1909), 504.

Netherlands, worked closely with trade unions and dedicated her life to running a free clinic specifically for destitute women and children; she often recommended the Mensinga diaphragm and was responsible for its popularity in the Netherlands.

The beginnings of sex reform

The large moral purity and abolitionist movements that mobilized at the turn from the nineteenth to the twentieth centuries were thus soon confronted with fledgling new movements which challenged the sexual double standard from the opposite direction, as it were. Rather than calling for men to be more chaste and controlled, these activists sought to make sex more pleasurable and less dangerous for women. Many simply took the position that it was only just and fair that poor women's lives not be crushed by near-constant pregnancy and that women's experience of sex not be continually dominated by this fear.

While sometimes these pro-contraception activists otherwise maintained fairly conventional views of gender and social relations, and simply sought to improve women's lot within marriage, others floated a variety of more radical ideas. Some of these new sex reform activists believed that capitalism needed to be overthrown before sex could be truly free. Some advanced the ideal of free love between equals as an alternative to what they saw as the grossly hypocritical system which maintained widespread prostitution alongside – manifestly inegalitarian – marriages, and they defended women's equal right to sex outside of marriage. Yet others believed sexuality in general needed to be more thoroughly investigated and understood and also that sexual minorities should be protected and accepted rather than persecuted and ostracized – and so some early sex reform organizations called for decriminalization and cultural acceptance of homosexuality as well as the decriminalization of contraception. Many of the doctors and activists involved in sex reform also researched varieties of sexual dysfunction and unhappiness and sought to provide insight and advice not only on birth control information and products but also on how to deal with such matters as impotence, premature ejaculation, frigidity, or anxieties about masturbation or sexual incompatibility within marriage.

Yet just as sex reform got underway as a movement, with transnational connections forged and clinics and counseling centers established in larger cities, many medical doctors were turning away from their earlier comfort with either openly or discreetly dispensing abortifacient and birth control information. Increasingly, many doctors transformed eugenic impulses initially aimed at improving individuals' lives into wider programs for "racial hygiene." Whether to bear children or not, and if yes how many, was no longer understood as an individual decision but rather one best left to medical experts who argued they had the good of society as a whole in view. In this context, physicians also began to lend their official support to the legal suppression of contraceptives as part of a more general move to take over from clergymen the task of professional moralizer – albeit using secular health-based and nationalist-racialized arguments.

Doctors started to take aim not just at mechanical or chemical birth control but also at coitus interruptus, claiming suddenly that it was unhealthy and could lead to impotence in men and incomplete satisfaction and hence generalized nervous disorders in women. Specifically women's hope for greater satisfaction due to lessened fear of pregnancy was thus insidiously manipulated by the reverse argument that it was the practice of withdrawal that left women unsatisfied. Individuals' and couples' interest in birth control was frequently decried not only by clergymen but now also by doctors, the new self-appointed experts in the area, as "selfish" and "egotistical." Almost as soon as they had gone public, then, defenders of contraception were put on the defensive. Arguing for freedom from suffering and ill health, or arguing for spacing of births so that children could be better cared for, also turned out to be far easier than arguing for women's rights to pleasure.

Pleasure remained a delicate subject. On the one hand, the fledgling sciences of psychoanalysis and sexology sought to investigate issues of desire, pleasure, practices, and orientation in detail – and the sex reform movement, with its complicated mix of eugenic and social-democratic or anarchist impulses, launched journals in various nations which brought the new insights and speculations about sex to a wider interested audience. On the other hand, pleasure without reproductive consequences remained a focus for intense ambivalence – with complex effects not only on how women's sexuality was interpreted but also on how the newly publicly visible issue of homosexuality was discussed.

Rethinking sexual orientation

The unmistakable trend toward separating sex from reproduction called ever more attention to questions about the nature and purpose of sex. Were human beings driven by an instinct to reproduce or were they above all moved to seek physical sexual pleasure? Did they seek emotional intimacy and connection as well? In fact, was sex a *push* or a *pull* – a drive, an urgency, a tension erupting *out* of an individual, or something drawing them *toward* another, specific individual? And were the desires of women and men similar or were there major differences between what women and men sought – and found – in their sexual encounters? Did men seek (preferably hasty and emotionally unencumbered) coitus but women seek babies and providers for them? Could women have orgasms also? Were men capable of monogamy? Were men even capable of love? Doctors wrote about all these matters based on the extant medical knowledge and presumptions, as well as their own experiences, but also based on what their patients shared with them. These accounts inevitably got increasingly explicit (though not therefore necessarily more accurate) as patients not only sought information on fertility management, but also increasingly saw themselves as beings with a right to the alleviation of sexual dysfunctions – even as what was dysfunctional and what was routine would remain matters of the most heated discussion.

Masturbation, for instance, remained almost universally condemned, even as it was, at least for young unpartnered men, almost universally practiced. When challenged to explain what made coitus healthy but masturbation unhealthy, a number of doctors argued that what was wrong with masturbation was that it depended on the individual generating sexual fantasies, which made them poor family men and poor citizens. In the nineteenth century, arguments had been put forward that masturbation was dangerous not only to the individual man or woman, but to entire nations. Men would be too feeble to defend or serve their country; pale, nervous women would be incapable of being effective mothers. And yet although many doctors at the turn to the twentieth century questioned the notion that masturbation could ruin societies or cause something as extreme as insanity in an individual, they continued to hold masturbation responsible for a wide range of troubles, especially in men – including impotence or fickle and inadequate erections, overall weakness and lassitude, acne and sweating, gastrointestinal and urological difficulties, hysteria, and possibly homosexual inclinations as well. Doctors and other self-styled experts simply presumed it to be self-evident that masturbation was awful. The effect of the constant condemnation, however, was not to stop the practice but rather to make it a source of inner conflict and hypochondria – and to burden additionally with enduring taboo and conflictedness the very acts of mutual masturbation within marriage that might have been useful as contraceptive technique.

Yet the ensuing closer investigation into the nature of what people sought and found in sex brought into view as well the remarkable range of human desires, and the differences not only between the genders but within each gender. Already the raging public debates about whether or not to tolerate prostitution had stimulated more attention to the apparent vagaries of human desire. When feminists argued not just that there was a "cesspool of sexual vice underlying society at the present time," but also that men were *inferior* to women because they were "slaves to the sex instinct" and apparently haplessly at the mercy of their genitals (to quote two female British activists) not only the defenders of prostitution felt obliged to respond with their own theories.[17] Also men who were just as uncomfortable with or repulsed by the prostitution-preferring habits of their fellow men started to speak up. Not just the mechanics of sex, in short, but also the emotions involved became matters for closer scrutiny. Nothing was any longer presumed to be self-evident.

Nowhere were the debates over the nature of sex more raucous and open than in Germany and the German-speaking areas of Switzerland and Austria-Hungary. Central Europe was home to the birth of sex research and sex reform alike. Many female sex reform activists were dubious about men's ability to combine physical passion and enduring affection. The German feminist and sex reform activist Johanna Elberskirchen, for instance, wrote in 1908 that "the male's capacity for love is essentially very poorly developed." A man, she wrote, was "basically satisfied, or exhausted, with the act of intercourse . . . basically incapable of loving woman," and whereas the "woman's soul joyously rushes out to meet the man she loves . . . Oh what a cruel delusion! . . . Her soul, drunk with love, thirsting for love, crashes against a dark, impenetrable wall of complete incomprehension." The most prominent male medical doctors agreed with this assessment but saw the differences between the genders as simply inalterably rooted in nature. Men, opined Albert Moll in 1904, sought "detumescence," or release; women sought "contrectation" – touch and connection. Numerous male doctors concurred, variously amplifying the point to argue that men's interest in sex was "superficial and episodic," and that for a man "love fades into the background as soon as his thoughts are claimed by his profession." Moreover, they contended, from the male point of view, monogamous marriage was a "pointless utopia"; men were "by nature polygamous and inclined to sexual 'snacking,'" and the very notion of monogamy "simply contradicts the inner experience of millions of men." But female sex reformers, while concurring that "the two sexes are driven apart like the different nations at the building of the tower of Babel," argued that this was not because men were somehow "naturally" brutish but rather because their socialization and their legal privilege and power allowed them to be so. In fact, many female reformers argued that women could be just as sexually

[17] Quoted in Lesley Hall, "Hauling Down the Double Standard: Feminism, Social Purity, and Sexual Science in Late Nineteenth Century Britain," *Gender and History* 16 (April 2004), 42, 45.

interested as men. They too wanted orgasms, not babies. Käthe Schir-macher even contended in 1909 that women were no less polygamous than men – they had merely been trained to monogamy by force and threat. If women were to regain economic independence, she said, "the old polygamous natural drives of women awaken again quite readily."[18]

The concept of homosexuality

In the midst of ever more heated conflicts over heterosexual relations, the concept of homosexuality was just in the process of being born. Homosexuality was not yet seen as the unmistakable counterpart to het-erosexuality. There were a number of reasons for this.

First, the crime on the books in many nations was not homosexu-ality but rather sodomy, and sodomy was a rather broad category. It could encompass male–female oral–genital and anal–genital contact as well as human–animal contact. Second, sodomy was for centuries seen as an *act* that anyone could in principle engage in, not the sign of an *identity* that saturated the individual in his or her entirety. Third, and although the words "homosexual" and "heterosexual" had been coined (by the Hungarian litterateur Karl Maria Kertbeny) in the 1860s, and the term "homosexual" was soon joined by other coinages like "invert", "uranian," member of the "intermediate sex," "third-sexer," or someone who had "contrary sexual sensations," this very proliferation of terms also suggests some of the difficulties contemporaries were having. Was what was unusual about the people they were naming their divergence from their *own gender role* (by feeling themselves to have a "woman's soul in a man's body," or vice versa, "a man's soul in a woman's body")? Or was what made them distinctive the gender of their preferred *choice of object*? And it would take yet more time for doctors to make distinctions between those who sought to change their own anatomical sex and those who sought same-sex relations. (Although the first partial sex-change surgeries took place in the 1910s–1920s, mostly in Germany, it would not be until the 1930s that the wider public became aware of the pos-sibility of transsexuality.) And meanwhile, what on earth the three-way relationship might possibly be between one's own sense of one's gender role, the gender of the object choices, and the *activities* one might like to engage in with those other people, was most thoroughly muddled. It was,

---

[18] Johanna Elberskirchen, Albert Moll, Max Marcuse, Hugo Sellheim, Christian Ehren-fels, Paul Näcke, Helene Lange, and Käthe Schirmacher, all quoted in Edward Ross Dickinson, "'A Dark, Impenetrable Wall of Complete Incomprehension': The Impossi-bility of Heterosexual Love in Imperial Germany," *Central European History* 40 (2007), 470–95.

after all, as late as 1905 that the Viennese doctor Sigmund Freud in his *Three Essays on the Theory of Sexuality* proposed that it might be useful to distinguish conceptually between sexual object (the person) and sexual aim (the activity). And it was also Freud who helpfully pointed out – though this hardly endeared him to many of his contemporaries – that there was quite apparently a tremendous blur between what was deemed perversion and what counted as normalcy. After all, did not kissing and caressing, as well as fixation on particular body parts or types of fabric or other props, continue to animate and intensify also supposedly "mature" genitally focused relations between men and women? What was passion without at least a little bit of perversion in it?

Among other things, and fourth, quite a lot of men in the early twentieth century had sex with both other men (or older boys) and with women, and did not see themselves as particularly unusual in doing so. The interest in sex with other men did not inevitably touch these men's self-concept. Nor was the gender of their partner necessarily what most outraged their contemporaries, either.

Indeed, and strikingly, for many moral purity activists, homosexual sex was best classed with prostitution as yet another sign of men's excessive sex drive and inability to restrict their own sexual activity properly to the institution of reproduction-oriented marriage, as "decent" women were expected to do. This notion that homosexual sex deserved punishment primarily because it was *non-marital* and *non-reproductive* (as opposed to simply non-heterosexual) was rooted in a tenacious tangle of associations that only started to unravel as more married couples strove for non-reproductivity. (The term "heterosexual" was in some quarters initially used not to designate someone interested in the so-called opposite sex, but someone "too" interested in the opposite sex for the purpose of sex alone and not primarily for the purpose of reproduction. Indicatively, moreover, the term "unnatural crimes" could be applied to same-sex activities and birth control alike.)

And in fact, there were yet more similarities between *some* men's same-sex activities and activities with female prostitutes: a tendency for the relationships or encounters, and the desire animating them, to cross the class divide – as well as a tendency for the sex to be transactional rather than rooted in mutual affection. Class differences rather than similarity in status were often the very basis for the strength of sexual desire. Indeed, the eventual shift from a power-differential-based understanding of desire to a concept of desire based in egalitarianism and approximately similar status between partners would take many decades to gain wide hold.

Certainly, sincere affection and economic transaction were not necessarily mutually exclusive. But there was in all large European cities a

phenomenon of young working-class men, soldiers, sailors, and laborers, servants and bathhouse attendants, who traded their sexual services
for money, goods, or benefits. Some of them preferred only men; some
of them dressed in flamboyant "feminine" style; some continued to be
interested also in women but wore lipstick and dressed as "queans" when
they went to gay clubs. But many of these men who were "to be had"
were "rough trade" whose self-understanding was by no means either
effeminate in gender role or exclusively homosexual in object choice. As
the historian Matt Houlbrook put it aptly in describing London: "The
most remarkable thing about queer urban culture is that it was, to a large
extent, composed of and created by men who never thought themselves
queer."[19] Or as historian Dan Healey noted with respect to St. Peters-
burg and Moscow in the early twentieth century, while "fleeting, mer-
cenary, and sometimes emotionless encounters by no means exhausts
the spectrum of same-sex love in Russian experience," plenty of men
had "lively appetites for casual sexual encounters" and within "Russia's
nascent male homosexual subculture, with its argot and a repertoire of
gestures and symbols . . . the men, youths, and boys who made themselves
sexually available in this environment exploited this cultural repertoire
without necessarily thinking of themselves as homosexual."[20] But it was
not just the young men offering sexual services for remuneration who
did not think of themselves as queer; many of their customers did not,
either. Meanwhile, travel to the Middle East, South Asia, the Orient, and
the European colonies on the African continent also provided numerous
opportunities for men seeking same-sex encounters away from the watch-
ful eyes of their communities of origin – encounters whose excitement
was often heightened by the sense of exoticism surrounding the partners
and suffusing the environment. Nonetheless, also in the overseas enclaves
of Europeans, conflicts arose over respectability and comportment, and
pressure was put to bear on European men to behave in such a way that
would legitimate European rule rather than undermine it.

For some men, the relationships with other men were most profoundly
rooted in passionate mutual affection, and for an even larger group the
attraction to other men was understood as suffusing all aspects of their
lives. Since at least the seventeenth century if not earlier, there had been
subcultures of men seeking sex with other men (and sometimes also
cross-dressing as women) in major European cities, including London

[19] Matt Houlbrook, *Queer London: Perils and Pleasures in the Sexual Metropolis, 1918–1957*
(University of Chicago Press, 2005), 7.
[20] Dan Healey, "Masculine Purity and 'Gentlemen's Mischief': Sexual Exchange and
Prostitution between Russian Men, 1861–1941," *Slavic Review* 60 (2001), 237.

and Amsterdam. But from the perspectives of outsiders – whether the police or the general public – and also from the perspectives of many of the participating men themselves, there was up until the late nineteenth century no clear sense of these men who loved and/or sought sex with men as some kind of distinct species.

Meanwhile, however, fifth, and crucially, there was no direct parallelism in either the experts' or the public's minds – or in the own minds of individuals who sought same-sex sex – between men who sought sex with men and women who sought sex with women. This was in part due to the fact that same-sex sex between women was in most countries not illegal. Austria, Hungary, and Sweden were three of the few whose gender-neutral language in the laws criminalizing sodomy left open the possibility that women could in principle be prosecuted, although in practice the numbers were far lower than they were for men. But it was also very much due to prevailing beliefs about differences between male and female sexuality.

Although references to lesbianism existed in obscure learned tomes and in some medical texts, lesbianism (or "tribadism" or "sapphism") was at the start of the twentieth century hardly a familiar concept to most Europeans. One argument scholars have made is that because women, especially "respectable" women, were often not seen as particularly sexual beings, what women did with other women could thus not seem terribly suspect. Neither did a masculine style imply a sexual preference. Even when in the early twentieth century increasing numbers of women adopted more masculine styles of dress, for instance, this was not immediately read as any indication of what they might or might not prefer to do in bed. Only in the course of the 1920s would "mannish" dress come to be seen as a decisive sign of female homosexuality. And only as research into sexual variety proceeded, and feminist sex reformers joined medical doctors in debating the nature of female desire, did a concept of lesbian relationships take shape.

The longstanding invisibility of lesbianism was also not least due to the fact that women lacked economic and social independence from men. Only the wealthiest women could afford to live on their own and it took major feminist campaigns for higher education and access to the professions to make financial independence from men a possibility for middle-class women. It was also typically not considered safe, and certainly not considered decent, for a woman to walk city streets alone at night. There was thus as well not much opportunity for women who might seek sex with other women to create an infrastructure of bars or other meeting places. Nor did women – in this way quite unlike men – show any tendency to have sex in public spaces like parks or public toilets. It was exactly when lesbianism eventually, and not least due to a series of public scandals in the 1910s–1920s, became a subject of mass fascination and speculation, that women-only institutions like female colleges became places in which lesbianism was suspected of being rampant.

Yet at the same time, many women had passionate romantic and also what we would now describe as physically sexual relationships with other women. Sometimes they lived openly together as a couple, in what they themselves referred to as a marriage. More often, at least one of the women was also married to a man. Yet turn-of-the-century culture conceived of these women's relationships differently than we do now, even as scholars continue to disagree on how to interpret them. Some contend that physical passion between women was not imaginable for most people and thus the public simply didn't "see" it; others argue that physical passion between women was in fact seen, but that it was understood as normal and unproblematic, in fact proper – especially in an era when female–female friendships were often far more emotionally sustaining to women than their marriages were. Again, as with married men who sought sex with men, it was the coexistence of what we would now call homosexual and heterosexual tendencies that allowed female homosexuality to stay under the radar of frenetically pathologizing public attention. Lesbophobia, like homophobia, must thus be interpreted not as some kind of time-transcending tradition, but as a *new* invention of the early twentieth century – one that emerged in tandem with, indeed in dialectical interaction with, the increasingly public self-declaration of same-sex desire among women.

Sixth, and finally, at the turn of the century, as more and more doctors turned their gaze to studying what they called sexual perversions, same-sex attraction was only one of a rich smorgasbord of predilections that also included masochism and sadism, voyeurism and exhibitionism, algolagnia (love of pain) and fetishism (whether for boots or fur, metal screws or rosebuds). No one could have guessed around 1900 that homosexuality and heterosexuality would emerge as the great contrast pair organizing the sexual universe. There were so many other non-normative human intensities to puzzle over. After all, heterosexual relations themselves were undergoing massive contestation and reconceptualization.

Activism, scandals, identities

What made homosexuality ultimately take shape as a visible identity? Three factors were vital. One was a growing campaign of sex reformers, some working individually, some in associations, across many nations, to decriminalize sodomy. Another was a series of scandals that brought the subject of same-sex-desiring individuals to the attention of a sensation-obsessed penny press-reading public. Some of these scandals involved ordinary citizens, some concerned literary and artistic milieus, and some reached into the highest echelons of diplomacy, military, and government; all triggered a welter of sniggering, mocking, and panicked articulations of what we would now call homophobia. But what finally was most decisive was the "feedback loop" by which, in the context of legal reform activism, scandals, and increasing medical interest in sexual variation, same-sex-desiring individuals began to express a sense of themselves as having a distinctive identity (perhaps inborn though of unclear origin) *and* a shared lot with one another. Each scandal and trial was an occasion for massive shaming and condemnation. All demonstrated the cost of deviance and were occasions for powerfully demarcating lines between normalcy and abnormalcy. Yet, and importantly, the scandals also provided opportunities for identification and self-definition. As the prominent English sex researcher Havelock Ellis, for instance (himself married to a lesbian), noted with respect to the scandal and sensational trials of playwright Oscar Wilde in the 1890s, the trials seemed "to have generally contributed to give definiteness and self-consciousness to the manifestations of homosexuality, and to have aroused inverts to take up a definite stand."[21]

What was the state of the law around 1900? Since 1810, when the Napoleonic Code was promulgated, France – in keeping with the French Revolution's more general anti-church impulses and desire to make firm distinctions between religion and law, sin and crime – had decriminalized sodomy along with fornication and prostitution. Many other countries which patterned their laws on the Napoleonic Code – including predominantly Catholic countries like Italy, Belgium, and Spain as well as mixed-confessional countries like the Netherlands (which had been under French occupation and only became an independent nation in the first third of the nineteenth century) – did not criminalize sodomy. However, predominantly Protestant countries like Denmark and Sweden, as well as mixed-confessional but Protestant-dominated nations like Britain and Germany, did criminalize sodomy. And Austria and Hungary, although predominantly Catholic, were the exceptions to the general rule about separation between religion and law in Catholic countries, and criminalized sodomy as well; so did several of the cantons in mixed-confessional Switzerland. In 1845 Russia, Tsar Nicholas I had introduced the criminalization of "muzhelozhstvo" – which the courts

21 Ellis quoted in Jeffrey Weeks, *Sex, Politics, and Society: The Regulation of Sexuality Since 1880* (New York: Longman, 1989), 103.

tended to interpret narrowly as anal sex between men, leaving consensual oral sex in private unprosecuted, but which could lead to seizure of property and four to five years of hard labor in Siberia; in 1903 a revised criminal code mitigated the punishment to three months' imprisonment.

Exactly this diversity of legal regulations across Europe created an opening for activists to argue for decriminalization on the grounds that consensual same-sex activity between adults was a victimless crime, but criminalization made those who sought same-sex sex vulnerable to exposure, blackmail, and destroyed livelihoods and lives. Many decriminalization activists also turned to medical experts for support of their theories that homosexual desire was "constitutional" – i.e. innate, inborn – as opposed to either a sign of sin or a condition acquired through seduction. Homosexuality was simply a minority but nonetheless natural variant of sexual expression. Yet other medical experts, however, used their authority to argue just the opposite: that while homosexual desire might be inborn or initially innocently acquired, it was nonetheless dangerous and criminal; some indeed argued that homosexuals tended toward criminality more generally. Both the state of the law and the import of medical findings for the law were in a state of profound flux. This led legal theorists and medical theorists alike to write ever more detailed ruminations on the intricacies of same-sex activities.

A long string of variables came under scrutiny, as the state of the law was compared across national boundaries. In some countries, only "coitus-like" activities were criminalized (although whether this made intercrural rubbing and oral sex or only mutual touching acceptable was open to frequent debate – so too whether this rubric could apply to women), but the punishment applied to both human sodomy and bestiality. In some countries, long prison terms were the norm; in others, shorter jail sentences were more typical (in Hungary for instance the punishments were somewhat less harsh than in Austria). In some countries, the motive of seeking sexual satisfaction was a matter for legal consideration. And in some other countries, for instance Sweden, only the "active," penetrating partner was punished, not the "passive" receiver – as male homosexuality, in this largely rural society, was interpreted very much within a bestiality paradigm (where the animal also was of course understood as passive). Importantly, here, penetration was understood as something done *to*, not *with*, another person. Same-sex mutual masturbation was considered irrelevant and in no way a sign of the self-concept of the individuals engaging in it; in Sweden it was not until the 1920s that homosexuality became conceptually detached from bestiality.

Meanwhile, also in countries like Italy and France in which consenting adult same-sex acts in private were legal (though by no means socially acceptable, nonetheless not prosecuted), there were still provisions for prosecuting same-sex acts involving a minor (the age of consent varied from 12 in Italy to 15 in France). There were also provisions for prosecuting acts involving: the use of force or threat of force; an abuse of relations of dependency (employer–employee, officer–soldier, teacher–student, guardian–ward); or an abuse of conditions (like drunkenness or mental deficiency) which cast doubt on the ability to give consent. Along related lines, with the amelioration of the provisions against homosexual acts between consenting adults in the Russian law code in 1903, an interesting intermediate category was additionally formulated which distinguished, for youths between the ages of 14 and 16, between those who were sexually experienced and "knowing" (and thus had no innocence to abuse or exploit) and those who were sexually inexperienced. Significantly, what all these diverse provisions expressed were the beginnings of a way of conceiving of sexual morality and sex-related law as based on the values of self-determination and consent rather than on notions of sin or deviance from norms.

Yet adherents to older notions of punitive treatment of deviance were not deterred easily and, as they began to be challenged by decriminalization activists, defenders of criminalization formulated new arguments about the purported dangers of homosexuality. The interlocking nature of developments that led to the emergence of new concepts of homosexuality is well exemplified in the case of Germany. The decriminalization movement was launched in Germany in 1897, under the leadership of the medical doctor Magnus Hirschfeld together with publisher Max Spohr and the government official Erich Oberg. They formed the "Scientific Humanitarian Committee" and already within three years had launched a journal, *Jahrbuch für sexuelle Zwischenstufen* (Yearbook for Sexually Intermediate Types), and published over twenty pamphlets criticizing Paragraph 175, the law which criminalized male same-sex activities. But just as the movement against Paragraph 175 was gaining support from many prominent people across the political spectrum, it was abruptly derailed by a series of scandals erupting in 1907 over homosexuality in Kaiser Wilhelm II's cabinet and entourage and additional scandals about homosexuality in the military.

The German and international media riveted onto the titillating details and suggestive cartoons which threatened German national honor at a critical moment in the arms race that eventually exploded into World War I. Both the Kaiser himself and his intimate friend Philipp Eulenburg were married men, and the libel suit brought by Eulenburg against the (Jewish) journalist Maximilian Harden, who initiated the scandal, brought to public view the uncomfortable possibility that the government

Fig. 1.3 "New Prussian Coat of Arms." Cartoon mocking the homosexual entourage surrounding Kaiser Wilhelm II. Published in *Jugend* 45 (October 28, 1907). Artist: Albert Weisgerber (1878–1915).

was run by queers who much rather preferred to go hunting and yachting with each other than be the upstanding family men they pretended to be. Shaken by the initial disclosures, in 1908 the Kaiser compounded his own problems by giving an inopportune interview to the London *Daily Telegraph* about German strategy in the arms race with its arch-rival Britain – and then, in the wake of the furious reaction of many politicians in the Reichstag, fleeing to a forest retreat with aristocratic friends. In

Fig. 1.4 Maud Allen. The American dancer performed the "Vision of Salomé" to great acclaim in several European cities. She was "the toast of London" in 1908 – ten years before the public scandal surrounding her libel trial against the editor of a xenophobic British journal declaring her a lesbian.

a bizarre twist, a leading military official at the retreat suffered a fatal heart attack while dancing in a ballerina tutu. The impact of the ensuing flood of press coverage and national embarrassment was incalculable. But without question it gave definite shape *both* to anti-Semitic backlash (not least as the exposures were retrospectively treated by the Kaiser as a Jewish conspiracy that subsequently led to Germany's defeat in World War I and his own abdication in 1918) *and* to novel expressions of homophobia. Already in 1909, when the proposal for a new German criminal code was being debated, the Kaiser's scandals were clearly alluded to when jurists found new language to explain why male homosexual acts needed to be criminalized.

At the same time, in a peculiar but revealing footnote to the 1909 criminal code discussions, an effort to extend the criminalization of male homosexual acts to same-sex acts between women – while oddly gaining support from some feminist groups on the grounds that it would mark an advance in gender equality (a move likely also motivated by discomfort with lesbianism within the feminist movement) – was quickly suppressed on the grounds that whatever women did with each other was not easily identifiable as "coitus-like" and was in any event too difficult to distinguish from the physical affections exchanged also between "normal" women. It would not be until several years later, with the lesbianism libel scandal surrounding the British dancer Maud Allen, that somewhat more defined notions of lesbianism began to capture the public imagination.

It has often been argued that the cataclysm of World War I shattered forever the Victorian code of sexual mores that reigned not only in Britain but on the Continent as well. But as the proliferating welter of debates over sex that rocked Europeans between 1900 and 1914 suggest – ranging as they did across the complexly intersecting topics of the double standard, prostitution, trafficking, venereal disease, marriage, contraception, abortion, eugenics, masturbation, perversions, and sexual orientations – new notions of sexual rights, dysfunctions, values, behaviors, and identities were already taking shape well before the first shots were fired.

Further reading

Aldrich, Robert, *Colonialism and Homosexuality* (New York: Routledge, 2003).
Arni, Caroline, "Simultaneous Love: An Argument on Love, Modernity and the Feminist Subject at the Beginning of the Twentieth Century," *European Review of History* 11, no. 2 (2004), 185–205.
Beachy, Robert, "The German Invention of Homosexuality," *Journal of Modern History* 82 (December 2010), 801–38.

Bernstein, Laurie, *Sonia's Daughters: Prostitutes and their Regulation in Imperial Russia* (Berkeley: University of California Press, 1995).

Bleys, Rudi C., *The Geography of Perversion: Male-to-Male Sexual Behavior Outside the West and the Ethnographic Imagination, 1750–1918* (New York University Press, 1996).

Brady, Sean, "Homosexuality: European and Colonial Encounters" in Chiara Beccalossi and Ivan Crozier (eds.), *A Cultural History of Sexuality in the Age of Empire* (Oxford and New York: Berg, 2011), 43–62.

Brandhorst, Henny, "From Neo-Malthusianism to Sexual Reform: The Dutch Section of the World League for Sexual Reform," *Journal of the History of Sexuality* 12 (January 2003), 38–67.

Cleminson, Richard, *Anarchism, Science and Sex: Eugenics in Eastern Spain, 1900–1937* (Oxford: Peter Lang, 2000).

Cook, Hera, *The Long Sexual Revolution: English Women, Sex, and Contraception, 1800–1975* (Oxford University Press, 2005).

Corbin, Alain, "Commercial Sexuality in Nineteenth-Century France: A System of Images and Regulations" in Catherine Gallagher and Thomas Walter Laqueur (eds.), *The Making of the Modern Body: Sexuality and Society in the Nineteenth Century* (Berkeley: University of California Press, 1987), 209–19.

Dickinson, Edward Ross, "'A Dark, Impenetrable Wall of Complete Incomprehension': The Impossibility of Heterosexual Love in Imperial Germany," *Central European History* 40 (September 2007), 467–97.

Doan, Laura L., *Fashioning Sapphism: The Origins of a Modern English Lesbian Culture* (New York: Columbia University Press, 2001).

Fisher, Kate, *Birth Control, Sex and Marriage in Britain, 1918–1960* (Oxford University Press, 2006).

Gibson, Mary, *Prostitution and the State in Italy, 1860–1915*, 2nd edn (Columbus: Ohio State University Press, 1999).

Harsin, Jill, "Syphilis, Wives, and Physicians: Medical Ethics and the Family in Late Nineteenth Century France," *French Historical Studies* 16 (Spring 1989), 72–95.

Healey, Dan, "Masculine Purity and 'Gentlemen's Mischief': Sexual Exchange and Prostitution between Russian Men, 1861–1941," *Slavic Review* 60 (2001), 233–65.

Houlbrook, Matt, *Queer London: Perils and Pleasures in the Sexual Metropolis, 1918–1957* (University of Chicago Press, 2005).

Hunt, Alan, "The Great Masturbation Panic and the Discourses of Moral Regulation in Nineteenth- and Early Twentieth-Century Britain," *Journal of the History of Sexuality* 8 (April 1998), 575–615.

Juette, Robert, *Contraception: A History* (Cambridge University Press, 2008).

Jušek, Karin, "Sexual Morality and the Meaning of Prostitution in Fin-de-Siècle Vienna" in Jan Bremmer (ed.), *From Sappho to Sade: Moments in the History of Sexuality* (London: Routledge, 1989), 123–43.

Laqueur, Thomas W., *Solitary Sex: A Cultural History of Masturbation* (Cambridge, MA: The MIT Press, 2003).

Levine, Philippa, *Prostitution, Race and Politics: Policing Venereal Disease in the British Empire* (New York: Routledge, 2003).

Makari, George, "Between Seduction and Libido: Sigmund Freud's Masturbation Hypotheses and the Realignment of His Etiologic Thinking, 1897–1905," *Bulletin of the History of Medicine* 72 (1998), 638–62.

Marcus, Sharon, *Between Women: Friendship, Desire and Marriage in Victorian England* (Princeton University Press, 2007).

Matysik, Tracie, *Reforming the Moral Subject: Ethics and Sexuality in Central Europe, 1890–1930* (Ithaca, NY: Cornell University Press, 2008).

Meyerowitz, Joanne, *How Sex Changed: A History of Transsexuality in the United States* (Cambridge, MA: Harvard University Press, 2002).

Nye, Robert A. (ed.), *Sexuality* (Oxford University Press, 1999).

Proschan, Frank, "'Syphilis, Opiomania, and Pederasty': Colonial Constructions of Vietnamese (and French) Social Diseases," *Journal of the History of Sexuality* 11 (October 2002), 610–36.

Rowbotham, Sheila, *Edward Carpenter: A Life of Liberty and Love* (London: Verso, 2008).

Rydström, Jens, *Sinners and Citizens: Bestiality and Homosexuality in Sweden, 1880–1950* (University of Chicago Press, 2003).

Rydström, Jens, and Kati Mustola (eds.), *Criminally Queer: Homosexuality and Criminal Law in Scandinavia, 1842–1999* (Amsterdam: Aksant, 2007).

Sinclair, Alison, "The World League for Sexual Reform in Spain: Founding, Infighting, and the Role of Hildegart Rodríguez," *Journal of the History of Sexuality* 12 (January 2003), 98–109.

Spector, Scott, "The Wrath of the 'Countess Merviola': Tabloid Exposé and the Emergence of Homosexual Subjects in Vienna in 1907" in Günter Bischof, Anton Pelinka, and Dagmar Herzog (eds.), *Sexuality in Austria*. Contemporary Austrian Studies 15 (New Brunswick, NJ: Transaction Publishers, 2007), 31–47.

Stauter-Halsted, Keely, "'A Generation of Monsters': Jews, Prostitution, and Racial Purity in the 1892 L'viv White Slavery Trial," *Austrian History Yearbook* 38 (2007), 25–35.

Stoler, Ann Laura, *Carnal Knowledge and Imperial Power: Race and the Intimate in Colonial Rule* (Berkeley: University of California Press, 2002).

Surkis, Judith, *Sexing the Citizen: Morality and Masculinity in France, 1870–1920* (Ithaca, NY: Cornell University Press, 2006).

"Enemies Within: Venereal Disease and the Defense of French Masculinity between the Wars" in Christopher Forth and Bertrand Taithe (eds.), *French Masculinities: History, Culture and Politics* (Basingstoke: Palgrave Macmillan, 2007), 102–22.

Szreter, Simon, "Falling Fertilities and Changing Sexualities in Europe since c. 1850: A Comparative Survey of National Demographic Patterns" in Franz Eder, Gert Hekma, and Lesley A. Hall (eds.), *Sexual Cultures in Europe: Themes in Sexuality* (Manchester University Press, 1999), 159–94.

Vance, Carole, "Thinking Trafficking, Thinking Sex," *GLQ*, 17, no. 1 (2010), 135–43.

Vicinus, Martha, *Intimate Friends: Women Who Loved Women, 1778–1928* (University of Chicago Press, 2006).

Walkowitz, Judith R., *City of Dreadful Delight: Narratives of Sexual Danger in Late-Victorian London* (University of Chicago Press, 1992).

"The 'Vision of Salome': Cosmopolitanism and Erotic Dancing in Central London, 1908–1918," *American Historical Review* 108 (April 2003), 337–76.

Wingfield, Nancy, "Echoes of the Riehl Trial in Fin-de-Siècle Cisleithania," *Austrian History Yearbook* 38 (2007), 36–47.

Walther, Daniel Joseph, "Racializing Sex: Same-Sex Relations, German Colonial Authority, and *Deutschtum,*" *Journal of the History of Sexuality* 17 (January 2008), 11–24.

2   State interventions 1914–1945

The pre-World War I period had already seen a growing publicity around sexual matters, and an upwelling of ordinary people's interest in improving their own experiences of sex as well as avidly monitoring and theorizing about the choices made by others. Yet the impact of World War I on sexual politics and sexual mores and practices was to be tremendous. The war dramatically quickened changes in the organization and understanding of sexuality that had been underway since the turn of the century. In many nations, the interwar period would then be a time of considerably greater loosening of sexual customs. The interwar period, however, would also be marked by unprecedented efforts on the part of national and local governments to intervene in their citizens' private lives. This would be true both for those nations that turned to fascism and for those that remained democratic. But no changes would be as convulsive and consequential as those wrought by the slaughter unleashed by Nazi Germany across the European continent in World War II.

World War I and its aftermath: violence and opportunity

World War I accelerated longer-term trends toward greater equality between the sexes, as well as toward heightened mobility of individuals – not just from countryside to towns, but also across many national borders within Europe. The war witnessed extensive traffic across Europe's external boundaries, too, as colonial troops from India, for instance, were drafted to fight on the side of Britain, and troops from Senegal, Tunisia, and Indochina were mobilized on behalf of France.

More devastatingly, the war divided couples for long periods of time, if not forever. Women on the home fronts often managed households on their own while they also did men's jobs and demonstrated that they were quite competent to do so. Yet in the meantime, the opposing sides' rivalrous race to develop and use new military technology, far from expediting the war's end, extended its duration and exponentially expanded the

Fig. 2.1 "A Wise Man." French colonial soldier with adoring French woman. This German caricature from World War I mocked the prevalence of consensual sexual and romantic relationships between French women and French colonial soldiers from North and West Africa in order to destabilize further the French authorities already made anxious by the relationships themselves. The drawing shows the white French officer trying to get the soldier to march to battle, but the soldier, Ibrahim, is "wise" and would prefer to stay with his lady-friend.

ensuing carnage. More than 6 million soldiers died in combat; another 2 million died from disease or in accidents or as prisoners of war.

Those men who did return were all too often shell-shocked or maimed. Even in cases where there was no grievous physical harm, psychological damage could be lasting – and inevitably had consequences for intimate partnerships. In short, the war separated the genders, but at the same time it blurred boundaries between them, as women took over formerly male responsibilities while men found their self-confidence and prerogatives shaken by the horrors of battle and the reorganization of social roles alike.

War's impact on sexuality soon showed its Janus face. The war brought both trauma and thrill. Theretofore unimaginable violence gripped the continent; war, as Sigmund Freud pointed out, altered human nature, brought out the sadistic and regressive elements that were kept more effectively under wraps in peacetime. Quite apart from the libidinal elements evident in violence more generally, the war also brought with it a terrifying array of specifically sexual violences, including rape, gang rape, and genital mutilation – phenomena reaching their most heinous manifestation in the mass incidence of sexual torture as well as sexual enslavement by Turkish troops of Armenian women in the course of the Armenian genocide of 1915–18.

Yet we will never understand the complex interconnections between war and sex if we focus only on the negative manifestations. For the war also offered numerous opportunities for new sexual pleasures, experiences, and relationships – often including the transgression of boundaries of nation, color, sexual orientation, and class. Precisely the anonymity and mass mobility facilitated by war, and the disruption of traditional constraints and communal and familial monitoring mechanisms, offered countless chances for consensual delights. The consequences were not just temporary but potentially momentous, as military mobilization, for instance, highlighted the need for far more effective venereal disease control and public health programming, or as the remarkable (and to government observers shocking) prevalence of romantic relationships between white women in European metropoles and the colonial men of color conscripted into European armies threatened to capsize the entire colonial order – along with the presumptive privilege of *European men* to partner with *colonized women* – and the pretense of white female purity on which that order rested.

It is important, however, both in the case of sexual violences and in the case of consensual pleasures, not to assume some sort of transhistorical sex drive erupting (either dangerously or happily) at those moments when constraints are removed – even as we take seriously the often

Fig. 2.2 "Next Gentleman, Please!" Brothel in Belgium in
World War I. Drawing by Heinrich Zille (1858–1929).

heightened intensity of sexual encounters in times of war, due either
to the impending separation of lovers or to the imminent threat of
death. Instead, sex in wartime brings into view even more clearly than
in peacetime just how extraordinarily variable a phenomenon sexuality

can be. Thus, for instance, military brothels encouraged an even more depersonalized, conveyor-belt quality of sex than had been typical in prewar prostitution.

At the same time, the outbreak of revolution in Russia in 1917 altered the course of the war – even as it altered the course of the history of sexuality as well. The idea that the Russian Revolution had, seemingly overnight, swept away a repressive culture and then subsequently instituted the decriminalization of both abortion and homosexuality (in 1920) was in some ways a convenient fiction, covering over as it did the trend toward liberal reforms of sex-related law in Russia in the pre-revolutionary years. But the symbolic significance of those decriminalizations made them a focus for the most elated inspiration and horrified alarm, respectively, for sexual liberalization enthusiasts and anti-Bolshevik conservatives elsewhere in Europe.

The Russian Revolution in all its dimensions proved especially disturbing to church authorities and – taken together with the inescapable evidence of growing secularization throughout Europe, particularly rising distrust of church teachings on sexual morality and family planning – it provoked the churches into developing a panoply of counter-strategies. These eventually included not only the Catholic church's forceful repudiation of contraception and abortion and the Anglican and other Protestant churches' more ambivalent combination of acquiescence to contraception and hostility to abortion. The counter-strategies developed by both Catholic and Protestant churches included as well efforts to present Christian teaching as not only compatible with sexual happiness within marriage but also as the *best* guarantor of a mutually loving, personalized (indeed the Catholic term was "personalist") – as opposed to depersonalized – sexuality. Personalism, as it was developed especially by French Catholics, was a deliberate contrast to Marxism and other forms of materialism. The argument constituted a modern defense of religion as best able to acknowledge also the spiritual aspects of human beings, in contrast to what was perceived of as an overly shallow, emotionally empty, and self-interested individualism. The clergy's hostility to Russian Bolshevism and other kinds of socialism and anarchism was complexly entangled with hostility to the growing interest in sexual freedoms and sexual pleasures of their own congregations.

The churches' evolving efforts to present Christian marriage as no longer a patriarchal or prudish but rather a companionate and joyfully sensual project were clearly intended to take the sting out of sex radicals' critiques and to adapt the growing popular interest in eroticizing marriage to an ongoing defense of the institution of marriage. The

Catholic church resisted all artificial interference with the possibility of procreation, but also began to emphasize more strongly than before – as Pope Pius XI would subsequently summarize it in 1931 – that sexual intercourse within marriage had additional purposes of "mutual aid, the cultivating of mutual love, and the quieting of concupiscence."[1] Protestants, too, while less strict, continued to express considerable ambivalence about contraception, considering it "selfish," while nonetheless celebrating marital mutuality.

In view of the cacophony of conflicting perspectives, the market for marital sex guidance – from expert books to counseling clinics – expanded accordingly. The most admired advice book of the era, the Dutch gynecologist Theodor van de Velde's *Ideal Marriage: Its Physiology and Technique*, published in 1926, was put on the Catholic church's index of prohibited books, but was also translated into numerous languages, went through over forty printings, and sold millions of copies. It contributed to the emergent modern consensus that happiness within marriage depended on sex being fulfilling for both partners.

Church hostility to contraception and abortion and to the more general pursuit of pleasure for its own sake created deep anxieties and conflicts for many believers. But many other Europeans in the post-World War I era began to articulate – or at the very least to practice – alternative visions of sexuality unhinged from any concern with church teachings or with (what was increasingly referred to disdainfully as) "bourgeois" respectability. The collapse of certainties of all kinds created a novel postwar climate of openness to experimentation – a climate which, while deeply threatening to some, was bracingly exciting to others.

Gender relations in the interwar period

The interwar era saw a rich burgeoning of bohemian and other ventures in non-traditional sexual arrangements among hetero- and homosexuals alike (many of which also demonstrated the still quite unsolidified boundaries between hetero- and homosexuality). These ventures ranged from openly acknowledged love triangles in artistic and intellectual milieus to classy urban clubs catering to lesbians and homosexual men to outdoors-oriented organizations dedicated to health reform and naturist nudity (often accompanied by paeans to nudism's

---

[1] Pius XI, *Casti Connubii*, www.vatican.va/holy_father/pius_xi/encyclicals/documents/hf_p-xi_enc_31121930_casti-connubii_en.html.

non-erotic chaste intentions but also often overlapping with challenges to Christian, especially Catholic, sexual conservatism). These more daring and ostentatiously visible (and to their critics distressing) manifestations of experimentalism were matched by a more quiet evolution in mores at the grassroots – not least because contraceptive products and information were more readily available, but also because in the course of the war years time-honored authorities had been shaken and habits loosened.

Divisions in values ran *through* as well as between national and regional cultures. Moreover, the south was not uniformly conservative, nor was the north of Europe entirely liberal. Also, in the southern Catholic nations of Spain and Italy, for instance, there were bohemian experiments, whether in the context of anarchist and socialist politics or for their own sake. Thus, Spanish anarchist women in the 1920s and early 1930s not only advocated for the use of contraceptives and criticized the institution of marriage and the sexual double standard, but called for both "free love" and "plural love" (more than one lover at the same time), also for women. As anarchists, they believed that it was not nature but rather the power imbalance structuring male–female relations that pushed men toward prostitutes and left wives sexually unhappy. Writing in journals like *Estudios*, *La Revista Blanca*, and *Mujeres Libres*, anarchist women like Amparo Poch y Gascón, Etta Federn, María Lacerda de Moura, and Federica Montseny argued that monogamy "does not mean 'forever', but [only] as long as . . . the will and feelings of the lovers lasts", that love and sex should be distinguished and one should struggle "against the widely accepted, but false, belief, that sexual satisfaction without love is a symptom of moral perversion – especially in the case of a woman." But while several of these women also practiced at least some of what they preached (many anarchist activists were involved in free unions, and birth control was used), already during the years of the civil war, 1936–39, many anarchist women had turned away from open advocacy of free love. This was above all because of the war itself and the fact that training and empowerment of women became the most pressing concerns. But it was not least also because, as Montseny's mother, Soledad Gustavo, had observed already in 1923, "Men find women's freedom a good idea, but they are not so pleased when women actually exercise that freedom."[2]

---

[2] Anarchist women quoted in Martha Ackelsberg, "Mujeres Libres: Identity, Community, Sexuality, and Power," *Anarchist Studies* 8 (2000), 101–11.

Fig. 2.3 Magnus Hirschfeld. The renowned medical doctor and sexual rights activist (with glasses, center) and friends. Nudism was broadly practiced in Germany and neighboring countries in the 1920s and was inseparable from a wider back-to-nature health reform movement; its adherents traversed the ideological spectrum from Left to Right. Hirschfeld was to become the most prominent advocate for decriminalization of homosexuality in pre-Nazi Germany, and also one of the most important early advocates for the scientific study of sexuality as well as the development of a sexual morality based on self-determination and consent. Hirschfeld would be driven into exile and his internationally renowned Institute for Sexual Science destroyed by the Nazis.

Meanwhile, in the north also, there were plenty of ongoing defenders of the traditional sexual double standard. In the British debates of the interwar years, for example, while there were certainly those who loudly celebrated free love as well as those who, with just as much fervor, offered more moderate paeans to greater affection and equality within marriage, there were also numerous commentators who contended that misty visions of mutuality, whether inside or outside of marriage, were idealistic nonsense. Men and women really were by nature profoundly different; a marriage based on aspirations for loving closeness and regular exchange of ideas was an absurdity. Women were disinclined to adultery and were most interested in finding a good provider for their children; as long as the family's financial situation was stable, they did not much concern themselves with their husbands' other activities, whether sexual or professional. British anti-feminist Boswell King, in his *Sex and Human Nature* (1933), opined that real men were emphatically not domestically inclined. A "comforting but innocuous wife" who did not cramp the man's freedom was best; what a man most needed was regularly to "get away from his family, and from women altogether, and foregather in the communion of men."[3] Men had roving eyes, enjoyed non-emotional sex with a variety of women in addition to their wives, and otherwise infinitely preferred the company of other males.

Sex reform goes transnational

It was against not just punitive and restrictive laws but also against this kind of unapologetic misogyny that sex reform as a transnational movement rebelled in the interwar years. The 1920s and early 1930s marked the heyday of sex reform organizations – from Britain and Scandinavia to the Netherlands, Austria, and Spain, as well as across the newly created nations of post-World War I eastern Europe. The aim was to rethink the entire complex of issues relating to marriage, reproduction, gender relations, and the very idea of what sex was and could be. Promoting contraception seemed inseparable from challenging inherited ideas about dynamics within marriage as well as the dividing line between the married and the unmarried. It is indicative that the now-famous words of the Norwegian-born, later Swedish feminist and sex reformer Elise Ottesen-Jensen, cofounder in 1933 of the Swedish Association for Sexuality Education (*Riksförbundet för Sexuell Upplysning*, RFSU) – "I dream of the day when every new born child is welcome, when men and

---

[3] King quoted in Marcus Collins, *Modern Love: An Intimate History of Men and Women in Twentieth-Century Britain* (London: Atlantic Books, 2003), 52–3.

women are equal, and when sexuality is an expression of intimacy, joy and tenderness" – could seem in their day both sentimentally utopian and strikingly controversial.[4] And while local initiatives ran the gamut from contraceptive-dispensing clinics (among the earliest of these was one opened in Vienna in 1922 by Johann Ferch and one launched in Oslo in 1924 by Katti Anker Möller) to a petition drive lobbying for legal changes in the status of homosexuality to proposals for sex education in schools, there was a growing effort to coordinate across national boundaries and develop a coherent vision for transforming sexual politics and cultures alike.

The most significant transnational activist efforts included not only the international conferences of birth control and population policy advocates coordinated by the American Margaret Sanger and the gatherings of sex researchers organized at the initiative of the German psychiatrist Albert Moll, but also the founding of the World League for Sexual Reform (under the leadership of German physician Magnus Hirschfeld, the English sex researcher Havelock Ellis, and the Swiss psychiatrist Auguste Forel) at a congress of sex rights activists in Copenhagen in 1928. Subsequent congresses were held in London (1929), Vienna (1930), and Brno, Czechoslovakia (1932). While the League may not have encompassed the "world," its members certainly spanned the European continent. Among those involved in the League's leadership, both in national chapters and at international gatherings, were the Russian physician Grigorij Batkis and the revolutionary feminist Alexandra Kollontai, Polish poet and doctor Tadeusz Boy-Żeleński and physician and birth control activist Henryk Rubinraut, French feminist, and birth control and abortion rights activist Berty Albrecht, Dutch physician Bernard Premsela, British gynecologist Norman Haire and socialist feminist Dora Russell, Spanish activist Hildegart Rodriguez, German Marxist Freudian Wilhelm Reich, and Austrian pediatrician and psychoanalyst Josef Friedjung. There were a remarkable 190,000 people associated with the World League through their membership in officially affiliated organizations. The World League's demands included the right to divorce, the equality of women with men, the promotion of safe birth control, and the equal rights of those "unsuited to marriage" (they meant homosexuals). It called for a reorganization of sex-related law based above all on the principle of consent and "the mutual sexual will of grown-up persons."

Yet while the League's demands were understood as militantly courageous, and openly in contravention to the laws on the books in many

---

[4] The Swedish Association for Sexuality Education (RFSU), "Our History," www.rfsu.se/our_history.asp.

nations, sexuality-related activism in the interwar era could take many forms and not all of it was risky. Quite a lot of it was in fact tolerated or even welcomed by state governments, political parties, and trade unions. And while some sex reformers spent their time fighting governments and deliberately courting prosecution, a growing number found their projects funded by governments, both municipal and federal.

At the same time, and in the midst of constant cross-referencing across the boundaries between Western and Eastern Europe, the tensions and overlaps between sex reform and eugenics became even more difficult to disentangle than previously. Polish eugenics, for instance, led by the physician Leon Wernic (who was also strongly involved in feminist causes and efforts to abolish prostitution), was most deeply influenced by Swiss and Scandinavian models, while Czechs, who described their efforts as "democratic" and motivated by "humanitarianism," expressly opposed themselves to the most overtly racialist German eugenicists and opted to present their orientation as pro-French. The Bulgarians, by contrast, were strongly inspired specifically by racist German versions of eugenics. In Hungary, in the rightward shift that followed the communist experiment of 1919, self-appointed expert activists and public health officials alike would only entertain the topic of birth control in the context of eugenic measures and efforts to prevent the hereditarily ill or mentally deficient from propagating, and had absolutely no interest in contraception as a means toward female sexual self-determination. In other nations – France was a key example – the aftermath of the war saw the abrupt criminalization of all contraception through a law passed in 1920; more threatening even than further depopulation was the very possibility for women of making motherhood into a choice – civilization itself seemed to be at stake.

Nearly all European state governments had been prompted by the experience of World War I to expand welfare and health care and administrative systems which intervened – in both restrictive and supportive ways – in the private lives and even directly in the bodies of citizens. The results ranged from the state financing of academic research institutes in demography and eugenics to the passage (or at least debating) of laws concerning either compulsory or voluntary sterilization of criminals, the mentally ill, and those suffering from hereditary disease (one of the first such laws was passed in Switzerland in 1928, in the canton of Vaud – it was understood as "progressive" and "reformist"), to the setting up of clinics at which couples wishing to marry were encouraged to get certificates attesting that they did not suffer from mental illness or deficiency, tuberculosis, or venereal disease, or clinics which provided prenatal care for women and classes in infant care. In some nations, sex reform activists and eugenicists were hired into the newly formed ministries of health and public hygiene. Yet at the same time, sex reform remained contested and the demands of its most radical activists were soon met by fierce conservative opposition from church leaders and right-wing politicians alike.

Pursuing pleasure

The conservative backlash would also be directed against the broader spread of a culture of pleasure. Not all the heightened visibility and scandal surrounding sex in the interwar era involved activism. Some of it was engaged in for the sheer sake of fun.

A particularly pertinent example might be the prevalence of overt homosexuality in the posh public schools of Britain, where the future diplomatic, economic, and intellectual elite of the nation was trained. As numerous retrospective accounts make clear, in the interwar era same-sex practices were not only pervasive but fashionable. One alumnus of the prestigious Oundle School in Northamptonshire remembered with fond nostalgia: "There was an enormous amount of sex, enormous. I had my share of it, but I would have liked even more." There were passionate romantic affairs and chaste adorations-from-afar, there was wild promiscuity and there were intense rivalries between boys. And while there was in some cases brutal exploitation and violation of younger or weaker boys, there were also schools in which the pairing of an older and a younger boy who served him was encouraged by the school itself. Meanwhile, it was not at all clear that these boys and young men remained or became self-identified homosexuals. While the list of illustrious Britons who discovered their homosexuality at public school is extensive, there were definitely also counterexamples, men for whom the boyhood experiences with other boys would come to be seen as nothing more than "stupid prelude." As one Haileybury alumnus recalled: "Oh yes, there were tons of sex. Does that make you a fag? – certainly not. The most active person that I knew at that time became a formidable womanizer."[5]

Experimentation was not just for the elite, however. The interwar era saw the flourishing of open homosexual subcultures in most major European cities – a phenomenon that would be taken as particularly offensive by the guardians of traditionalism. Paris, for instance, was home to a growing community of women who self-identified as lesbian, and carved out a life of professional and personal independence from men. And while

---

[5] Quoted in Florence Tamagne, *A History of Homosexuality in Europe*, 2 vols. (New York: Algora Publishing, 2004), vol. I, 148–57.

all major cities in the interwar era were full of opportunities, in the public imagination no place was wilder or more flamboyant than Weimar-era Berlin. There were bars and clubs catering to every imaginable preference and fetish – which attracted enthusiastic tourists as well. One travel guide explained to interested heterosexual male visitors where the most noteworthy lesbian clubs, like the Damenklub Violetta or the Café Olala, could be found – but there was also a guidebook just for lesbians that described fourteen clubs, and there were venues like the Confetti Club that appealed to gay men and lesbians both. There were underground and above-ground lesbian and homosexual magazines. There were clubs supplying services for transvestites, and for those interested in sadomasochism. There was an explosion of porn production.

In trying, then, to discern whether the interwar era should be understood as a time of sexual revolution – as some contemporaries thought it was and as many scholars have argued – it is important to identify what exactly was changing. Certainly there was the new level of visibility to homosexuality, especially among men but increasingly also women – a growing refusal to hide one's predilections, a greater comfort with defining oneself as inclined to same-sex attractions (even when heterosexual marriages were officially maintained). In addition to practical experimentation, the interwar years saw an extraordinary surge in literary publications dedicated to exploring both self-laceratingly surreptitious and defiantly ecstatic homosexuality, and a growing publicity around the topic in general – in Britain, France, and Germany especially, though also, albeit to a lesser extent, in Switzerland, Sweden, and Spain – which also caused the idea of what homosexuality exactly was (an inversion in one's own gender identity or a preference for lovers of the same gender or some – at least partial – combination of both?) to take firmer shape in the mind of the public and in the minds of self-identified homosexual men and lesbians alike.

With regard to lesbianism, no event had a more enduring impact than the obscenity trial surrounding British author Radclyffe Hall's "mannish lesbian" novel *The Well of Loneliness* (1926). The book based its defense of lesbianism on emergent sexological medical arguments about homosexuality as an unfortunate but nonetheless not immoral form of gender inversion. And although initially banned in Britain, the novel was translated into numerous languages. The consequences above all for the self-understandings of women who discovered they desired women would be incalculable. (Among many other instances, one woman who read it in Polish later said she survived the Nazi concentration camps in the 1940s just hanging on to the dream that someday she would get to experience kissing another woman.)

Fig. 2.4 *Die Freundin*, April 30, 1930. The headline reads: "This paper may be openly displayed everywhere!" Weimar-era Berlin did not just boast a flourishing lesbian club life, but also was the first home of an uncensored lesbian press – although authorities had managed to suspend publication of *Die Freundin* for twelve months in 1928–29. *Die Freundin* helped develop lesbian community in numerous ways, exploring a multiplicity of possible lesbian identities and relationships, covering a wide variety of political issues of the day, and alerting its readership to the launching of "ladies' clubs" in cities such as Zurich in Switzerland and Hamburg, Cologne, Frankfurt, Leipzig, and Breslau in Germany.

A BOOK THAT MUST BE SUPPRESSED.

By THE EDITOR OF THE "SUNDAY EXPRESS."

Fig. 2.5 "A Book That Must Be Suppressed." *Sunday Express* headline against Radclyffe Hall's (at the time scandalous, now iconic) lesbian love story, *The Well of Loneliness* (1926). *Sunday Express*, August 19, 1928.

Yet also for heterosexuals, popular mores and practices were loosening – but what primarily made that dramatic was that they were loosening *for women*. Men had already had considerable freedoms before. What was being challenged was the inequality of heterosexual relations.

Just to take the example of Germany: There were, in Berlin alone, more than three dozen sex counseling centers serving the local populace (there were hundreds of sex counseling centers, both independent and government-sponsored, in Weimar Germany as a whole). The German pharmaceutical industry produced over 80 million condoms annually; the Berlin factory of Julius Fromm, which received the first condom patent in 1916, led the market with ever more sensation-sensitive and reliable prophylactics. Numerous members of the medical profession and a plethora of sex reform activists made frank talk about sexual technique and the alleviation of female frigidity a topic of nationwide concern. In addition, there was a massive insurgent movement, involving hundreds of thousands of Germans but centered primarily in Berlin, that demanded the decriminalization of abortion.

Finally, then, what was distinctive about the post-World War I years and what made it appear to be an era of revolution was the *openness* of public discussions about sex, the willingness of progressive activists and literati to challenge restrictive laws and social codes and the growing popular flaunting of those codes. And ultimately, it was precisely this openness and publicity around sex – most particularly with regard to the issues of contraception and abortion that were essential to women's sexual equality as well as the issue of publicly visible male and female homosexuality – that would provide fodder for the terrorizing backlash against the whole notion of individuals as having sexual rights that would become such a major feature of the sexual politics of German Nazism, Vichy France, and the fascist regimes of Italy and Spain (as well as, strikingly, of Stalin's reign in the Soviet Union). Hostility to contraception and abortion and to homosexuality (although in each case with distinctive national variations in the timing and force – and even the meanings – of the crackdowns) would become *the* distinctive markers of fascist sexual politics – and not least a particularly easy way for fascists to garner support from religious conservatives.

In retrospect, what is most notable about all of the notions of sexuality and sexual rights expressed by the small handful of pioneering sex reform activists in the 1920s and early 1930s – with the important exception of the eugenic impulse, which would finally, after a long post-fascist hiatus of ongoing contempt for the disabled, be subjected to fiercely eloquent moral criticism from the 1980s on – is that it would not be until the major and much larger sexual revolutions of the 1960s and 1970s that such notions would become cultural common sense in most Western European nations and serve as the basis for important progressive reformulations of sex-related law. For the rise of fascism brought an abrupt end to the pro-feminist and pro-homosexual elements of sex reform – even as the eugenic impulse that sex reform had also shared was taken in new and horrifyingly brutal directions.

Fascism: masculinism and reproduction

Male ambivalence about female sexual emancipation turns out to have been a surprisingly significant key to the rise of European fascist movements. In Italy, where fascism was born (in 1919) and where a fascist movement first acquired the reins of government, under the leadership of Benito Mussolini (in 1922), connections between the ascendancy of the political Right and attempts to restore masculine sexual predominance were especially clear. Central were efforts to restore a masculinity believed to have been undermined by the triple trauma of widespread bloodshed in World War I, by the displacements and injustices of capitalist economies (a concern that would become especially acute after the Great Depression of 1929), and by the transformation of gender roles and the growing sexual, emotional, and economic independence of women.

For self-maintenance, fascisms rely not only on brute suppression of political dissent, censorship, and the dismantling of parliamentary democracy, but also on charismatic leadership and relentlessly repetitive propaganda. In the case of Italy, Mussolini both sought to be the model of the new heroic Superman and inundated Italian men with injunctions to develop a dynamic, athletic, and bellicose masculinity. Italian men were taught to worry that they had been emasculated under the impact of women's emancipation, and Italian fascism claimed explicitly that it could provide therapies for male insecurity and restore masculine privilege. In the words of a contemporary, writing in the journal *Il Selvaggio* in 1924: "It is a question . . . of giving back to all classes of Italian society a sense of force, virility and willfulness. It is a question of defending the warrior tradition of our race: to make Italian males, considered by foreigners as pasta eaters, mandolin players, etc. into men." This made the onset of a new war an exciting prospect. As another writer of the era effused, "war is something sublime . . . the brutal discriminator that distinguishes man from man": on the one side, "the effeminate, the cry-babies, the mommy's boys; on the other . . . the hot-blooded heroes."[6] The idea was to remake (male) human nature, to create a new type of man.

What did this mean for women? It was not so easy to turn a typical Italian man, whether a peasant or a "pathetic little petit-bourgeois office worker, perhaps a bit chubby," into the ideal "fascist male." Thus, "to lend some verisimilitude to this virile image," a contrast was needed: "a modest and submissive wife, who at least by her behavior in public and social role would confirm that fragile superiority."[7] Yet submissiveness alone was not enough. High fertility was also essential. The demographic campaign pioneered in Italy from the late 1920s onward insisted on a neopatriarchal restoration: Women were to be driven out of the world of work and independence of any kind, while *repeated* impregnation of the wife was understood – with astonishing explicitness – as a man's best revenge against modernity. Men had been demoralized by the loss of authority when a wife worked outside the home (working the fields was considered an acceptable exception; working in a store or office was a problem). "Women's work," Mussolini announced, "distracts from procreation" and "foments independence." It would be better for a family to lose the additional income. The journalist Umberto Notari warned that "man must decide. If he wants the woman to be fertile, in the Biblical sense and according to the commands of the Race and the Nation, he alone must assume, by himself, all the responsibilities of their common sustenance."[8] Notari took most offense at the new modern woman who was neither a robust mother nor an old-fashioned femme fatale, but rather a slender and attractive office worker, uninterested in having more than one or two children, and inadequately respectful of her husband.

This context of widespread anxiety about the decline of male predominance also helps to explain why the fascisms of the 1920s–1940s characteristically, and indicatively, tended to criminalize contraception and to intensify the suppression of women's access to abortion as well as male homosexuality. Women's inability to control their own reproductive life-choices made them dependent and vulnerable by definition; declining birthrates had been interpreted, in every nation, as a weakening of the nation's strength. And homosexuality among men was perceived as a

---

[6] Mino Maccari and Mario Carli quoted in Sandro Bellassai, "The Masculine Mystique: Anti-Modernism and Virility in Fascist Italy," *Journal of Modern Italian Studies* 10 (2005), 317, 331.

[7] Chiara Saraceno, "Costruzione della maternità e della paternità" in Angelo Del Boca, Massimo Legnani, and Mario G. Rossi (eds.), *Il regime fascista: storia e storiografia* (Rome and Bari: Laterza, 1995), 482.

[8] Mussolini and Notari quoted in Bellassai, "The Masculine Mystique," 328–9.

dangerous degeneracy. Yet the backlash against individual sexual rights that would come to define fascist sexual politics did not emerge overnight, but rather had older origins, and played out differently in each national context. The post-World War I anxiety about depopulation that explains the intensified prosecution of contraception and abortion in many European nations, like the discomfort with the increasing publicity surrounding homosexuality, also had a far broader political base than fascism per se. This had the counterintuitive consequence that the exacerbated prosecutions initiated by fascist and collaborationist regimes could initially seem like not necessarily such a radical departure from prior trends and could count also on wide popular support.

Vichy France and Franco's Spain

In France, the law of 1920, which had passed almost unanimously, criminalized the sale of contraceptives as well as "propaganda" on behalf of contraception, and also made abortion an imprisonable offense with a minimum sentence of six months. In 1942, under Marshal Philippe Pétain's Vichy government, a far harsher new law allowed abortionists to be tried before the Tribunal d'État. Abortion became a crime against the state, and could incur the death penalty. In addition, also in 1942, and despite the fact that consensual homosexual acts had been decriminalized in France since the French Revolution, Pétain's government reintroduced the long-disappeared category of "unnatural acts" and acted on longstanding requests of the Parisian police and the French naval authorities in moving to criminalize sexual acts between an adult over 21 and an individual of the same sex under the age of 21. What had concerned the Navy leadership as well as the police was the widespread phenomenon of young sailors in their teens and early twenties making easy money prostituting themselves to sex tourists in port cities and Paris alike. The ascent of Pétain, in short, permitted police and military authorities finally to intervene in a situation that had frustrated them for quite some time. It was not so much that there was quantitatively more homosexual activity after World War I than before as rather that it was becoming a more inescapably conspicuous part of the urban streetscape. Again, then, the issue was public visibility.

In Spain, by contrast, the liberal moment arrived only in the early 1930s – just as right-wing countermovements were already taking shape in France and Germany. Anarchists were part of the government of the Second Spanish Republic formed in 1931 and they sought to put their views on female sexual self-determination, but also on the need for improved prenatal, maternal, and infant care, into policy and practice. In the anarchist-ruled region of Catalonia, abortion had been legalized in 1936, for "therapeutic, eugenic, or ethical reasons." At the national level, too, the Republican government formed in 1936 – with anarchist feminist Federica Montseny as the new Minister of Health – implemented a similar abortion policy, while also inaugurating new hospitals and services for maternity and pediatrics. All of this would come to an abrupt end with the crushing of the Republic and the triumph of Francisco Franco in 1939.

Franco's government was alarmed at the decline of the birthrate (from 33.8 per thousand in 1900 to 28.2 per thousand in 1930) and convinced that abortion and the "leprosy" of contraception were the cause. The government was especially eager to garner the support of the Catholic church and generally hostile to all the increasing freedoms acquired by women in the years of the Republic (including the right to divorce and the greater tendency to work outside the home). In 1941 the government not only made all sale or advertisement of contraception illegal but also declared abortion a crime against the state. The government actively mobilized doctors to turn in all cases of suspected abortion that came to their attention, and set high prison terms (in some cases over ten years) on those who performed or abetted abortions. Yet certainly popular mores and practices remained at variance with government policy, and women, not least because of the shame traditionally attached to active female sexuality and the desire to avoid dishonor in cases of extramarital pregnancy but also because of the suppression of contraception, continued to seek and find illegal abortions. By some estimates there continued to be hundreds of thousands of illegal abortions a year, of which hundreds of cases were brought before the Supreme Court and were punished severely.

Homosexuality was, at least initially, handled with less harshness. As in France, same-sex acts had simply not been mentioned in the Spanish criminal code. Some scholars have speculated that homosexuality was perceived as less of a threat because in traditional Spanish culture the figure of the *marica*, or effeminate passive homosexual male, was an object more of humor or pity than of hatred, someone who could service a macho heterosexual man, the *hombre de verdad*, or real man – typically married, and with children – without denting that man's self-concept. Yet while that may well be a generalizing cliché rather than a genuine insight, there is no question that openly defiant homosexuality had been far less of a presence in 1920s–1930s Spanish culture than it was in interwar Germany, France, or Britain. There had been isolated efforts to reform attitudes toward homosexuality in the 1920s and the slightly greater openness of homosexual lives and literary production that had briefly been possible during the liberal window of the years of the Republic was definitively shut with Franco's victory in 1939. Yet while as early as the onset of the Spanish civil war in 1936, the leading general and close friend of Franco's Gonzalo Queipo de Llano let it be known in a radio address that "every fairy or pervert that brings any kind of shame to this movement should, I say to you, be killed like a dog," it would in fact not be until the 1970s that the Franco regime explicitly criminalized male homosexuality and sent men accused of same-sex acts to reeducation camps.[9]

Ambiguities of Italian fascism

As Mussolini continued to consolidate power, the sale of contraceptive devices was criminalized in 1926, and, subsequently, the Rocco Code of 1930–31 prescribed heavy jail penalties for abetting, procuring, and performing abortions. But fascism could also be perceived as modernizing; it had a double edge. It is difficult nowadays to imagine under what conditions women in the 1930s in the most rural areas gave birth – often in squalor, on hay or rags, with only a midwife or "handywoman" to assist. Mussolini's government both sought to upgrade professionally the skills and services provided by midwives and attempted to draw midwives into the work of reporting "miscarriages" – as well as to give free rein to the police to monitor midwives closely (since many also provided abortions). The police carefully tracked regional and local variations in birthrates in order to ascertain whether abortion was being heavily used in a particular area. And yet all through, while the pro-natalist campaign ended up producing far less than the hoped-for results, the promises of restored patriarchalism and martial masculinity that accompanied it were received with enormous enthusiasm and functioned as important factors in social integration and support for fascism. Although many rural peasant women, like their more "modern" middle-class urban counterparts, sought ways to control their fertility (that is, couples continued to rely on coitus interruptus, and women continued to seek abortions), they shared the views of men of their class that large families were a sign of strength. Often, then, these women were both proud that they had more children than the "decadent," "skinny," and "sterile" professional women who restricted their fertility to just one or two children if any at all, and at the same time resented their poverty and the regime's inadequate support.

Under Mussolini, male homosexuality also began to be aggressively prosecuted and punished. Although the commission formulating the Rocco Code initially proposed adding an article criminalizing same-sex

---

[9] Queipo de Llano quoted in Werner Altmann, "Zwischen Diktatur und Demokratie. Homosexuelle Emanzipation in Spanien nach Francos Tod," *Invertito* 4 (2002), 150.

activities between men (these had not been previously criminalized in Italy – as in France and Spain, the law had simply made no mention of them), the article was removed from the final version of the code as jurists worried that outside observers might think same-sex vice was on the rise in Italy. Silence was thought preferable. Still, the Italian police had broad jurisdiction in surveillance and incarceration of men deemed gender deviants or caught engaging in homosexual activity, and they kept a close watch on cafés, dance halls, and resort towns where homosexual men gathered. Homosexuals were seen as undermining Mussolini's intended anthropological revolution and doing damage to the Italian "race" or "stock."

Between 1926, when new police prerogatives were introduced, and 1943, when Italian fascism was defeated, several thousand men (the exact numbers will never be known) were incarcerated for homosexuality in penal colonies – both in those designed for common criminals (*confino commune*) and in those designated for political opponents of the regime (*confino politico*) – as well as in local jails. Arrests did not require evidence and the accused were not provided with any opportunity for defense. Policemen's decisions were driven by their own prejudices especially against effeminate men, but also against those taking the "passive" position in sex, as well as by beliefs that homosexuals were intrinsically criminal, given to prostitution and extortion. But despite the lack of formal criminalization, outside observers knew homosexual men were being targeted. In a revealing remark, a conservative French politician declared in 1933 his admiration for Nazi Germany and fascist Italy in tandem: "Far be it from me to want to turn to fascism either today or tomorrow... but all the same, we have to agree that in some things those regimes have sometimes done good... One day Hitler and Mussolini woke up and said, 'Honestly, the scandal has gone on long enough; the streets are dirty and smell bad; we need a radical cleansing'... The inverts... were chased out of Germany and Italy the very next day."[10]

The repressive reorganization of sexual politics in fascist Italy, or in Pétain's France or Franco's Spain, however, ultimately in no way compared with the grotesque extremity of Nazi Germany. No regime before or since did so much to intervene violently in the bodies and intimate relationships of its citizens, and of citizens of all the conquered and occupied and collaborating nations – while at the same time promising rapturous enjoyment and the right to break taboos to its own followers. The crucial

[10] Lionel Nastorp in 1933 quoted in Michael Sibalis, "Homophobia, Vichy France and the 'Crime of Homosexuality': The Origins of the Ordinance of 6 August 1942," *GLQ: A Journal of Gay and Lesbian Studies* 8 (2002), 307.

point to grasp about Nazi sexual politics is the way that it combined subjugation with disinhibition.

Nazism: human engineering and the promise of pleasure

Far from being a trivial side matter, the reorganization of sexuality was at the heart of the Nazi project. During the late years of Weimar, malicious sexual innuendo was a vital element of Nazi anti-Semitism and the mobilization of popular animus against Jews – as well as a key factor in the early support of the Christian churches for the Nazi regime. While not all of the sex reform and sex rights activists in Weimar Germany were Jewish, many were, and their leadership in the campaigns against Paragraph 175, which criminalized homosexual acts between men, and Paragraph 218, which criminalized abortion, made them easy targets. And as the years of the Third Reich unfolded, there were countless sexually repressive and cruel phenomena, some directed by the regime, others spontaneously invented by its supporters and beneficiaries: from the forced sterilization of proletarian women whose purported promiscuity was taken as a sign of mental deficiency to the hounding, torture, and murder of homosexual men (numbers of whom came to the attention of the law because they were denounced by neighbors or co-workers), from the aggressive prosecution of Jewish–gentile sex in the so-called "race defilement" trials to the monstrous reproductive experiments and sexual sadism practiced on Jewish and other prisoners in the concentration camps and death factories.

Yet in the end, none of these horrific facts justifies the conclusion that the Third Reich was repressive for everyone. For avowedly heterosexual, non-disabled non-Jews – i.e. the majority of the population – Nazi policy and practice turned out to be anything but sexually repressive. Certainly, there was under Nazism a cacophony of conflicting injunctions, and throughout the Third Reich a wealth of regime-endorsed writings advanced the arguments that racial purity and national recovery depended on premarital chastity, monogamous and prolifically procreative marriage, and wholesome family life. Traditionalist constituencies could always find texts that reflected their concerns and that described Weimar as a "Jews' republic" and a hothouse of decadence and promiscuity, a time of the most "vulgar stimulation of steamy, debauched eroticism."[11] But the overall goal of Nazi sexual politics was not so much to suppress sexuality. Rather, the aim was to reinvent it as an "Aryan"

[11] Georg Schliebe, "Die Reifezeit und ihre Erziehungsprobleme" in Martin Löpelmann (ed.), *Wege und Ziele der Kindererziehung unserer Zeit*, 3rd edn (Leipzig: Hesse und Becker, 1936), 148.

(a)

Figs. 2.6a and 2.6b "Shameless Business" versus "Beautiful and Pure." The Nazi SS journal *Das schwarze Korps* in 1938 deliberately contrasted what it considered the dirty "Jewish" sensuality of the Weimar era and its cabaret culture (including an image of the African American dancer Josephine Baker) with what it deemed the healthy and attractive nudity promoted by Nazism.

(b)

Fig. 2.6 (*cont.*)

privilege – all the while claiming to be "cleaning up" sexual morality in Germany and overcoming the "Jewish" legacy of Weimar.

While racism of any kind has necessarily always been also about sex, this was especially true for National Socialism. The Third Reich was an immense venture in reproductive engineering. This was powerfully apparent in the vigor with which Nazis pursued the project not only of encouraging and enforcing the reproduction of those prized as "healthy" (through financial incentives, propagandistic enticements, and restrictions on contraception and abortion) but also, and crucially, of prohibiting (through sterilization, involuntary abortion, and, eventually, mass murder) the reproduction of those deemed "undesirable." The Reich Office for Combating Abortion and Homosexuality was created in 1936, the sale of all contraceptives aside from condoms was outlawed in 1941, and the penalties on abortion providers were expanded in 1943 to include the death penalty. Yet the other side of the coin of abortion rights denied to the majority of German women was the coercive abortions violently imposed on women deemed likely to have "hereditarily diseased offspring," Jewish and Sinti and Roma women as well as forced laborers brought into the Reich. In addition, there was throughout in Nazism a strong impulse to penetrate the mysteries of the human organism, a ferocious "will to know" about the functioning of psyches and bodies that also, over and over again, crossed the border into violence. Some of the patients in their regular practices and the inmates of prisons and camps provided medical doctors with human "material" for an array of invasive investigations into sexual variability, desire and response, drive and dysfunction. No less significant were efforts to pursue fantasies of selective breeding with cooperative volunteers – including via artificial insemination but also through voluntary coupling – or to determine whether hormonal supplementation during pregnancy could affect the gender of the fetus.

The Nazi regime displayed as well a manifest effort to manipulate – in quite sophisticated ways – the range of (so often profoundly conflicting) psychological and physiological reactions that sexuality can evoke: arousal and anxiety, attachment and repulsion, ennui or envy as well as ecstasy. Nazism, after all, came to power in 1933 at a time of competing tendencies toward ongoing liberalization, on the one hand, and, on the other, fierce backlash and demands for renewed restraint. The stimulation of contradictory affects and sensations was used both to bind people to the regime and to mobilize anti-Semitic and other forms of racist and eugenic sentiment, including discomfort and revulsion at the disabled. For instance, when the Nazis launched their campaign to sterilize the disabled (ultimately between 300,000 and 400,000 individuals were sterilized against their will), they accompanied this campaign with strategic arguments that included flattery of the sensual sex appeal of women who produced "healthy" children.

Moreover, integral to the effectiveness of these emotional strategies was the special usefulness of sexual politics as a device for reworking moral languages. Not only did Nazis both attack Christian values and, simultaneously, appropriate them for their own purposes, speaking constantly of the "sanctity" of racial purity, the "salvation" of Germany, and "guilt" and "sin" against the race or the *Volk*. They also drew on profound (and strongly church-fostered) associations between sex and evil – and between sex and Jews – to make the early systematic disenfranchisement of Jews appear morally legitimate. The initial hearty support of both the Catholic and Protestant churches for Nazism was based on the (as it turned out, false) presumption that the Nazis would purify German sexual mores and reinstitute respect for family values.

Church leaders energetically supported the Nazis. They especially welcomed early Nazi actions to shut down brothels, gay and lesbian bars, and nudist organizations, and to scour city streets of pornography. Thus Protestant activists could gush over how "Overnight things got different in Germany. All smut and trash disappeared from public view. The streets of our cities became clean again," while a Catholic paper could effuse about these "sharp measures against different forms of public immorality" and declare that "we stand behind the efforts of the government 100 percent."[12] Pius XI himself was "warmly" impressed with the "resolution and purposefulness" which the new regime was demonstrating in the battle against pornography: "The Vatican welcomes the struggle of National Germany against obscene material."[13] Within Germany, many clergymen shared the view that Jews were somehow responsible for the sexual immorality that purportedly pervaded Weimar culture. They praised Hitler as a "marvelous gift from God" and celebrated the Nazis' rise to power as a "miracle." The "immense power of international Jewry" was deemed a "frightening" threat, while Hitler was providential: "It is absolutely certain that God sent us this man and through him protected us from a great danger."[14]

---

[12] Adolf Sellmann quoted in Hans-Georg Stümke, *Homosexuelle in Deutschland* (Munich: Beck, 1989), 92; *Kirche im Volk: Monatsschrift für die katholische Pfarrgemeinde*, January 1934, 31.

[13] *Deutsche Allgemeine Zeitung*, April 6, 1933.

[14] Quoted in Hartmut Lehmann, "Hitlers protestantische Wähler" in *Protestantische Weltsichten: Transformationen seit dem 17. Jahrhundert* (Göttingen: Vandenhoeck und Ruprecht, 1998), 136–9.

However, within just two to three years, Christian spokespersons found reasons to feel disillusionment over the Third Reich's sexual politics. Far from being afraid to criticize the government, they openly assailed the regime's apparent intention to reintroduce the very "culture of naked-ness" it had claimed it would abolish. In reaction, pro-sex Nazi commen-tators directly attacked the Christian churches as they advanced their own particular brand of racist libertinism. They argued that "sexual activity is not sinful, it is sacred."[15] Pro-sex Nazis were just as anti-Semitic as sexually conservative Nazis, but they used anti-Semitic rhetoric as a way to distract attention from their own incitements to premarital and extra-marital sex.

And these incitements were many, as the regime became increasingly bold. By 1935 at the latest there was nothing particularly secret about what went on in some of the local chapters of the Hitler Youth and the Federation of German Girls – and while there were chapters in which, as contemporaries remember, premarital purity was maintained as a cherished aspiration, there were dozens of popular jokes and much earnest outrage about the prevalence of teen sex in others. The interna-tional press also reported that parents were frequently devastated by news of what went on in the Reich Labor Service, and the encour-agement to pair off for sexual encounters that young people received while away from home. By the early 1940s, the regime was so uncon-cerned with international opinion on these matters that it was openly publicizing its encouragement of marital infidelity as well, and not just for the elite. And again, the point of the officially endorsed extramar-ital sex was not only reproduction but also the pursuit of pleasure. At the same time, pro-Nazi doctors (putting themselves in the place, as it were, of the Jewish sex rights activists of Weimar who had been driven into exile or deported and murdered) lavished attention on the topic of improving marital sexual satisfaction. There was more detailed discussion of the best techniques for enhancing female orgasm under Nazism than there would be in the far more conservative decade of the 1950s.

The encouragement to cheerful heterosexual activity – both within and outside of marriage – for those racially approved by the regime was the other side of the coin of vicious, eventually lethal, homophobia. The crackdown happened in stages that varied by region and was often in response to popular enmity toward homosexuality. A big turning point came early, in 1934, when Hitler instigated the murder of his old friend

---

[15] Alfred Zeplin, *Sexualpädagogik als Grundlage des Familienglücks und des Volkswohls* (Rostock: Carl Hinstorffs, 1938), 24.

Ernst Röhm, the head of the SA (the "brown-shirts") and an open homo-sexual, and a few other political rivals, in order to gain the support of the army. Until that time, quite a few SA bars were well known also as homosexual bars, a significant number of right-wing homosexual men were attracted to the Nazi party, and there had been no perceived con-tradiction between right-wing politics and homosexual rights activism. All of that changed dramatically when the virulently homophobic Hein-rich Himmler, eventually head of the SS, the Gestapo, and of the entire concentration camp system, became, next to Hitler himself, the most powerful person in the Reich.

In 1935, the Nazis sharpened the existing law, Paragraph 175, which criminalized male (but not female) homosexuality, not only expand-ing it to include 175a, with its special provisions against seduction of minors and abuse of relations of dependency (like teacher–student, boss–employee, officer–soldier), but also widening the law's application. Pre-viously, only "intercourse-like" actions had been criminalized; as of 1935 not only mutual masturbation but even parallel individual masturbation and even "erotic" glances could fall under the law's purview. By 1937, prosecutions for homosexuality escalated considerably.

One thing that bothered Nazi homophobes about homosexuals was their purported refusal to live up to Nazi ideals of manliness; another was their purported refusal to reproduce. But just as important was a third factor: The Nazi leadership was tremendously anxious that *it* not be per-ceived as "queer," internationally or domestically. This anxiety was fed not only by the high-profile Röhm case and the well-known phenomenon of a "virilist" strand of homosexual rights activism compatible with right-wing politics, along with a strong association in the popular mind between Nazism and homosexuality (which was played up constantly by left-wing critics of the Nazis both within Germany and in exile). It was spurred also by the way the prevalence of same-sex Nazi institutions like the Hitler Youth, the SS, and the army inevitably fostered popular speculation that homoerotic activity was a constant tempting possibility – and hence the regime sought over and over brutally to prove Nazism's straightness. In addition, the same fear evident also in other nations that the incidence of homosexuality was actually spreading in the wake of World War I – as though homosexuality was contagious – rather than merely becoming less furtively hidden and more frequently adopted as part of an openly claimed identity rather than an activity occasionally engaged in, fueled the regime's worry that consistent heterosexuality was all too often an only fragile achievement.

By the end of the war approximately 100,000 men had been prosecuted for same-sex activities. Close to half (between 46,000 and 50,000) had been convicted and usually sent to prisons or penitentiaries, or to concentration camps where they were made to do impossibly hard labor in rock quarries and often tortured, treated as among the most despicable of the prisoners, and at Buchenwald subjected to medical experiments and at other camps forced intercourse with female prostitutes. Several hundred were castrated. And although the majority – perhaps 70 percent – survived these torments, only often to be drafted into the *Wehrmacht*, it is estimated that somewhere between 5,000 and 10,000 died. The killing fields included not only concentration camps and prisons but also mental institutions and *Wehrmacht* cannon fodder units in suicide missions.

Intensified prosecution of men caught in same-sex acts was also extended to lands occupied by the *Wehrmacht* in the course of World War II, including parts of Belgium and the parts of France under direct German occupation, as well as both annexed and occupied Poland, and annexed portions of Czechoslovakia. In the Nazi-occupied Netherlands the law in place since 1911, Paragraph 248bis, which resembled the law of Vichy France in criminalizing sexual acts engaged in by an adult over 21 with a person of the same sex under 21, was retained, while an additional decree, 81/1940, prohibited also consensual adult homosexuality – although prosecutions did not grow dramatically. In Nazi-annexed Austria, however, the technically gender-neutral language of the inherited law maintained by the Nazis criminalized not only male homosexuality but also lesbianism, and men and women were both aggressively prosecuted under the auspices of the Austrian criminal code Paragraph 129. In 1940, the Nazis expanded the Austrian Paragraph 129, parallel to their earlier expansion of the German Paragraph 175, to incorporate also fleeting touches.

In short, the distinctive innovation of Nazi sexual politics was the attempt to harness the popular groundswell of growing preoccupation with sex and liberalization of heterosexual mores to a racist and homophobic agenda. Thus, while Nazism was the ultimate example of fascist sexual politics in its aggressive suppression of both abortion and homosexuality, it differed from all other fascisms in its overtly expressed hostility to traditional Christian sexual mores. None of the other fascisms would contain the ribald, decisively pro-sex and distinctively anti-church impulses that Nazism so clearly did. (In the meantime, Joseph Stalin's sexual politics as well turned out to be more conservative than Adolf Hitler's. The Soviet Union's own particular variant of intensified homophobic persecution was justified not as an emulation of the murderous homophobia implemented by Nazism but rather as a contrast to the homoeroticism insinuated to be at the heart of Nazism; communist propaganda referred to homosexuality as "fascist perversion.") The other three – largely Catholic – western European fascist regimes of Italy, Vichy France, and Spain, like the right-wing dictatorship that António de Oliveira Salazar created after his coup d'état in Portugal, were far more concerned than the Nazis ever were to reinforce rather than to challenge Catholic church teachings on sex and reproduction (also in Salazar's Portugal abortion and homosexuality would be suppressed). Mussolini may have started out with anticlerical impulses – and he continued to have extramarital affairs – but he wanted the Catholic church's support, not its enmity. The uniqueness of the German situation, and especially the fierce contest that raged in the course of the Third Reich between the Christian churches and the Nazis over sexual values and practices, would eventually emerge as an especially important determining factor in the evolution of sexual politics in Europe after the Nazis were defeated in 1945 – and the churches gained renewed prestige under the auspices of the American occupiers in particular.

Democratic welfare states: liberality and ambivalence

While nations with right-wing regimes escalated the prosecution of both homosexuality and abortion, and as Stalin's Soviet Union too recriminalized homosexuality in 1933 and then also, expressly in hopes of increasing the birthrate, recriminalized abortion in 1936, democratic nations showed more contradictory pictures. Great Britain maintained its criminalization of male homosexuality (in fact, the interwar era saw heightened prosecution) and – while lifting restrictions on the distribution of contraceptive information in 1930 – only ever so slightly loosened restrictions on access to abortion in 1929, with an additional modification in 1939. Democratic Switzerland offered the opposite trajectories: criminalizing abortion while decriminalizing consensual adult homosexuality. But the democratic nations of Denmark and Sweden moved their sexual politics toward greater liberality. As it turned out, the Scandinavian developments were unique.

In Britain, the Infant Life Preservation Act of 1929 actually created a new crime: the killing of a viable fetus (after twenty-eight weeks' gestation), but it did make an exception in cases where the woman's life was at risk. After strenuous campaigning by women's rights activists involved in the Abortion Law Reform Association (founded 1936) and a government-sponsored investigative report on the shocking extent of maternal mortality due to self-induced abortions (published 1937), the issue was brought to a head by physician Aleck Bourne, at that point one of Britain's most renowned gynecologists and in 1938–39 president of the Ob-Gyn section of the Royal Society of Medicine. (Among other things, the government report had found that fully one third of maternal deaths in Scotland in the 1930s were due to septic abortion.) Although married women who were already mothers sought the vast majority of abortions at that time, the case chosen to challenge the law concerned a minor who was a victim of gang rape. In 1938, at the encouragement of women's rights activists, Bourne deliberately invited prosecution by performing an illegal abortion on a 14-year-old girl who had been assaulted and raped by five soldiers. (One doctor had already refused to perform an abortion, despite the parents' pleas, saying that since the girl had been "raped by officers, she might be carrying a future prime minister of England.")[16] Bourne wrote openly to the Attorney General of his intentions. He was charged and pleaded not guilty, arguing that he had provided the termination in order to save the girl from "mental collapse." Bourne's acquittal in 1939 created a case precedent which permitted mental health considerations to be taken into account when doctors decided whether carrying a pregnancy to term would be a threat to a woman's health. But the law itself did not change, and women seeking abortions and the doctors they turned to both remained vulnerable to prosecution. (Bourne himself would later join an anti-abortion organization; he did not believe in abortion rights except in extreme circumstances.)

The contrast between Britain and the Scandinavian countries was stark. In 1930, Denmark – which had a large illegal abortion industry, with medical doctors providing the service off the books – officially reduced the prison sentences for providing illegal abortions from eight years to two, while police also seldom prosecuted the women seeking the abortions. In 1932, a Danish government-appointed commission of medical experts, lawyers, and politicians was formed to consider possible changes in the law. Not least on the grounds that the law was being ignored, the commission recommended that abortion be officially legalized on the basis of four possible "indications": medical (danger to the woman's life or health); ethical (rape or incest); eugenic (the possibility of fetal anomalies); and social (designating those situations in which having the baby would be a social or economic burden on the woman). Ultimately, the law passed in 1939 recognized only the first three of these indications. Yet the medical indication could be – and was – "stretched" by some doctors to include the negative impact on the woman's physical and mental health of socio-economic stress. In the interim, Iceland (since 1918 its own sovereign nation but still part of the Danish kingdom) had

---

[16] Summary of the doctor's views in Wendy Holden, *Unlawful Carnal Knowledge: Irish Abortion Case that Shocked the World and Changed the Law* (New York: HarperCollins, 1994).

in 1935 permitted legal abortions under some limited circumstances. And in 1938, Sweden became the first western nation (and the second nation in the world after the Soviet Union in 1920) significantly to liberalize its abortion law (recognizing the first three indications, as well as a fourth category, referred to as "worn-out mothers"). In 1946, the Swedish law would be liberalized yet further, when an additional indication was formally added for any cases in which carrying a pregnancy to term could potentially cause impairment of the woman's physical or emotional well-being.

Denmark also moved to decriminalize homosexuality as early as in 1933. Sweden would eventually follow suit in 1944. The Danish and Swedish cases both, but in different ways, exemplified the complexity of the relationship between the emergence of "modern" notions of homosexuality, transnational flows of ideas, and the shifting contours of national legal systems.

In the early twentieth century, in reaction to conservative politicians' discovery of the phenomenon of homosexual prostitution in Copenhagen, the Danish government in 1905 had promulgated a statute making male homosexual prostitution illegal. The years that followed saw a major scandal over roundups and trials of men accused of homosexuality, sensational press coverage, flights into exile, including to the USA – and also suicides. Danish homosexuals (experts estimated they numbered "several thousands"), as well as their outraged detractors, looked to Germany, and especially Berlin, where Magnus Hirschfeld was promoting ideas of homosexuality as innate rather than acquired as grounds for decriminalization. In the wake of a number of imprisonments for sodomy in 1907, professional debates recommenced, and medical experts and lawyers, basing themselves specifically on the argument that homosexuality was congenital and thus a medical and not a criminal matter, argued for legalization – and in 1912 the government's Royal Commission on a New Criminal Code concurred and a government bill decriminalized both same-sex acts and bestiality. However, it would not be until 1933 that the new code was fully put into effect; a similar code was adopted in Iceland in 1940. Moreover, and strikingly, in a pattern that resembled the developments in other nations but with an additional time lag, while the first Danish novel alluding to (chaste and tragic) male homosexual love, Christian Houmark's *For Guds Aasyn* (In the Eye of God), appeared in 1910, it would not be until 1941 that the first lesbian novel, *Et Vildskud* (Strange Friends), was published (under the pseudonym Agnete Holk).

Interestingly, Sweden was perceived as a less liberal nation. When the Swedish homosexual rights activist Eric Thorsell wrote in 1932 to the

Swedish physician Torsten Amundson (who lived with his male lover most of his adult life – though his lover was also his secretary and this may have been successful enough as a cover story) about how best to pursue the decriminalization of homosexuality in Sweden, and how best to draw on the expertise developed by Magnus Hirschfeld in Germany (whom Amundson also knew), Amundson responded:

> I have always maintained, and pointed out for the *Sanitätsrat* [Hirschfeld] as well, my opinion that it would be best if no propaganda were made in Sweden, since the Swedes resemble the English in their hypocrisy regarding this matter, and that I hoped that a law reform as in Denmark or Norway would be more easily brought about if agitation did not influence the general public to, as would seem likely, thwart a successful reform in every possible way.[17]

(Norway's law looked harsh, but in practice things there were better. While in the new Norwegian Penal Code of 1905 the ban on same-sex sexual acts had been retained, a provision had additionally been introduced which said that same-sex acts could be prosecuted solely "when general conditions so demand," and practically, that meant that the law was almost never applied to consenting adults, but only in cases in which a minor was involved.) Thorsell was thus on his own in the Swedish context and, undeterred, he spent several months in Berlin at Hirschfeld's Institute for Sexual Science. Back home, in 1933, he gave one of the first public talks ever given on homosexuality in Sweden, under the title: "Are Homosexuals Criminals with No Rights?" Amundson's skepticism about his countrymen turned out to be both wrong and right. By the mid-to-late 1930s, the transnationally networked sex reform movement – with its very specific ideas about gender equality, abortion, contraception, and tolerance for varieties in sexual orientation – had developed a good working relationship with the Social Democratic government of Sweden (in power since 1932), and in 1944 the country did finally move to decriminalize homosexuality.

Yet there were considerable ambiguities and complexities in the evolution of discussions in Sweden in the course of the 1930s. Thus, for instance, while in 1932 leading scholars had advocated decriminalization not least on the grounds that homosexuals were so frequently victimized by blackmailers – often aggressive gangs of young male prostitutes – already by the later 1930s the boys were themselves conceived as the victims who needed protection from male homosexuals. Thus, and tellingly, when the 1944 Swedish law finally decriminalized

---

[17] Amundson to Thorsell, quoted in Jens Rydström, *Sinners and Citizens: Bestiality and Homosexuality in Sweden, 1880–1950* (University of Chicago Press, 2003), 52.

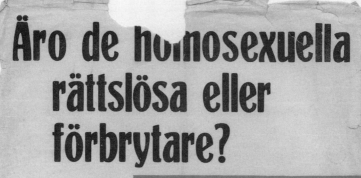

Fig. 2.7 "Are Homosexuals Criminals with No Rights?" Poster for a talk given in 1933 by the Swedish homosexual rights activist Eric Thorsell. Thorsell was inspired by Magnus Hirschfeld. While Hirschfeld was driven into exile and homosexuals were brutally persecuted and murdered in Nazi Germany, the sex reform movement in Sweden succeeded in getting homosexuality decriminalized in 1944.

consensual adult homosexuality, it also ensconced in law elaborate provisions for punishing same-sex acts with "minors" (including not just those between the ages of 15 and 18 but also those between 18 and 21 if the act involved taking advantage of their "inexperience or dependent position"). But there was a clear homophobic element in this decision, not just a concern to restrict youth sexuality in general. As in Denmark, the age of consent for homosexual acts was set higher than that for heterosexual acts. Although more comparative research is needed, the 1930s–1940s do appear to be a moment when, in countries with starkly divergent legal frameworks, sexual orientation was being reconceptualized as highly vulnerable in the teen years, and the older concept of the "knowing" teen was giving way to a more protectionist outlook.

Furthermore, developments among homosexual men and lesbian women were drawn into greater parallelism than they might have been without the publicity and legal disputes. In Sweden, as in so many other countries, the British lesbian novel by Radclyffe Hall, *The Well of Loneliness* – translated into Swedish in 1932 – shaped the self-perception of women who discovered that they loved and desired women. The many letters received by Elise Ottesen-Jensen at the RFSU throughout the 1930s and 1940s make clear not only how lonely and isolated many same-sex-loving women continued to feel, but also how greatly they struggled to make sense of their own feelings and confusions – and worries about what had caused their homosexuality and whether in fact it was innate – in the midst of the shifting matrices of discursive knowledge about homosexuality that were being created in the debates over the nature and rights of homosexual men. For example, a Swedish woman writing to Ottesen-Jensen in 1935 acknowledged that she loved women but also suffered from that, and begged for "Mrs. Jensen" to "write to me and give me an acknowledgment that I cannot help it by myself." Ottesen-Jensen met with her and advised her to read *The Well of Loneliness*, and the woman said about the book: "Here I recognize myself." She had lost one woman to a man, but now had a new possible friend, yet still sought advice about how best to "explain homosexuality" to the new lover. "It would be good for her to get to know something about this, but cautiously." Another young woman wrote to Ottesen-Jensen about how she felt she had a "male disposition," but no interest in men. When she had feelings about a girl, however, "it was as if my heart wanted to stop beating." And when the co-worker girl she was interested in accidentally touched her, "it is as if I get all dizzy."[18] Meanwhile, and although the lawmakers

[18]   Quoted in Rydström, *Sinners and Citizens*, 297–8.

certainly were clueless about lesbianism, they nonetheless did their part to shape lesbian self-understanding when they formulated the 1944 law in such a way that, for women too, consensual adult same-sex behavior was decriminalized while the age of consent for same-sex acts was again higher than the age of consent for heterosexual activity.

Different – albeit similarly complex – dynamics played out in the case of Switzerland. While anal intercourse had been criminalized in the German-language cantons but not the Romance-language speaking ones, in the context of a long process of coordinating the legal systems of the various cantons, Switzerland in 1942 finally decriminalized all homosexual acts between consenting adults in private. (At the same time, however, a new provision specifically criminalizing homosexual prostitution was introduced – a provision that would remain on the books until 1992.) Yet the relationship between the debates over sexual orientation in politically neutral Switzerland and its fascist neighboring nations remained complicated.

After the National Socialists took over in Germany and banned all homosexually oriented publications, those published in Switzerland were the only ones left in the world. But the editors felt they had to tread cautiously. As of 1932, for instance, the newly founded *Freundschafts-Banner*, the first openly pro-homosexual periodical in Switzerland, had been calling for self-outing of homosexual men even though it also from the start had recurrently reminded its readers to act respectably. But a year later, coinciding with the Nazis' ascent, the journal began constantly cautioning its constituency to make more of an effort not to give offense, to blend in, and to avoid openly lived homosexuality as well as any "effeminate" behavior. Secrecy and discretion were advised. This was not only a reaction to the rise of Nazism next door (although it is noteworthy as well that the Swiss border town of Basel became a haven for homosexual men fleeing the Nazis during World War II). It was also a response to a defamation campaign against homosexuals and their organizations led by the Swiss boulevard scandal paper, *Scheinwerfer* – and not least a desperate effort to avoid giving the lawmakers any potential excuse for keeping anti-homosexual legislation on the books. In 1934, the journal – which also attracted a lesbian readership (in the first decades of the twentieth century Switzerland was a magnet for women seeking university education, many of them feminists, and quite a few lesbian or bisexual) – was subjected to repeated legal harassment over both its personal ads section and its display at kiosks. (The personal ads were attacked under the legal premise that they constituted "pimping," i.e. solicitation for sex; the open sale was deemed to violate laws against public obscenity.) It would not be until the 1960s that the terms of discussion about homosexuality in Switzerland would change, and the apologetic tone be overcome.

Meanwhile, moreover, although the Swiss Penal Code formulated in 1937 and coming into force in 1942 decriminalized adult homosexuality, it expressly criminalized abortion, with stiff penalties (up to five years' imprisonment) for those performing abortions. The only exception granted was in cases of danger to the life or severe danger to the health of the woman. Nonetheless, the handling of the law varied by canton, and in some places doctors could be found who interpreted the concept of danger to health broadly to encompass also threats to mental health and/or socio-economic welfare.

Eugenics in democratic nations

State interventions into bodies and private lives in Scandinavia and Switzerland in the 1930s and 1940s were also infused with eugenic concepts. Sweden had an extensive program for sterilizing mental patients; under a law passed in 1934 and supported both by the Social Democratic government and by the Lutheran church, the sterilizations were technically "voluntary," though frequently not entirely freely chosen. More than 62,000 people would be sterilized from 1934 to 1975 – Sweden sterilized more people than any other European state aside from Nazi Germany. And although Denmark's and Norway's programs were smaller, they too practiced sterilizations.

Denmark passed the first castration law in the world, in 1929, as a component of its first sterilization law, and over the next forty years 1,012 men would be castrated (often on the grounds of a diagnosis as "sex offenders"). The only opposition to the sterilization law of 1929 came from a popular conservative clergyman within the parliament, Alfred Bindslev, who argued that eugenic science had not developed fully enough yet to be sure that correct decisions were being made, and he expressed his "instinctive aversion . . . toward this type of experiment, which interferes with the most secret riddles of life itself."[19] Nonetheless, the law passed and sterilizations commenced.

More than 90 percent of the individuals sterilized in Denmark between 1929 and 1934 had been deemed mentally handicapped. A new law concerning the mentally handicapped was passed in Denmark in 1934, which

---

[19] Bindslev quoted in Bent Sigurd Hansen, "Something Rotten in the State of Denmark: Eugenics and the Ascent of the Welfare State" in Gunnar Broberg and Nils Roll-Hansen (eds.), *Eugenics and the Welfare State: Sterilization Policy in Denmark, Sweden, Norway, and Finland* (East Lansing: Michigan State University Press, 1996), 38.

superseded the previous sterilization law (which in turn would be revised in 1935). Sterilizations of the mentally handicapped could now be undertaken without the individual's consent; the argument could either be that the individual was not capable of raising children, or that sterilization could facilitate release from confinement or placement in a less restrictive environment. But the law also permitted forcible confinement from the onset of puberty. More sterilizations occurred under this law than under the revised sterilization law; and more than twice as many women as men were sterilized.

In Switzerland, by contrast, sterilizations were more typically undertaken off than on the books. In the fifty years that the sole sterilization law (in the canton of Vaud) was in effect, "only" 187 sterilizations were carried out. In other cantons, where there was no law shaping the practice, clinics carried out many hundreds more – about half in cases in which a patient, most often female, had been diagnosed with "feeblemindedness," but often also in conjunction with an abortion (for which two medical doctors needed to provide endorsement assessments). Psychiatrists became the arbiters of female sexuality, as they presented women with the options of sterilization, workhouse, or a warning that poor relief would be withheld, or refused to permit an abortion or grant a marriage license unless a woman consented to "voluntary" sterilization. Alcoholism, social conspicuousness, inappropriate public comportment were all seen by professionals as signs of mental health problems that could warrant sterilization. Ironically, in the mixed-confessional country of Switzerland, in which both Protestant and Catholic churches were active in politics, it was the passionate ethical resistance of Catholic conservatives to putting eugenic notions formally into law that allowed medical experts to keep matters in their own hands – but also allowed Swiss eugenic practices to weather the pall cast on eugenics by Nazi abuses and thus to continue unchallenged for a long time into the post-World War II era as well.

Holocaust and World War II

Already World War I had shown war's intrinsically contradictory impact on sex, and World War II amplified those countervailing tendencies exponentially. On the one hand, there was unimaginable brutality and terror, a continent covered in blood, human beings set loose on each other like feral beasts, and a system of concentration, labor and death camps in which sadism, both banal and inventive, was routine. On the other, the war, through the theretofore unprecedented mobility of masses of peoples, not to mention an increasingly anarchic atmosphere, created enormous opportunities for exhilarating amorous experimentation and, even more frequently, countless occasions for sexual encounters that were more prosaic – consensual, but also, and above all, commercial or instrumental.

Violence soaked into the most intimate areas. The Nazis followed their sterilization program with a program for mass murder of the disabled. A month after Germany started World War II by attacking Poland, systematic murder of handicapped children began. Midwives, nurses and doctors were obliged to report all cases of mental and physical disability and parents were urged to turn children over to clinics in Germany and Austria (which were actually killing centers). Children were killed by lethal medication overdose or by starvation. Six killing centers for cognitively disabled and mentally ill adults (including those suffering from schizophrenia and epilepsy as well as those deemed criminally insane) were established as well. Grey buses took the victims to their deaths. Ultimately, and despite protests and resistance from the general public and clergymen and caregivers, over 5,000 German children and eventually more than 210,000 disabled and mentally ill individuals in total would be killed (70,000 of these at the six main killing facilities in 1940–41). An additional 80,000 patients of psychiatric facilities would be murdered in the occupied parts of Poland, France, and the Soviet Union.

The killing of the disabled and the Holocaust of European Jewry, as well as the mass murder of Roma and Sinti, were complexly intertwined, not only in the technology and personnel but also in the attitude toward "lives unworthy of life." And the perpetrators were hardly remorseful later. Nor were the doctors and nurses particularly miserable during the killing sprees. Sexual liaisons among the staff, wild parties with extensive alcohol consumption, and pilfering of victims' property were routine.

Scholarship on concentration camps in Germany and Austria also makes clear that the guards there routinely dated the young women in the local population. In some camps in Poland, wives and children of guards lived on the premises. At some of the death camps in Poland, prostitution was common around the camp – not least because the prostitutes could acquire goods stolen from the murdered victims. And in some camps which had both male and female staff, for instance at Ravensbrück and Auschwitz, there were affairs between guards. In general, the concentration and death camps provided cushy positions for guards – a way of avoiding the stresses of military service. The Catholic leftist journalist Eugen Kogon, who was imprisoned in Buchenwald, commented after the war on how "fond of promiscuity" and of "drinking and whoremongering" were the SS officers and guards working in that "paradise of shirkers," the concentration camp system.[20] But those were consensual relationships – the mundane continuities of daily life in wartime in areas not subjected to battle – and not to be compared to what else went on inside the camps, nor on the battlefields themselves.

Within the concentration camps, guards sometimes chose prisoners as sexual servants; in some cases the more powerful prisoners, the *Kapos* (frequently, though not always, those who had been criminals in the outside world), had other prisoners as sexual servants (generally of the same sex). Within ghettos and labor camps, sexual affairs – heterosexual or homosexual – could mean reprieve from deportation or selection. Within concentration camps, sex could be exchanged for a scrap of food or some needed object. In general, sex could mean survival.

There were also brothels – for non-Jewish prisoners only – established by Himmler within ten of the concentration camps. These were conceived as a spur to prisoner-worker productivity – and occasionally as a site for testing whether men imprisoned for homosexuality could perform heterosexually. The peepholes of the brothel rooms served as a focus for guard voyeurism and amusement. The women prisoners coerced to work in these brothels as sexual slaves received slightly better rations, but were usually murdered after a few months rather than released.

Sexual humiliation of prisoners by the guards was constant, sexualized torture frequent. Women entering Auschwitz – whether driven into "showers" and about to be killed or spared from immediate death and stripped and shaved and paraded for selections – were subjected to riding crops jabbed into breasts, ugly mocking commentary, defloration with fingers. Beatings and random killings were simply daily activities, but there was also a surfeit of terror that was specifically aimed at destroying the sexuality of the victims. The camps were laboratories in domination, and perpetrators clearly took pleasure in tormenting victims, or forcing them to abuse each other. Killing was not enough; the death of the soul was aimed at – and in the assault on their sexuality, the victims were targeted in their innermost selfhood.

And there is yet a further way to think about the sexualized violence within the camps. In the camps, the guards had total power, and they were frequently bored. They were eager to entertain each other – and competed with each other. When a mother at one of the killing centers in Poland was forced to watch while trained dogs violated her daughter; when, at Flossenbürg, a man accused of homosexuality had his testicles

[20] Eugen Kogon, *The Theory and Practice of Hell: The German Concentration Camps and the System Behind Them*, trans. Heinz Norden (New York: Berkley Medallion, 1968), 285–6.

pushed alternately into scalding and cold water and then was raped with a broomstick; or when, at Buchenwald, rope was tied around a prisoner's genitals and he was hung upside down from a door: The grotesquerie of the violence became an end in itself, part of an escalating competition of mutual performance and diversionary entertainment among the guards.

In addition, there was in the camps obscene intimate violence in the name of scientific inquiry. At Ravensbrück, Polish as well as Roma and Sinti women prisoners were subjected to "experiments" not only in bone grafting and injection of bacteria into the limbs (on the argument that the knowledge acquired could help in treating soldiers' wounds), but also injections into the uterus and fallopian tubes. At Auschwitz, survivor Olga Lengyel, a physician's assistant, describes the sterilization experiments carried out on both women and men – with X-rays and short-wave rays, surgeries, or caustic substances injected into the genitals – and notes that they were "cruel games rather than serious quests for truth": "Everyone has heard of heartless children who amuse themselves by tearing off the legs and wings of insects. Here there was one difference: the insects were human beings." At times, women sterilized with short-wave rays ("which caused unbearable pains in the lower part of the abdomen") would be cut open so doctors could observe the lesions. But also included in the "cruel games" was the demand that women whose bodies were already burned from extreme levels of X-ray radiation be forced to copulate, and that boys who had been sterilized were forcibly massaged on the prostate glands and masturbated with a metal instrument in order to determine the remaining extent of their ability to have an erection.[21]

Battlefields and occupied territories

The war on the Eastern front was a war of annihilation and it too was accompanied by extensive sexual violence. Despite directives officially prohibiting or restricting sexual contact between German men and "ethnically alien women" or women considered "racially inferior," the authorities found that *Wehrmacht* soldiers constantly ignored the rules against "undesirable sexual intercourse" – both with rapes and sexual enslavement and with consensual encounters and liaisons. In any event, the authorities were also convinced that regular heterosexual intercourse was beneficial for soldier morale and performance. In this contradictory situation – with racist assumptions in conflict with beliefs about masculinity – the military sought to provide brothels and to admonish

[21] Olga Lengyel, "Scientific Experiments" in Carol Rittner and John K. Roth (eds.), *Different Voices: Women and the Holocaust* (St. Paul, MN: Paragon Press, 1993), 120.

soldiers to be attentive to the "racial" qualities of women with whom they had contact. Military authorities literally assumed that when brothels were available – and they made sure both to rely on extant local brothels and to set up their own everywhere the German army went – there would be less "need" for men to rape. At the same time, the military leadership was continually concerned with preventing the spread of venereal disease (hence again the preference for brothels, where some kind of overview and disease control efforts could be maintained) as well as with preventing personalized intimacy and attachment with women of the local populations (so as to curtail the opportunities for enemy espionage and prevent any breakdown of the emotional boundaries between Germans and their enemies). And there was yet another concern: The leadership worried that out-of-control sexual violence could affect military discipline adversely.

Nonetheless, sexual violence was ubiquitous. It included mutilation of body parts – cutting off breasts, and letting women bleed to death. It included rapes followed by murders, and it included necrophiliac violation of women already killed. And it included gang rapes. (Gang rapes and other kinds of group sexual violence were also engaged in by local collaborators of various nationalities fighting in SS contingents.) Unlike in the camps, in which perpetrators were protected, the battlefields were dangerous territory, and the men were deeply dependent on each other in a hostile environment, and continually afraid for their own lives. Certainly the sexual brutalities terrorized the local populations and sent a message to the men of the enemy: *You cannot protect your own women.* But in addition there were the messages that the soldiers sent to each other – as well as to themselves. In sharing in horrific violence, they reaffirmed their bonds with one another (as well as the hierarchies that structured those bonds). While a few cases of rape and gang rape were brought to trial, convictions usually only resulted in cases where there was a concern for military discipline or the reputation of the *Wehrmacht*.

That the men had had contact with "women of alien races" rarely caused a stir. So too was it simply taken in stride that the vast majority of women either choosing to, or forced to, work in the hastily assembled and heavily trafficked brothels (the lines of soldiers waiting their turn at the lunch hour or in the evenings snaked down many a city street across Latvia, Russia, the Ukraine, and other Eastern lands) were not exactly "Aryan." Himmler himself had in 1942 formally approved of such intercourse between German men and Polish women, as long as the women were not Jewish, on the grounds that these encounters did not involve "personal attachment and reproduction." (There is a revealing and instructive parallel here with earlier shifts in fascist Italian sexual politics in the course of the war in Ethiopia in 1937. While previously, Ethiopian women had been eroticized and their charms and appeal for Italian men described in the most glowing terms – the right to conquer these exotic beauties was dangled as one of the benefits of participating in the imperial project in northern Africa – after the declaration of the fascist empire in 1936 and the subsequent turn to racism and concern with miscegenation, with an abruptness that was remarkable, long-term and especially loving and passionately attached relationships between white men and Ethiopian women were deemed an "obscenity" and disgrace to Italian racial dignity. In 1937, love and attachment were criminalized, as police and courts alike worked to distinguish between legally tolerable, emotionally uninvolving "episodic" relations like an occasional visit to a prostitute and the now suddenly unacceptable cohabitation or any kind of romantic or caring commitment to a specific individual woman.)

The German army and the SS both tried to provide occasions for German men to have contact with German women with whom they did share attachment. Not only were soldiers granted leaves to go home (often also in the hope that they would impregnate their wives or girlfriends). There were also numerous instances in which wives and girlfriends were given opportunities to visit SS men when they were stationed in the occupied areas, and even while mass killings of Jews by shooting were occurring daily. And sometimes German men did fall in love with women in the Eastern territories, although fraternization with affection was far less frequent on the Eastern front than the Western front. For those Soviet women who consorted with the Nazi occupiers, it is less clear whether the relationship with an enemy male was a strategy for self-protection in a deadly environment or a genuine expression of affection. Or perhaps it was – as one Belorussian woman remembered – just an opportunity for "a little amusement... That was simply pure human," while "around us the war raged."[22]

While, on the Eastern front, battles were brutal and constant, battalions were continually on the move and the tide turned repeatedly both for and against Germany, on the Western front there were long stretches of time when occupation forces were not engaged in battle and thus had more opportunity for leisure. In almost all the Western nations, there were brothels for *Wehrmacht* soldiers (Denmark was an exception,

---

[22] Quoted in Regina Mühlhäuser, "Between 'Racial Awareness' and Fantasies of Potency: Nazi Sexual Politics in the Occupied Territories of the Soviet Union, 1942–1945" in Dagmar Herzog (ed.), *Brutality and Desire: War and Sexuality in Europe's Twentieth Century* (New York: Palgrave Macmillan, 2009), 209.

Fig. 2.8 Nazi *Wehrmacht* brothel established in a synagogue in Brest, France, in World War II. The hours of operation for the brothel are directly below the Star of David, blatantly reinforcing the violation of Jewish sacred space – after the majority of French Jews have been deported and tens of thousands murdered.

because it had a ban on brothels), as well as considerably more consensual relationships – while rapes were far less tolerated. The army was quite well organized, in many cases handing out condoms and insisting on post-coital "sanitation" (prophylactic injections with sulfonamides, precursors to antibiotics). In addition, there were fewer prohibitions, or in some countries like Norway or Denmark (whose populations were supposedly of kindred racial type) no formal prohibitions at all on consorting intimately and openly with the local population – the Danish ban on brothels certainly did not prohibit fraternization – and also in Belgium and the Netherlands fraternization was condoned.

Meanwhile, many men of the occupied nations were absent. Often they were imprisoned as POWs or had been conscripted into forced labor by the Nazis. Many had also volunteered themselves to work for the Nazis and had become members of the German armed forces, while others worked in the underground resistance in their own nations. (In France, for instance, approximately 2 million men between the ages of

20 and 40 were away from home, while more than half a million German soldiers were stationed in the country.) In any event, the local men were not at home – leaving their wives and lovers both with daunting new responsibilities and vulnerabilities, but also unprecedented freedoms. Women in the occupied nations negotiated carefully between attraction to the powerful new occupiers and the virulent hostility often directed at them by their countrymen for departing from national loyalty and the traditionally expected female sexual fidelity alike. In every language, the women were referred to as "tarts" and "sluts."

Estimates are that one in ten Danish and one in five Norwegian women under the age of 30 were at some point during the war romantically and sexually involved with German men. A percentage of these relationships, in turn, resulted in illegitimate offspring. Out of a total population of 3 million people, some 40,000 Norwegian women got involved with German soldiers, and at least 9,000, although likely more, Norwegian–German children were born. For Denmark, the officially recorded number of children is 5,500; in the Netherlands, the number of Dutch–German children is calculated at between 12,000 and 16,000. For France, the numbers are much higher. German officials estimated the number of illegitimate children of French women and German men at 85,000 already as of 1943, and for the entire occupation period scholars have calculated the total number of French–German children at 200,000. Meanwhile, German women on the home front often had romantic and sexual relationships as well – not just with other Germans but also with many among the close to 4 million forced laborers – from such countries as France, Italy, the Netherlands, Czechoslovakia – and almost 2 million prisoners of war brought into the Reich to work in agriculture and military industries to compensate for German men at war.

Fraternization and propaganda

The warring armies sought to use the ubiquity of fraternization against each other. Although probably less than 1 percent of the millions of flyers and leaflets dropped during World War II were sexual in nature, there were still dozens of leaflets with suggestive images and messages that were designed by "Psy-op" (psychological operations) staff in the USA, Britain, Germany, and the Soviet Union and then dropped en masse by plane in enemy territory. The images were generally of a fraternizing woman betraying her boyfriend or husband who was risking his life on the battlefield. Soldiers frequently found the images sexy or funny and saved them as pin-ups. But the hope of their creators was that they would be perceived as deeply threatening. The idea was always to divide and conquer – above all to turn Allies against each other. Thus, for example, a French woman would be found in the arms of a "Tommy" (i.e. an Englishman), or an English woman would land in the arms of an American GI. Or (in the case of Germans trying to divide the Free Polish Army from the Allies on whose side it was fighting in Italy), the propaganda suggested that wealthy Jews were stealing beautiful Polish women while Polish men were on the battlefield – the height of dreadful absurdity in view of the number of Polish Jews already murdered. In other cases the move was to turn soldiers against their officers or against slackers back home who had managed to avoid army service, or (and this was a Soviet as well as British propaganda strategy) to strike alarm in the hearts of German men that the German women and girls they had left behind were enjoying the sexual favors of foreign forced laborers. In one instance, playing on a patriotic song from the era of the German Kaiserreich ("Firm and true stands the watch on the Rhine"), a British leaflet from 1944 distributed among German soldiers stationed in Denmark was overtly pornographic, showing a voluptuous and lovely naked German woman enjoying being entered by a foreign worker ("Firm and true the foreign worker sticks it in [*Fest steckt's und treu der Fremdarbeiter rein*]").[23] In general, the idea was to demoralize the enemy soldier.

While many soldiers may well have been more amused and titillated than made anxious or alarmed by the flyers, there is no question that the logic which informed the flyers, no matter which nation's army was designing them, depended on a wholly transformed idea of female sexuality when compared with the assumptions still predominating before and during the First World War. What the flyers revealed was that the longstanding assumptions about vast differences between wives and prostitutes had collapsed. Wives had come to be understood as sexual beings who actively sought pleasure for themselves. There was no longer any difference in ardor between good girls and bad girls. And – no minor matter – from now on men would have to compete to be the objects of female desire. The rage at female disloyalty was measurable not least by the numerous humiliating hair croppings and head shavings meted out in the context of nationalist uprisings against the German occupiers (as in Denmark in August of 1943) and the tens of thousands of hair croppings and head shavings meted out in the wake of the Nazis' defeat all across the formerly occupied nations to women who were accused of "horizontal collaboration."

However, and just as important, the reality of unmistakably widespread fraternization and infidelities among both men and women would be a key factor in fueling the return to conservative sexual mores in the wake

---

[23] Leaflet from the collection of Dr. Rod Oakland, in Herbert A. Friedman, "Sex and Psychological Operations," www.psywarrior.com/sexandprop.html, 51.

(a)

Figs. 2.9a, 2.9b, and 2.9c Three Nazi "Psy-op" propaganda flyers from
World War II, each directed at a different nationality of enemy soldiers. Often the aim
was to divide Allies from each other. In the first, "Où le Tommy est-il resté?" ("Where is
Tommy staying?" Or "What happened to Tommy?"), the target audience is French
soldiers, who are encouraged to worry that while they are dying on the battlefield
(shown at the bottom of the image), their women are enjoying the ministrations of the
Allied British soldiers (Tommies). In other instances, the aim was to undermine soldier
morale by implying that slackers who had managed to avoid the war were helping
themselves to soldiers' sweethearts. For example, in the second image, the target
audience is American soldiers, urged to be anxious that their wives and girlfriends are
appreciating the romantic overtures of men left on the home front. This flyer was
dropped at the Battle of the Bulge, in the winter of 1944–45. Note the photo of the
soldier on the bedstand. The text reads: "It was a nice evening with drinks, kisses – and
then the gorgeous night . . . " The third image is directed at fighters in the Free Polish
Army fighting with the Allies in Italy in May 1944, being told to fear that Jews are
availing themselves of beautiful Polish women – a particularly noxious image in view of
the million Polish Jews who had already been murdered. The text says: "Polish friends!
Do you want to die for these?" The back of the leaflet blames the Jews for the war and
tells the Polish fighters that while they are "wandering far from your close ones, in a
far-away country," "the swindlers and imposers of the war are away from the front,
enjoying every comfort" and that "the Jews are getting the best of it."

(b)

(c)

Fig. 2.9 (*cont.*)

of the war. Sexuality had escaped from the marital framework in the years when the world turned upside down. Trying to repair ruptured relationships and restore a domesticated heterosexuality would become a project not only imposed from above by conservative governments and with the support of church leaders, but also a movement carried from below by the yearnings of countless ordinary people. That those countless ordinary people had, moreover, very often been witness to (or even participants in or at least beneficiaries of) barbaric persecutions and mass murder and horror on an unprecedented scale – that Europe had been convulsed by an existential cataclysm – as well as themselves suffering deprivation and loss, only intensified the desperate urgency of the search for a (however fragile) postwar normalcy.

Further reading

Accampo, Elinor, "The Gendered Nature of Contraception in France," *Journal of Interdisciplinary History* 34 (2003), 235–62.

Ackelsberg, Martha, "Mujeres Libres: Identity, Community, Sexuality, and Power," *Anarchist Studies* 8 (2000), 99–117.

Beadman, Clive, "Abortion in 1940s Spain: The Social Context," *Journal of Gender Studies* 11 (March 2002), 55–67.

Bellassai, Sandro, "The Masculine Mystique: Anti-Modernism and Virility in Fascist Italy," *Journal of Modern Italian Studies* 10 (2005), 314–35.

Bergen, Doris L., "Sexual Violence in the Holocaust: Unique and Typical?" in Dagmar Herzog (ed.), *Lessons and Legacies VII: The Holocaust in International Perspective* (Evanston, IL: Northwestern University Press, 2006), 179–200.

Broberg, Gunnar, and Nils Roll-Hansen (eds.), *Eugenics and the Welfare State: Sterilization Policy in Denmark, Sweden, Norway, and Finland* (East Lansing: Michigan State University Press, 1996).

Brooke, Stephen, "'A New World For Women'? Abortion Law Reform in Britain during the 1930s," *American Historical Review* 106 (2001), 431–59.

Cleminson, Richard, "'Science and Sympathy' or 'Sexual Subversion on a Human Basis'? Anarchists in Spain and the World League for Sexual Reform," *Journal of the History of Sexuality* 12 (January 2003), 110–21.

De Grazia, Victoria, *How Fascism Ruled Women: Italy, 1922–1945* (Berkeley: University of California Press, 1993).

Doan, Laura, *Disturbing Practices: Sexuality, History, and Women's Experience of Modern War, 1914–18* (University of Chicago Press, 2011), forthcoming.

Dose, Ralf, "The World League for Sexual Reform: Some Possible Approaches," *Journal of the History of Sexuality* 12 (January 2003), 1–15.

Espinaco-Virseda, Angeles, "'I feel that I belong to you': Subculture, *Die Freundin* and Lesbian Identities in Weimar Germany," *spacesofidentity.net* 4, no. 1 (2004), https://pi.library.yorku.ca/ojs/index.php/soi/article/view/8015/7176.

Gawin, Magdalena, "The Sex Reform Movement and Eugenics in Interwar Poland," *Studies in History and Philosophy of Biological and Biomedical Sciences* 39 (2008), 181–6.

Gerodetti, Natalia, *Modernising Sexualities: Toward a Socio-Historical Understanding of Sexualities in the Swiss Nation* (Berne and Oxford: Peter Lang, 2005).

Gori, Gigliola, "Model of Masculinity: Mussolini, the 'New Italian' of the Fascist Era," *International Journal of the History of Sport* 16 (December 1999), 27–61.

Grau, Günter, and Claudia Schoppmann, *Hidden Holocaust? Gay and Lesbian Persecution in Germany, 1933–45* (Chicago: Fitzroy Dearborn Publishers, 1995).

Herzog, Dagmar, *Sex after Fascism: Memory and Morality in Twentieth-Century Germany* (Princeton University Press, 2005).

(ed.), *Brutality and Desire: War and Sexuality in Europe's Twentieth Century* (New York: Palgrave Macmillan, 2009).

Latimer, Tirza True, *Women together/Women apart: Portraits of Lesbian Paris* (New Brunswick, NJ: Rutgers University Press, 2005).

Lybeck, Marti M., "Gender, Sexuality, and Belonging: Female Homosexuality in Germany, 1890–1933," *Bulletin of the GHI* 44 (Spring 2009), 29–41.

Rydström, Jens, *Sinners and Citizens: Bestiality and Homosexuality in Sweden, 1880–1950* (University of Chicago Press, 2003).

Rydström, Jens, and Kati Mustola (eds.), *Criminally Queer: Homosexuality and Criminal Law in Scandinavia 1842–1999* (Amsterdam: Aksant, 2007).

Sibalis, Michael, "Homophobia, Vichy France and the 'Crime of Homosexuality': The Origins of the Ordinance of 6 August 1942," *GLQ: A Journal of Gay and Lesbian Studies* 8 (2002), 301–18.

Sontheimer, Michael, and Götz Aly, *Fromms: How Julius Fromm's Condom Empire Fell to the Nazis*, trans. Shelly Frisch (New York: Other Press, LLC, 2009).

Snyder, David Raub, *Sex Crimes under the Wehrmacht* (Lincoln: University of Nebraska Press, 2007).

Tamagne, Florence, *A History of Homosexuality in Europe*, 2 vols. (New York: Algora Publishing, 2004).

Turda, Marius, and Paul Weindling (eds.), *Blood and Homeland: Eugenics and Racial Nationalism in Central and Southeast Europe, 1900–1940* (Budapest: Central European University Press, 2007).

Warring, Annette, "Intimate and Sexual Relations" in Robert Gildea, Olivier Wieviorka, and Anette Warring (eds.), *Surviving Hitler and Mussolini: Daily Life in Occupied Europe* (Oxford: Berg Publishers, 2006), 88–128.

Willson, Perry (ed.), *Gender, Family and Sexuality: The Private Sphere in Italy 1860–1945* (Basingstoke: Palgrave Macmillan, 2004).

3   Cold War cultures 1945–1965

What made sexual conservatism popularly appealing after the continent-wide carnage of World War II? Many factors converged. Guilt, fear, exhaustion, immeasurable loss, an elemental longing for stability and security in the wake of deprivation and disaster: all were contributory. So was sincere pleasure in daily calm ordinariness. But so too were the elaborate stratagems employed by postwar political and religious leaders to reinterpret the meaning of the recent apocalyptically horrendous past. The Cold War era would be one of great contradiction in the West: rising prosperity, but also ongoing ambivalence about pleasure as an end in itself. Skepticism about women's rights and the rights of sexual minorities was pervasive. Activists seeking to transform popular attitudes and to change laws were few; it would take many years before both the social context and the ways of thinking about sexuality changed enough for a framework based on the principles of privacy and consent to be in the ascendant.

Mass violence and the return to domesticity

After the metaphysical as well as literal catastrophes of total war and mass murder, there was initially an atmosphere of ongoing utter chaos. The war had ended in an avalanche of mass rapes. In the last weeks of the war, Soviet Red Army soldiers raped multiple hundreds of thousands (by some estimates 1 to 2 million) German and tens of thousands of Austrian and tens of thousands of Hungarian women. (Hungary was a Nazi ally.) A hundred thousand rapes occurred in the final assault on Berlin in April 1945, with many women raped repeatedly. Gang rapes were also common in the assault on Vienna. And an estimated 10 percent of women in Budapest were raped. Polish women (technically Soviet allies) and Jewish survivors of camps and life in hiding were raped along with non-Jewish Germans. Often the rapes were fueled by alcohol.

One young Soviet officer retrospectively described the scene in the eastern territories of the German Reich as the Red Army advanced:

"Women, mothers and their children, lie to the right and left along the route, and in front of each of them stands a raucous armada of men with their trousers down ... The women who are bleeding or losing consciousness get shoved to one side, and our men shoot the ones who try to save their children." As this was happening, officers were "grinning" and one was "directing – no, he was regulating it all. This was to make sure that every soldier without exception took part."[1]

Rapes by western Allies were more rare but also occurred. By some estimates American troops raped 10,000 German and other European women. In addition, there were an estimated 10,000 rapes of Italian women by French colonial troops – called "Moroccans" by the Italians, although there may have been other North African colonial soldiers involved. Because of difficulties with troop morale, French officers had deliberately given these soldiers license and encouragement to rape and pillage. Only when the situation began to be perceived as "out of control," the French commanders called it off and the officers switched to executing (by systematically shooting) the troops that had engaged in the rapes – while providing medical care to some of the violated women.

In the course of the war, 50 million people died worldwide. The USSR alone suffered 26 million of those deaths; Germany 5.5 million; Poland 5.8 million (90 percent of the prewar Jewish population of Poland had been murdered in the Holocaust, 10 percent of the prewar non-Jewish population). For those still alive in 1945, trauma was too weak and insufficiently differentiated a concept to cover the experiences of hundreds of millions of victims, perpetrators, and bystanders – and the many people who traversed those categories. Streams of refugees filled the European continent, fleeing or being expelled from various nations and locales; hunger, homelessness, and overwhelming terror were pervasive. Normalcy appeared a distant dream.

For countless women, voluntary prostitution with soldiers of the various Allied armies or – ideally – a long-term romantic relationship with one of the occupying soldiers rapidly came to seem like a sensible option and a possible escape from relentless daily misery. Millions of men of the Axis armies were dead. Hundreds of thousands remained in POW camps, with those in western Allied custody being the lucky ones since the conditions in Soviet POW camps were especially harsh. Within western and central Europe, the men who returned home, whether they were of French, Dutch, or Belgian provenance and had been forced laborers

---

[1] Leonid Rabichev quoted in Catherine Merridale, *Ivan's War: Life and Death in the Red Army, 1939–1945* (New York: Metropolitan Books, 2006), 309.

for the Germans, or whether they were Germans and Austrians who had been part of a genocidal war machinery, brutalized by what they had been through and seen (or in many cases also themselves done), were often devastated to find that the women of their home communities had been – or in the case of German and Austrian women suddenly were – consorting with the former enemies. As the presence of occupation troops became financially lucrative for local populations, many tensions over fraternization subsided – but the animus that remained (in a striking morphing of post-Nazi racism) was directed particularly at women who sought out relationships with African American GIs. Also, returning Soviet soldiers – often just as brutalized by the battles they had experienced and the sexual violence they had unleashed – were enraged to find wives who had been disloyal. Everywhere the women, toughened by the independence and the horrors they had had to survive on their own, often had difficulty subordinating themselves once again to a man they were no longer sure they loved and – in many ways correctly – felt that they now barely anymore knew. This was true also for those who had waited faithfully. Not only the rates of venereal diseases but also the divorce rates soared in the first postwar years.

Yet while millions struggled, some in relief and joy but others in anguish and only with great difficulty, to repair damaged relationships or to build up new ones, some commentators conceded that, at least once the violence was over, the wartime and immediate postwar anarchy had been not only awful, but also a chance for many a merry transgression. The war and its immediate aftermath had been the context in which millions of people had experienced premarital and extramarital sexuality, and crossed boundaries or experimented with relationships that might never have been possible in the more closely monitored and stable environments of peacetime towns. The first postwar years were thus filled with strikingly frank discussion – in popular culture, mainstream journalism, and professional advice literature alike – about the importance of forgiving one's partner's departures from fidelity, even as there were also widespread expressions of embarrassed discomfort and vituperative fury especially at female faithlessness (understood in both nationalist-patriotic and sexual terms). Specifically, because the postwar era often saw new occupation soldiers vying for the attention of local women, nationalist and masculinist resentment against these interlopers was yet another factor reinforcing trends toward more conservative sexual mores, and especially toward renewed restrictions on women's sexual freedoms.

Gradually, moreover, the ascendant tendency was to suppress and deny the reality of wartime and early postwar pleasures. While during the war, for instance, and in dawning dread awareness of Germany's impending comprehensive defeat, German soldiers and civilians had circulated the slogan "Enjoy the war, the peace will be awful," the predominant impulse prevailing a few years into the postwar period was to shut the door on such unguarded acknowledgment of what had transpired in the recent past. Especially for Germans (burdened but also angered by the moral revulsion of the entire globe at Nazism's crimes) and for Austrians (who succeeded with breathtaking efficiency in promoting themselves as Nazi Germany's first victims rather than often enthusiastic collaborators), the onset of the Cold War and the ensuing reconfiguration of ideological frameworks provided a useful occasion for promoting the importance of cleaning up sexual mores.

The postwar era saw a major displacement of moral discussion away from a focus on participation in the expropriation and genocide of European Jewry to a narrow notion of morality as solely concerned with sexual propriety. The initial restoration of sexual conservatism in the postwar West, then, was not just a reaction to postwar chaos and economic deprivation. It also had a great deal to do with the boost in prestige acquired by Christian Democratic parties. This was due not least to a (transnationally popular) postwar interpretation of Nazism as either a result of or a contributor to secularization processes – an interpretation especially well suited to erasing from view Christian church leaders' own profound complicity with Nazism and other forms of fascism. Far from being silent about Nazi crimes, religious leaders, politicians, and opinionmakers in the Federal Republic of Germany continually made references to "concentration camps," "gas chambers," and "Auschwitz" as they urged Germans to return to Christianity and to conservative sexual mores. In short – and not least because Nazism had been not just cruelly repressive in its sexual politics but also highly sexually inciting for those segments of the population favored by the regime – conservatives were able to present the re-establishment of traditional mores as a postfascist imperative and corrective, the best way to overcome the worst aspects of the nation's recent history. Associating Nazism with sexual libertinism, promiscuity, and excess, the churches presented the restoration of sexual conservatism as an anti-Nazi program. While there is no question that the Cold War provided the framework for the ideological renaissance of the domestic ideal, and that Western governments and opinionmakers eagerly presented the Eastern European socialist governments' demands that women work outside the home as an unattractive counterexample that highlighted the better lot of the stay-at-home wife and mother within the West, the complex legacies of the violent past were highly significant as well.

Conservatism, east and west

Moreover, also within the Soviet Union and in the Eastern European nations under Soviet tutelage and oppression, the postwar years saw desperate efforts to re-establish traditional family structures, paternal authority, and stricter mores. It has been argued that a major motivation was the Soviet government's desire to raise the Soviet birthrate (in the wake of the millions of war deaths) by denying access to contraception and by maintaining the 1936 recriminalization of abortion (although as of 1955 abortions were quietly once again permitted – in an effort to reduce maternal mortality due to widespread illegal abortions). But no less significant was that in the Stalinist era (and in this way in profound contrast with the minority of sex-radical Bolsheviks that had tried to set the tone in the 1920s), Soviet Communism relied on an intolerant and negative view of sex. Self-discipline and marital and family stability were demanded for the sake of both the nation and the Communist Party. The wider aim, according to the venerable Soviet sex researcher Igor Kon, included "totalitarian control over the personality." As Kon observed, "the practical message regarding sex remained the same: DON'T DO IT!"[2] Or, as he noted in another context, "The entire history of Soviet culture, from start to finish, consists of out-and-out campaigns and mandates in which sexophobia plays a leading part."[3] Over and over, also for Soviet-ruled Poland and Ukraine, commentators retrospectively observe that issues relating to the body and to sexuality were treated as taboo, passed over in silence – not just because sex was considered something problematic and "bad" that required suppression and control, but also because of a more general state hostility to individual autonomy and freedom in personal relations. In addition, as it has been remarked for Hungary, a major aim of postwar social policies restricting access to contraception and abortion was to restore a semblance of prewar normality by restoring gender hierarchies.

This does not mean that the population did not find its own path. Certainly the pro-natalist emphasis in Soviet family law, for instance, also created a space for women to become single mothers, and in the Soviet Union in the first decade after the war 9 million women did exactly that. And already by the 1960s there would be an evident relaxation of popular mores, accompanied also by an increase in debate about sexual matters

[2] Igor S. Kon, "Russia" in Robert T. Francoeur and Raymond J. Noonan (eds.), *Continuum Complete International Encyclopedia of Sexuality* (New York and London: Continuum, 2004), 890, 894.
[3] Igor S. Kon, *Sexual Revolution in Russia: From the Age of the Czars to Today* (New York: Free Press, 1995), 68.

among medical and social scientific professionals – trends particularly noticeable in East Germany and Czechoslovakia, which had older sex-positive traditions to build on. But there is no question that in the Cold War era the Eastern European and Soviet media were tight-lipped on the subject of pleasure.

Yet a further factor operative in Eastern Bloc countries, especially in the first ten to fifteen postwar years, was the extreme poverty and material privation, coupled with inadequate and extraordinarily overcrowded housing that made privacy and indulgence in extended intimacy all but impossible. From Belgrade to Budapest to Warsaw, multigenerational families packed into tiny, one- or at best two-bedroom apartments, often sharing the WC and kitchen with other families. Women were drawn into the workforce far more than in the West – and in this sense Eastern governments advanced gender egalitarianism and greater female independence. In most Eastern countries, more generous maternity leaves and a network of childcare facilities were meant to facilitate the balancing of reproduction and work outside the home. But in conditions of systemic shortages, women were also burdened by additional household labor and hours spent procuring food and other basic necessities. The impact of massive male deaths also meant that many households were headed by widows, even as, just as in the Soviet Union, the enormity of population losses (and hence worry about the size of a future labor force) continued to fuel the various Eastern governments' desires to promote pro-natalist policies.

These policies, however, only had mixed success, as women continued to seek illegal abortions. Thus, the reversal of the anti-abortion law in the Soviet Union in 1955 was followed also in other Eastern Bloc countries by loosened restrictions on legal abortions performed in clinics: 1956 not only in Poland (where there were an estimated 250,000 to 340,000 abortions annually) but also in Bulgaria and Hungary; 1957 Czechoslovakia; 1959 Yugoslavia. Yet in all cases, the aim was solely to counteract the damage done to women's bodies by illegal abortions. In Bulgaria, for example, the same law permitting clinic abortions also penalized pharmacists who sold hormonal or herbal abortifacients over the counter. Everywhere, provisions of contraception remained sparse to nonexistent. In 1950, the Yugoslav government announced plans to promote knowledge of contraception but as of 1961, as one Western Planned Parenthood-affiliated expert reported, not much progress had been made. In 1957 a "Society for Planned Parenthood" was officially founded in Poland, but the Western observer noted ongoing high resistance to contraceptive use, especially among Polish men.

Fig. 3.1 Haircropping in post-Liberation France. An estimated 20,000 French women accused of "horizontal collaboration" with the Germans had their hair shorn in front of jeering crowds in order to humiliate them. The emphasis on the women distracted from the far broader phenomenon of male political collaboration with the enemy occupiers.

Yet while the desire to restore something resembling normalcy profoundly shaped the sexual cultures in all nations affected by World War II, from West to East, there were nonetheless important national differences. In other words, although seemingly similar on the surface, the turn to sexual conservatism in the postwar era could actually have quite diverse causes, motivations, and functions in each national case. This is especially evident in the contrasts among Western national cultures. In post-Vichy, post-occupation France, for instance, the public shamings and head-shavings of French women who had had relationships with German occupation soldiers and the subsequent reinstallation of more conservative mores could be interpreted as a way to deflect attention from the greater shame of so many more French *men's* collaboration with the Nazi occupiers. But on a deeper level, the male shame may not have been so much over collaboration as over the prior disgrace and humiliation of having been so easily militarily defeated by the Germans.

In Italy, religion played an important role. The Catholic church had been profoundly enmeshed with the fascist regime; nonetheless, far from being embarrassed by the complicity, the defeat of fascism was perceived as a terrific opportunity to strengthen even further the church's role in public and private life. Eager to present themselves to the world as good people (*brava gente*), i.e. victims of fascism rather than its supporters, ordinary Italians, after the long-drawn-out chaos and suffering of a brutal civil war, accepted the imposed restoration of conservative mores as part of a return to stability. A law passed in 1946, for example, restricted the circulation of information about contraception even more than it had been restricted under fascism. Moreover, the Italian Communist party (the largest in western Europe) was so fearful of displeasing the Catholic church and offending its working-class constituency that it never challenged the sexual conservatism propounded by the postwar church. (Protest would be left to a minuscule handful of socialists and radicals.) Indeed, some scholars argue that, with the church's help, and despite the military and political defeat of Italian fascism and the establishment of a democratic republic, the rigidly conservative norms promoted (although not practiced) by fascist leaders persisted well into the 1960s and beyond. It was precisely the independence women acquired during the war years which became understood as a reason to encourage them to return to a subordinate status in the war's aftermath.

In Spain and Portugal, both of which had been neutral in World War II (although Franco had benefited greatly from support from both Hitler and Mussolini), the combination of authoritarian Catholicism and the perseverance of fascist regimes into and through the post-World War II decades together enforced highly restrictive sexual cultures, especially with respect to controls on female sexuality. The church strongly supported Franco's policies on reproduction. Birth control was seen as a great evil, a disturbing sign of "a decline in Christian resignation." Contraceptives were deemed the "social cancer of our times, a strike against biological duties, a dagger which is assassinating our civilization"; by restricting fertility, "women blacken their souls with the black crepe of mortal sin."[4] While most of the countries of Western Europe recovered economically in the 1950s from the ravages of war and entered a period of prosperity, Spain and Portugal remained largely agricultural and disconnected from global markets. This meant that the much-promoted birthrates did not actually rise until the economies improved in the early 1960s. But there is no question that the poverty and static nature of

---

[4] Demographer Severino Aznar and physician Vital Aza quoted in Mary Nash, "Pronatalism and Motherhood in Franco's Spain" in Gisela Bock and Pat Thane (eds.), *Maternity and Gender Policies: Women and the Rise of the European Welfare States, 1880s–1950s* (London: Routledge, 1994).

the society in these two nations contributed greatly to the persistence of conservative values. Part of that conservatism included the maintenance of a regulated brothel system – "a large part of the sexual space of male Spaniards" – and perceived as "an essential piece of the moral order, the safeguard of feminine virginity and the tranquility of the Christian family."[5] Upwards of 60 percent of male Spaniards, a retrospective survey conducted in the 1960s had found, had their first sexual experience with a prostitute – and going to the brothel was often a group experience for young men.

In post-Nazi Austria, the antagonism toward Austrian women over their relationships with American, British, French, or Soviet occupation troops could certainly be seen as a means for redirecting attention away from Austrian men's participation in the Nazi war machinery. But the anger was also a way of registering frustration over changing gender norms and the loss of unchallenged male privileges (and over a loosening of mores for which both Nazi policies and the practical exigencies of the war years had been responsible). For example, when an Austrian man in a local newspaper complained that the Austrian men no longer had a chance with Austrian girls and women because the American soldiers were apparently more attractive, an Austrian woman wrote back a fiery letter to the editor reminding the "poor" man that only a few years earlier things were apparently different. She mocked the returning men's sudden keen longing for quiet domesticity with a faithful modest Gretchen since, when the Axis still dominated the continent, the same men loved themselves in the role of "smart Don Juans" and were delighted to snuggle up with the likes of Yvonne in France, Sigrid in Norway, Rosje in Belgium, and Nelle in the Netherlands – not to mention indulging in the good wines and pretty women in Greece and Italy as well. But despite the perceptiveness of this rebuttal, the hostility to the "good-for-nothing broads" and "occupation whores" (as Austrian women who consorted with the victors were called) – carried both by religious authorities and by popular animus and sheer envy – unquestionably helped usher in a more conservative era.

Also in countries with extensive secularization and with no fascist past, however, as in continuously democratic Britain, there was a renewed turn to a preoccupation with sexual respectability and conservative mores. As of the late 1940s a survey showed that one in four Britons doubted the

[5] Jean-Louis Gereña, "Marginación, prostitución y delincuencia sexual: la represión de la moralidad en la España franquista (1939–1956)" in Conxita Mir, Carem Agustí, and Josep Gelonch (eds.), *Pobreza, marginación, delincuencia y políticas sociales bajo el franquismo* (Universitat de Lleida, 2005), 167.

Fig. 3.2 "Marriage Guidance." Masthead for the newsletter of the National Marriage Guidance Council, UK. The restoration of harmonious domesticity was an important goal in the aftermath of World War II.

existence of a deity and only one in ten went to church "fairly regularly," with two-thirds never going to church at all. Christianity was seen as "a not very interesting mystery" and "opinions as to Christ himself varied between the views that He did not exist, that He was 'just a carpenter' and that He was 'quite a good chap' but 'nothing extra.'"[6] Yet the early 1950s saw a revival in church attendance such as had not been seen since the nineteenth century, part and parcel of a broader endorsement of conventionality. The restoration of traditional gender roles held broad appeal far beyond church dictates. Above all, in postwar Britain many women, and most especially women in the working class, saw the opportunity to build a little haven of domestic bliss as the wonderful, fervently wished-for reward for having survived years of economic deprivation in prewar and wartime Britain. The British government, too, worked hard in the postwar era to make marriage and domesticity appealing – also for men. Especially significant was the government's effort to provide affordable housing for young couples; in general, the prospect of full employment, upward mobility, and welfare state support structures aided greatly in stabilizing postwar society. In addition, a private initiative initially launched in the 1930s, the National Marriage Guidance Council (NMGC), was revived after the war and received government aid from 1948 on. A few years later, in 1951, the government established the Royal

---

[6] "Secularism and Christianity," *Times Literary Supplement*, July 12, 1947.

Commission on Marriage and Divorce. Cultural authorities associated with the NMGC worked tirelessly to advance the new notion that men uninterested in marriage were "immature" and also put much effort into promoting the ideal of "companionate marriage," redescribing the role of devoted male breadwinner and considerate (as opposed to patriarchally authoritarian) husband not as dull but rather as "heroic." For while there were indisputably countless men who sought and enjoyed the domestic harmony they were able to build with their wives, the official postwar efforts to consolidate a culture of domesticity were also met by a fair amount of ambivalence specifically by men who yearned for the uncouth homosociability and the thrills of war and who considered marriage to a woman to be a kind of "trap."

The rise of romance

Meanwhile, the model of marital domesticity restored in the postwar years in most Western European nations was different in quality from what had gone before; above all, it was an eroticized model. From the beginning, the restoration of domesticity was accompanied by heightened expectations and standards of pleasure. The experiences of the war years had taught Western Europeans to think differently about wives' desires and reinforced the new conviction that reciprocally pleasurable sexuality was important for marital durability. While the family constellation was in many ways still conceived in patriarchal terms and both law and habit kept women in a subordinate status to their husbands (with regard to everything from how to raise the children to whether and in what profession or job a woman might work outside the home), new ideals of romance as the reason to marry and at once passionate and comradely companionship as the goal and the glue of marriage were avidly promoted and strongly competed with the older asymmetrical model.

In general, two strongly conflicting narratives could be told about the West in the Cold War era – and, however paradoxically, both are true. On the one hand, there is the story of lingering traditionalism in gender and sexual values, exacerbated further by a postwar restoration (and/or new invention) of an especially restrictive, even claustrophobic, version of heterosexual domesticity. On the other, there is the story of economic and cultural optimism, greater opportunities for consumerism, increased aspirations for fun, and the rise of a romantic model of marriage, accompanied by the growing acceptability of premarital sex. So successful was the economic recovery of the postwar era that in West Germany it was referred to as the "economic miracle" and in France as the "thirty glorious years." Numerous factors converged to lend to sex a more positive valuation. Indeed, even the Christian churches' ongoing efforts to resist the sexualization of mass culture involved an even stronger endorsement than previously of the importance of mutually satisfying marital sex – no longer only legitimated by reproduction, but also for its value in nurturing the marital bond.

An especially important factor in the ascent of the ideal of female "sex appeal" was its growing pervasiveness in film and advertising. For every religious or political or cultural leader's announcement that women should be dutiful housewives, there was a competing image or story that conveyed the allure and excitement of being an object of desire. The free sensuality of Silvana Mangano in Giuseppe de Santis' *Riso amaro* (1949) or Brigitte Bardot in Roger Vadim's *Et Dieu . . . créa la femme* (1956) was unreachable (or not even imaginable or desirable) for the vast majority of women. Nonetheless, movies as well as magazines following the lives of the film stars from marriages to affairs to divorces not only imparted new ideals of female attractiveness but also emphasized the importance of love (and not just marriage) as the key to justifying sex. No less significant was the prevalence of bombshell beauties in advertising of everything from soap to stockings to margarine. In a complicated interplay between intimidation and inspiration, women strove to navigate the conflicting injunctions to be both wholesome and sexy and learned to measure themselves with and against the circulating images and popular magazine chatter.

In addition, the 1950s were the first great era of the social survey. Western Europeans learned to be fascinated by averages and percentages and to worry about exactly how "normal" they were – and then to have their worries both soothed and pricked further by countless additional studies, both serious and superficial, about the values and habits of their fellow citizens as well as the citizens of other lands. The effects of the explosion of surveys, polls, and magazine quizzes were multiple and contradictory. They reassured readers that others too were breaking with inherited norms, and they expanded the horizon of the imagination by revealing a variety of behaviors and views that some readers may never have considered otherwise. But they additionally generated new pressures to conformity and restricted the imagination to a set menu of delineated activities. They also contributed both to the vague and fuzzy idealization of starry-eyed love and to the growing routing of personal emotions through constant comparisons with mass media generalizations. A survey conducted in Italy in 1954, for example, asked men questions such as: "What is love? What are its 'symptoms'? Would you forgive a woman who sinned and lied for the sole purpose of making you happy? Can love exist without passion and vice versa? Do you believe in love at first sight?

Fig. 3.3 Silvana Mangano. The Italian bombshell became an international icon in the postwar era. The poster is from the 1949 film *Riso amaro* (Bitter Rice).

What, above all else, do you notice about a woman who awakens your desire? Are you favorable to free love? What are your thoughts on today's women?"[7] A survey conducted in France in 1958 asked women questions like these: "What do you dream of?" "Whom do you find sexy?" and "Do your ideals come from the radio or the cinema?" As cultural theorist Jean Baudrillard once noted, polling could be defined as "continual voyeurism of the group in relation to itself."[8]

While cultural differences are certainly noticeable in the questions posed, just as noteworthy is the shift that the phenomenon of polling represented. No longer were medical or religious professionals the only orientation points in telling people what was right and wrong; for the first time, ordinary people learned about the sex lives and love lives of vast numbers of other ordinary people. At the same time, however, while some people evidently got lucky, as their lives seemed effortlessly to match the new norms, many, many others found themselves unsure how to negotiate the heightened expectations and find their way between media pronouncements on what was typical or desirable and their own hopes for happiness. (The author of the Italian survey, for example, found women on the whole unhappier than men. Women, she found, felt unappreciated by husbands, fathers, and brothers, and the author also opined that women did not betray husbands for fur coats, but because they felt ignored and misunderstood.) The constant pulse-taking and the racy and sensationalist exposés about just what percentage of individuals approved of, or had engaged in, this or that particular activity or shared this or that particular value did make clear, often titillatingly, just how many people diverged from what had once been considered the straight and narrow. But another inevitable effect was that people began to measure themselves against the findings and to doubt their own experiences and to wonder whether their own practices and attitudes or those of their partners could be improved.

In this context, marital sex was newly situated somewhere between mundane expected routine and aspirations for being "madly in love." When the British social science survey organization Mass-Observation in 1949 (taking its cue directly from the US-based Kinsey Report on *Sexual Behavior in the Human Male*, published in 1948) asked Britons about "current attitudes to sex and sexual behavior in this country," one respondent noted that while cultural leaders liked to conceive of marriage

---

[7] Anna Garofalo, "Undici domande per smentire Kinsey," *Epoca*, January 10, 1954, 25–6.
[8] *Elle* survey and Baudrillard quoted in Judith G. Coffin, "Between Opinion and Desire: *Elle* Magazine's Survey Research in 1950s France" in Kerstin Brückweh (ed.), *The Voice of the Citizen Consumer: A History of Market Research, Consumer Movements, and the Political Public Sphere* (Oxford University Press, 2011), 51–73.

as a "spiritual affair," the "man in the street" took a more "down to earth view, regarding it more as a matter of the sex act, and jobs around the house, and arguments over the children."[9] But there was no question that also in Britain ardent love was the new ideal.

Already during the war, it was apparent that British women had been navigating previously uncharted terrain. One author employed by Mass-Observation who studied young women serving in the British Women's Auxiliary Air Force noted that rivalry for prestige among the women all revolved around the "Man Chase," and "the longer you can keep your man, the higher you are in the competition." What were the young women looking for in these men? "Technique in kissing is of first importance." A man who was "wandering" from woman to woman was eyed with suspicion, and intercourse ("actual immorality") was frowned on. In short, "the most eligible men are those who kiss well, but 'know when to stop,'" while the highest prize was a man who was "falling violently in love with you for a long time."[10]

Yet while older standards disapproving of premarital sex persisted, they were increasingly shaken. One teacher from Wales told Mass-Observation that premarital sex "leads to loss of mutual self-respect," while an Englishman (a schoolmaster) declared "No man wants secondhand goods, and to the right minded man there is an exhilaration in his own purity." But others sought a balanced view on premarital intercourse. In one man's words: "Upbringing, and its prejudices, make me condemn it," but "personal experience inclines me to commend it as a means of acquiring technique!" And one medical doctor opined that prostitution was declining "on account of the increasing willingness of girls armed with a knowledge of contraception, to oblige their boyfriends." And yet another man (29 years old, a laundries manager) confided that he had been experimenting for quite a while, even though not all had gone smoothly: "Then with my first big love affair with a woman as inexperienced as myself, though we tried on numerous occasions I could never achieve proper penetration or orgasm. I think this was due to the fact that I was wearing a French letter and couldn't achieve a big erection at the right moment... I was 21 then." Later "I met another girl, a very lascivious type who was furious at my bad technique. She told me to read Van der Elde [*sic* – he meant the Dutch advice writer Theodor van de Velde] and cleared off. So I read him and it was some

---

[9] University of Sussex Mass-Observation Archive (hereafter M-O A). M-O A: FR 3110B 'Sex Survey,' 6.

[10] M-O A: TC 32 Box 3 File E, 'The Great Digby Man Chase,' December 28, 1941 (about the WAAF), 5–7.

considerable help as regards technique and so on." Then, "the third [girl] had a worse mastibation [*sic*] complex than I had, and we always had a row as to whether we should mastibate each other or fornicate, we finally parted after a major row on this issue." In conclusion, the respondent confessed that he continued to find condoms challenging and "if I can possibly persuade the girl to use a fitted plus a chemical pessary it makes an enormous difference." The interviewer noted at the end of the report with some astonishment: "Only two girls have refused to go to bed with him. He is not at all good looking."[11] Clearly, there was a strong relationship between the increasing familiarity with contraceptive possibilities and *both* the increasing eroticization of marriage *and* the growing acceptability of premarital sex.

Ambivalence about contraception

Nonetheless, it is essential to grasp the extraordinary ambivalence that continued to surround contraception. While in Eastern Europe, contraceptives were hardly available and withdrawal and abortion were the main methods of fertility control, in Western Europe the available methods remained as they had been before the war: the condom, spermicidal soluble pessaries or spermicide-soaked sponges, cervical caps, reliance on the "safe period," and postcoital douching. Reliance on withdrawal was still named in one British survey as a preferred technique by 36 percent of respondents. Needless to say, none of the available methods was ideal.

More significantly, birth control remained also in Western nations strongly associated with "selfishness" as well as unnaturalness. "Coitus interruptus the only method which prevents intercourse from degradation," asserted a clergyman from Gotham. Another man of the cloth declared: "Permissible under control by moral considerations . . . always vitiated by deliberately selfish use." And a medical doctor found none of the mechanical or chemical means acceptable: Birth control was "quite proper if it be by self restraint; but not by contraceptives."[12] Yet another medical doctor, writing in the *New Statesman*, had asserted that: "A well-balanced view seems to be that the use of contraceptives for a relatively short time – say, twelve months – in the case of a newly married

[11] M-O A: TC 12 Box 14/C, no. 83, May 1949; M-O A: TC 12/Box 14 File A (Teachers), no. 029; M-O A: TC 12 Box 14/C, no. 95, May 1949; M-O A: TC 12/Box 14 File D (Medical practitioners), no. 89, Liverpool; M-O A: TC 12/15/H, December 30, 1948, 2.

[12] M-O A: TC 12/Box 14 File C (Clergy), no. 022; M-O A: TC 12/Box 14 File C (Clergy), no. 024; M-O A: TC 12/Box 14 File D (Medical practitioners), no. 51.

couple, both of whom are healthy, can do little permanent harm; whereas the use of these measures over a number of years is almost certain to lead to degenerative changes in the genital organs of the woman, and to consequent sterility or at least impairment of fertility."[13]

The climate of official censorship surrounding the topic of birth control was evident not least in the fact that as of 1953 only three European nations had branches of Planned Parenthood: Sweden, the United Kingdom, and the Netherlands. Activists in West Germany would soon succeed in starting a branch there as well, although their efforts were hampered by the persistence of Nazi laws retained in some West German states. And in Switzerland contraception was not illegal and there were a number of marriage advice bureaus that couples could consult. But in nations like France and Italy in which advertising of contraception was criminalized, deep-seated hypocrisy among medical professionals and fear in the general populace were big factors in squelching open discussion of contraception. Illegal abortion remained the fertility control method of choice for most women when the most prevalent preventive strategies (rhythm method, postcoital douches, coitus interruptus) failed. In France, for instance, in the early 1950s, as one critic noted, "abortion is rife among all social classes and so easily escapes all sanction, that the question of contraception is, one knows not why, an 'off-limits' topic, especially among doctors; those who tackle the problem risk being discredited by others."[14] In Italy, even to talk about birth control in public settings remained illegal into the 1960s.

The ambivalence about contraception was, however, not just due to didactic moralizing disdain expressed by authorities, and not just to punitive legislation, but also for personal reasons both of emotional discomfort and physical awkwardness. French philosopher Simone de Beauvoir, in *The Second Sex* (1949), struggled to find an apt vocabulary for articulating the conflicting emotions aroused in women by the combination of yearning for ecstatic union and terror of pregnancy. A woman, she wrote, "must overcome a certain repugnance before she can treat her body as a thing." "Cold premeditation" and "hygienic procedure," being "stoppered" for a man's pleasure with a cervical cap or a spermicidal sponge, or monitoring anxiously to make sure the man withdrew in time and then rushing off to douche with chemicals: All of that, de Beauvoir pointed out, felt "surgical" and "indecent" and "contrasts rudely with the

---

[13] I. Geike-Cobb, "The Problem of the Falling Birth-Rate," *New Statesman and Nation*, March 11, 1944, 169.

[14] Marie-Andrée Lagroua Weill-Hallé, "Le contrôle des naissances à l'étranger et la loi française de 1920," *Semaine des Hôpitaux* 29 (1953), 145, 150.

sensuous magic of caresses" and the "fusion with the beloved" that "delights the woman in love."[15] Even manual stimulation to avoid impregnation seemed clumsy and uncomfortable also for many women; women, too, she insisted, longed for the merger of intercourse – and yet were constantly afraid. Nonetheless, and while noting that French women were still more likely to be virgins at marriage than American women, not least because of the dearth of easy and legal access to birth control in France, de Beauvoir observed as well that also in France the trend in the postwar years was toward higher rates of premarital sex and of women moving fairly quickly from necking and petting to intercourse. At the same time, and movingly, de Beauvoir sought to put into words what sex felt like for women, the ways in which the entire body's sensory apparatus was recalibrated in the experience of pleasurable intercourse – and differently than it was with clitoral stimulation. As with the sociological surveys and magazine quizzes, here too: No longer were only (mostly male) medical and religious experts the ones who could expound on female bodies and desires. The taboo on open popular discussion of the intricacies of female physical feelings had been transgressed.

Yet changes in the views expounded by religious authorities mattered as well. The Vatican's own stance was confusing for ordinary believers and clergy alike. On the one hand, as of 1951 (in the context of an address to Italian midwives), the Pope confirmed that he approved of the use of the rhythm method within marriage, i.e. periodic abstinence, if conception was to be avoided. On the other hand, and at the same time, the Pope declared that the method would not be permissible if the couple's intentions were to prevent births entirely. The rhythm method was only to be used for "serious" reasons, which could include the woman's physical or mental health or severe economic difficulties but could by no means simply be the couple's personal preference. In the ensuing interpretive wiggle room, compassionate clergy sought to help believers find arrangements that worked for them. In France and West Germany, a movement called *nouvelle théologie* developed in the 1950s that contributed important impulses to transnational Catholic debates about the permissibility of contraception, and attempted to formulate humane alternatives to the strict view that openness to reproduction must occur in every marital sex act. The concepts advanced by *nouvelle théologie* (which ultimately would also find expression in Vatican II) emphasized the integration of faith and daily life and suggested that dogmas that made sense in one historical context needed to be reconsidered as contexts changed – including

---

[15] Simone de Beauvoir, *The Second Sex*, trans. and ed. H. M. Parshley (New York: Alfred A. Knopf, 1953), 363–4, 368.

especially views on birth control. Were not economic and social justice issues as important as issues of sexual morality? Was it good for religion to be so narrowly fixated on sexual matters? French and West German clergymen, confronted by the agonies of couples striving to live in accordance with church teachings but miserable over the fear of pregnancy and confusion over the permissibility of various activities, were acutely aware that parishioners' difficulties in reconciling piety and fertility control contributed powerfully to popular secularization. Meanwhile, among British Roman Catholics surveyed in the late 1940s, 37 percent (almost two out of five) disagreed with church teachings and admitted to approving of the use of birth control.

Dutch society provides yet another exemplary case of transformations in attitudes about birth control *within* Catholicism in the course of the 1950s. In a 1987 study that analyzed several hundred letters written by mothers of large families about their experiences in prior decades, Dutch women reported that, well into the 1950s, they were required to hand to their family doctor a written statement from their parish priest that the priest had granted them permission to use the rhythm method before the doctor would explain the details of the method to them. In addition, there were yet more intrusions into the private sphere. Among other things, priests: visited families that had not had a child for several years; provided fire and brimstone preachments when a couple confessed to using withdrawal; and refused to absolve couples when they confessed to having used the rhythm method without permission. Meanwhile, large families were praised as God-pleasing. But over the course of the 1950s in the Netherlands, social workers and psychiatrists became important supplementary participants in the Catholic welfare system and clergymen who worked together with these other professionals helped to formulate a shift from an ethics based on procreation to an ethics based on quality of relationship; by the early 1960s, this ethical stance included a more understanding view of contraception, one that had also grown out of respectful dialogue with the laity. By 1958–59, even the Roman Catholic Society of Physicians, which had long insisted that a couple's goal should be to have as large a family as possible, declared that it was acceptable for couples to space the birth of their children. This turnaround greatly facilitated as well the subsequent acceptance of the birth control pill, as it became available in the early 1960s.

Nonetheless, the birth control pill was met with ambivalences – and not only because commentators feared that long-term hormone usage might cause health damage in women. There were more metaphysical worries expressed as well. A West German commentator summarized the fears in an essay "For and Against the Anti-Baby Pill" in 1962. As he phrased it with evocative circumlocution:

It is seriously worrisome that "the pill" could take from lovers a good part of what generates attraction between the sexes. Is not the secret of the relationship between two people that within it there is always a little bit of a game with life and death, a risk, a bit of irrevocability? And is this not in the first place how love becomes, unconsciously, the singular, amazing experience of our life? To release the drive for connection from its fateful context can thus hardly be without consequences for morality in general.[16]

Such concerns were far from unusual. The unhinging of female sexuality from the possibility of procreation (and thus also economic and emotional dependence on a man) would remain a major source of ambivalence for men (and not a few women) for years thereafter.

Birth control was, simply, a difficult topic. Strikingly, for instance, inquiries in Britain about views on contraception recurrently triggered responses which revealed the ongoing significance into the postwar era of eugenic attitudes and utter lack of self-consciousness in expressing those. One woman, headmistress of a school, in response to a query about "your attitude to birth control," spontaneously offered this: "Unaesthetic, but probably necessary in many cases. Proper social training should deter physically-unfits from having children. Mentally-deficients should be prevented if necessary." And a schoolmaster opined that birth control was "being used by the wrong people. Intelligent people should procreate and give us more of their sort. But it is the semi-morons who breed like rabbits."[17]

The British were certainly not alone in taking these views. Post-Nazi West Germans, as well as their Swiss neighbors, also retained eugenic convictions as they discussed birth control. Thus West German Catholic sociologist Werner Schoellgen in 1948 spoke of contraception as "biological suicide" and argued that "the eugenic idea" had not lost its value despite "the abuse in the Third Reich."[18] A contributor to the respected intellectual Catholic journal *Frankfurter Hefte* in 1951 declared that Catholic couples were obligated to conceive "the highest number of physically and psychologically valuable offspring" that they possibly could.[19] And the influential Swiss Protestant advice writer Theodor

---

[16] Theo Löbsack, "Für und wider die Anti-Baby-Pille," *Die Zeit*, January 19, 1962, 29.
[17] M-O A: TC 12 Box 14/C, no. 2028, May 1949; M-O A: TC 12/Box 14 File A (Teachers), no. 029.
[18] Werner Schöllgen, *Die Kirche in der Welt* 1 (1947–48), 160.
[19] Ernst Karl Winter, "Das grosse Geheimnis: Ehe und Familie in der christlichen Zivilisation," *Frankfurter Hefte*, October 1951, 716.

Bovet insisted in 1955 on the need to "be concerned with the healthy inheritance of our *Volk*" as he bemoaned the fact that "the less valuable elements, especially the mentally deficient, reproduce themselves approximately twice as much as healthy families. It is therefore absolutely necessary that, if we do not one day want to be completely flooded by those [elements], that everyone who feels himself to be healthy . . . give life to as many children as possible."[20]

This persistence also into the postfascist era of eugenic attitudes toward the lower classes within European nations was accompanied by a pronounced preoccupation with comparing birthrates globally – a trend that had just barely begun in earlier decades but was soon to explode. As early as 1944 a British commentator had noted that birthrates were declining almost everywhere in the world except for India and China. This author placed the blame directly on growing European contraceptive use and British rates in particular were plunging, he fretted. The World Health Organization, meeting in Geneva, Switzerland, in 1951, debated extensively the importance of providing contraceptive information to women around the world, while the delegate from Norway additionally called for propagandizing on behalf of birth control specifically in "overpopulated" countries. Yet critics, often religiously inspired, objected strenuously, demanding also the expeditious return home of the birth control emissaries already sent to India; the meeting ended without a vote on the matter, in the interests of maintaining transnational harmony. At the United Nations subdivision UNESCO as well, debate was vigorous, with the leadership furious at religious conservatives who acted as though "Providence" would take care of burgeoning world populations, and calling instead for contraceptive counsel to be seen as just as important a public health matter as advice on combating malaria or improving crop yields.

By 1953 the concept of "world hunger" and by 1954, at the latest, the notion of "global overpopulation" had come into general vogue – almost always with gestures to India and China specifically. There were certainly commentators who felt that what ailed the world was not the prospect of global overpopulation but rather the horrendously unjust distribution of material resources, but who nonetheless believed that contraceptives should be made available to anyone who wanted them. But these more balanced observers found themselves without much of an audience.

As illogical as it may seem in hindsight, in a cultural atmosphere of apparent inability directly to defend sexual pleasure as a value in its

---

[20] Theodor Bovet, *Von Mann zu Mann: Eine Einführung ins Reifealter fur junge Männer* (Tübingen: Katzmann-Verlag, 1955), 47.

own right, commentators seeking to promote contraceptive use within Western European nations reached for arguments about the potential dangers of global overpopulation to make their case. Indeed, so concerned was the Catholic church by the spread of this particular strand of pro-contraception rhetoric that it was already by the mid-1950s attempting to respond preemptively. A Belgian Catholic journal in 1954 not only chastised those European couples who gestured to "the specter of global overpopulation" and especially the growing populations of India and China to justify their own contraceptive use, asserting that "nothing" could ever justify using something that was "in itself immoral." It also mocked those who thought they could define as "ecstasy" the "physical quivering" that was orgasm once they had separated it from the "the grandeur of parenthood" and thus turned that quivering into a "sacrilegious and basely voluptuous parody of the gift that is love."[21]

The persecution of homosexuals

Another important manifestation of the restored conservatism of the postwar era was the contempt directed especially at male homosexuals. World War II had two (opposing) consequences for popular thinking about male homosexuality. On the one hand, the war had provided countless occasions for men to experiment with homosexual sex; this was true both for those men who otherwise thought of themselves as attracted to women but had turned to men in the largely female-free context of the armed forces and for those men who preferred men in any event. Yet on the other hand, once the war ended, the very familiarity with and prevalence of male–male sexual activities during the war served as a basis not for developing sympathetic attitudes but rather as a source of discomfort, an excuse to avert one's gaze from the reality of ongoing persecution of men who continued to seek same-sex encounters. Lesbianism, by contrast, remained far less visible. When remarked upon at all, it was more often with amused pity than with a sense of threat. In some cases it was seen as a "second best" arrangement arising due to the dearth of men; very rarely was it imagined as titillating.

For men who sought same-sex encounters, the postwar years would be harsh. In France, the Vichy-era innovation criminalizing same-sex encounters between those over 21 and those under 21 was retained by General Charles de Gaulle into the postwar decades. In the Netherlands, although the more restrictive law that had been added under Nazi

---

[21] M. Kuppens, "Problèmes actuels concernant la fécondité humaine," *Revue Ecclésiastique de Liége* 41 (1954), 25.

Fig. 3.4 "A Kiss between Soldiers." Male French soldier couple laughingly wearing *Wehrmacht* uniforms and celebrating the defeat of Nazism at the end of World War II.

occupation was not maintained, the preexisting law from 1911, Paragraph 248bis, continued to criminalize sexual activity between men over 21 and those under 21, and castrations as well as imprisonments remained common in the Netherlands through the first postwar decades. In fact, the persecution of homosexual men actually escalated in the postwar years. Paragraph 248bis was used by the police to register and monitor anyone they suspected of homosexual activity. Close to 1 percent of the entire Dutch male population over age 16 was registered and more than 1 percent of the male population of Amsterdam. Many men lived in constant fear of blackmailers.

In West Germany and Austria, the added devastation of having tens of thousands of men accused of homosexuality brutally persecuted under Nazism, and somewhere in the vicinity of 7,000 murdered for their homosexuality, coupled with the retention of the repressive laws from the Nazi era, left an indelible mark and made work on behalf of decriminalization extraordinarily difficult. Men who had been imprisoned for homosexual sex in the Third Reich found themselves not only denied reparations for time spent in concentration camps, but also denied their pensions and reinstatement in their former jobs – and in many cases found themselves reimprisoned for renewed infractions against Paragraph 175 or 175a. Conditions for openly lived homosexuality, to say nothing of activism, were not auspicious. Only in a continuously democratic nation like Switzerland, which had decriminalized consensual adult homosexuality in 1942, was more open activism feasible. But also in Switzerland, the fears imbued in homosexual men in view of what had happened in neighboring Nazi Germany, along with the aggressive homophobia continuing to be spouted by Swiss moral purity organizations, made activists exceptionally wary of provoking backlash.

Strategies of resistance

In the 1950s, it took extraordinary courage to challenge the laws criminalizing homosexuality as well as the popular homophobia, and the tiny handful of individuals in every nation who took these challenges upon themselves faced constant opprobrium and harassment. Strategic caution was necessary at all times. The result was that also in France, where adult homosexuality was not illegal, activists were extremely circumspect in their activities. When the former Catholic seminarian André Baudry, inspired by the Swiss homosexual rights journal Der Kreis, launched the French journal Arcadie in January 1954 and subsequently a group by the same name (a group that would eventually turn into a movement, with branches in provincial cities and specialized groups for lesbians,

Christians, married men, and men attracted to teen boys), any sexual contact between someone over and someone under 21 was punishable by six months to three years in prison, and sanctions were placed on any club that permitted dancing between men. By 1957, the journal had 4,000 subscribers (by the late 1960s it would be 10,000). Together with the writer Roger Peyrefitte and the right-wing Catholic aristocrat Jacques de Ricaumont, as well as a higher government official who used the pseudonym Marc Daniel, *Arcadie* dedicated itself to respectability. Baudry rejected the word "homosexual" and opted for the less-likely-to-offend term "homophile," which put the emphasis on emotions and attractions rather than activities. Yet despite these maneuvers, the Ministry of the Interior forbade the open display of the journal as well as its sale to minors (a prohibition that would remain in place until 1975). More devastatingly, in 1960, a leftist deputy named Paul Mirguet proposed to the French Assemblée Nationale that a law be passed that categorized homosexuality as a "social scourge" akin to alcoholism or prostitution, that the youth of France needed to be protected from this scourge, and that the government should be authorized to take measures to combat homosexuality. The proposal passed, almost unanimously, and without any discussion – and apparently in the midst of general laughter among the parliamentarians. The result of the Mirguet Amendment was that, a few months later, the government raised significantly the penalties for so-called public offenses against decency when these involved "an act against nature." This law would not be repealed until 1980, and although it did not directly affect most homosexuals in their daily lives, it contributed significantly to their stigmatization.

In Britain and West Germany, where male homosexuality continued to be formally criminalized into the postwar decades, men who had engaged in same-sex activities were constantly vulnerable to blackmailers. Numerous men paid large sums of money over many years in order to keep their tormentors quiet. Many men spent repeated bouts in prison. Indicatively, so pervasive was popular homophobia believed to be in Britain that the Mass-Observation Sex Survey conducted in 1949 in emulation of Alfred Kinsey's research in the USA opted not even to ask the citizens stopped on the street about their opinions on the topic. In Allied-occupied Germany, in the immediate post-Nazi years, there had been an atmosphere of flux and confusion in the law, and sometimes more liberal judges handed down fines rather than prison sentences, or noted that time served while awaiting trial was adequate. Activists hoped that the US military occupiers could be convinced to rescind Paragraph 175 and the Nazi addition of 175a the way they had undone other Nazi racial laws. But the Americans refused, and, as of 1950, aggressive prosecutions resumed – even as the judiciary had been inadequately de-Nazified. The first major case of the postwar era, in Frankfurt am Main, was a massive police and court action which brought 700 investigations and 140 prosecutions (many of them based on denunciations proffered by one young male prostitute); furthermore, the defendants faced the same man as judge who had also been their prosecutor during the Third Reich. The action ended in numerous prison sentences and at least six suicides.

Activists who sought to challenge the law in West Germany on the grounds of its unconstitutionality (arguing that criminalizing homosexual activity conflicted with West Germany's Basic Law guaranteeing each individual's right to "free development of the personality" and that the criminalization of male but not female homosexuality was discriminatory on the basis of gender) were repeatedly rebuffed. Among other things, a West German court in 1957 directly announced the law should stay, on the grounds that male homosexuality was far more dangerous to society than lesbianism. Meanwhile, the European Court of Human Rights, which began its work in 1959, recurrently refused cases concerning homosexuality through the 1960s. This was despite the fact that Articles 8, 12, and 14 of the European Declaration of Human Rights formulated in 1948 (the Court's legal basis) had been designed not least in reaction against Nazism's brutal invasions of the private sphere and intimate relationships, and expressly guaranteed the individual's right to privacy, to form a family by marriage, and to non-discrimination. It would not be until 1975 – notably in the midst of the wider sexual revolution sweeping Western Europe at that time – that the European Commission, which regulated the access of cases to the Court, would acknowledge that sexuality could be considered an "important" part of private life. And it would not be until 1981, in the context of a case concerning homosexual rights in Britain, that the Court ruled in favor of the plaintiffs.

In West Germany in the wake of Nazism, moreover, homophobic attitudes, far from being widely challenged, were actively refurbished and updated by leading self-appointed experts. Church leaders and activist conservative laity argued vigorously that sexual orientation was vulnerable, that homosexuality was a contagious condition, and that young people needed to be protected "during the time of their bisexual lability and homosexual receptiveness," while "those who disdain marriage must be punished."[22] But prominent secular individuals also played their part. The eminent sociologist Helmut Schelsky, for instance, by no means a sexual conservative in general, in his *Sociology of Sexuality* published

---

[22] A. Ohm, "Homosexualität als Neurose," *Der Weg zur Seele* 5 (1953), 56, and "Literatur-Umschau," *Kriminalistik* 6 (1952), 167–8.

in 1955 did not rely on traditional religious objections to homosexuality, but rather built on newer arguments that had been developed under Nazism. While homosexual rights activists emphasized the harm done to homosexual men by homophobia, Schelsky presented homosexual men as suffering from a "deficit" of heterosexual vitality and maturity – a "failure to build up a complete opposite-sex partnership." Homosexuals, Schelsky opined, really were incapable of citizenship, because their level of personhood was not high enough. Their tendency toward "solipsism," this "staying with one's own body," caused homosexuals to remain stuck at an "autistic" level, in a "sexuality of only pleasure-seeking." The idea that homophobic prejudice caused difficulties for homosexuals' acceptance in society reversed cause and effect, Schelsky thought: "The abnormals are not condemned to an outsider role only through some arbitrary norm-placement of society . . . Rather, the normative verdict constitutes the assessment of a culture that these groups are not capable of reaching the higher states of being."[23]

The rise of reform

Yet gradually, the tide was turning. In the postwar Netherlands, Bob Angelo (pseudonym for Nick Engelschman) restarted the magazine *Levensrecht* (Right to Life) he had first founded in 1940 with Jaap van Leeuwen (only three issues had appeared before the Nazis marched in); in 1946 Angelo launched a social organization for homosexuals, soon to be called COC (Cultuur en Ontspanningscentrum, Culture and Recreation Center), which attracted a small number of lesbians and a larger number of homosexual men. The police – not least because Angelo carefully maintained an age limit of 21 – opted for monitoring rather than outright repression. Working to maintain good relations with the government advisory committee concerned with identifying porn, Angelo also kept the content of *Levensrecht* deliberately innocent. He launched one dance club in 1952, and a second in 1955. As scholar and activist Gert Hekma has put it, with just a touch of sarcasm, "the police now preferred seeing homosexuals concentrated in a respectable club behind closed doors rather than swarming over the streets asking unsuspecting heterosexuals for sex at public urinals."[24] Chapters of COC spread to several other larger cities, although in one town (Groningen) police intervention did trigger suicides.

[23] Helmut Schelsky, *Soziologie der Sexualität* (Reinbek: Rowohlt, 1955), 62–83.
[24] Gert Hekma, *Homoseksualiteit in Nederland van 1730 tot de moderne tijd* (Amsterdam: Meulenhoff, 2004), 103.

In addition to providing support and socializing, one of COC's most successful initiatives was the work of activist Henri Methorst, a publisher and translator, who between 1953 and 1958 organized discussions between homosexuals and "experts" (such as lawyers, doctors, and clergymen). The long-term positive result was that most of the professionals involved in the conversations eventually, in the 1960s, published texts which humanized gays and lesbians. The Catholic psychiatrist Kees Trimbos and Dutch Reformed psychiatrist F. J. Tolsma became especially important advocates for tolerance. Just as with the discussions about birth control, so also with homosexuality, then, it was the conversion to a more sympathetic stance among professionals, also specifically religious ones, that ultimately paved the way for a transformed legal situation and more accepting popular attitudes. At the same time, the postwar shift in Dutch homosexual life from the streets to clubs turned Amsterdam into the new international "gay capital" that once, in the 1920s, had been the role of Berlin.

This shift toward greater tolerance in the Netherlands also brought a change in the organization of homosexual encounters. Pick-ups on the streets had often involved men who did not consider themselves homosexuals; those who understood themselves as homosexuals (*nichten*) had tended to go for "straight" men (*tules*). Now a new type of homosexuality evolved, one in which homosexual men both developed a more masculine personal style while at the same time seeking encounters and relationships no longer with heterosexuals but with other men who shared their orientation. No longer was *difference* (of age, class, or gender behavior) the erotic draw; similarity and equality were no longer felt as a hindrance to desire. At the same time, this shift within homosexuality accompanied a stronger delineation of the boundaries between homosexual and heterosexual, as self-defined heterosexual men who might in the past have enjoyed an occasional homosexual adventure on the side increasingly avoided male–male sex for fear of being labeled homosexual themselves.

Significantly, in short, precisely the loosening of restrictions on premarital heterosexual sex contributed even more to the stricter divisions between homo- and heterosexuality. Homophobia changed form. Sexual orientations became less fluid, more rigid. At the same time, the idea that sexuality was acceptable for married and unmarried heterosexual people alike created a new climate also for homosexual rights activism.

In Britain, too, transformed attitudes about heterosexual sex contributed to a climate in which a rethinking of the laws criminalizing male homosexuality was possible (even as the coincidentally concurrent reconceptualization of the laws surrounding heterosexual prostitution brought new

difficulties for prostitutes). A committee convened by the British government in 1954, headed by Sir John Wolfenden, the vice-chancellor of
the University of Reading, and including twelve others (three of them
women), mostly lawyers, clergy, and medical doctors, was assigned the
task of considering the state of the law surrounding both male homosexuality and female prostitution. While under Nazism and fascism homosexuality was often conceptually paired with abortion not least since the
emphasis lay in the *control of reproduction*, in the post-World War II era,
with the transnational shift to a preoccupation with *nurturing the domestic marital ideal*, it made some sense that the British government would
pair male homosexuality with heterosexual prostitution as two key forms
of deviation from the norm. Specifically, however, the conjunction happened to be the result of the British government's double embarrassment
in the face of pressures, on the one hand, from leading proponents of
decriminalization that pointed to the lack of anti-homosexual laws for
adults in France and Italy and, on the other, a growing sense of public
outrage over the perceived rise of visibility in street prostitution in the
postwar years, which was becoming a matter of international embarrassment; prostitution itself was not illegal but causing public annoyance by
soliciting was.

After years of deliberation, the Wolfenden Report was published in
1957, accompanied by massive journalistic coverage and expert discussion, both in Britain and internationally. The outcomes of the Wolfenden
committee's deliberations with respect to female prostitution were highly
problematic. The crackdown on public soliciting that Wolfenden recommended was motivated by quite overt misogyny; once the new legislation
was put in place, the result for prostitutes was exacerbated vulnerability.
However, the Wolfenden committee's recommendations with respect to
male homosexuality – urging the decriminalization of consensual homosexual relations in private for adults over the age of 21, a recommendation
finally turned into law in 1967 – is rightly celebrated as one of the great
turning points in the history of homosexual rights in the modern era.

It was not least a recognition that premarital and extramarital sex
among heterosexuals was pervasive but not criminalized that caused not
only Wolfenden's committee, but also leading spokespeople for both the
Anglican Protestant and the Roman Catholic churches, to suggest that
the law of the land should not be based on theological notions of morality. Premarital and extramarital heterosexual sex, after all, was also condemned by the churches, but it was not prosecuted by law. As *The Times*
of London summarized the point, criticizing those prominent clergymen
who wished to retain criminalization while praising those church leaders
(like the Archbishop of York and the Archbishop of Canterbury) who had

opted against "theocratic" legislation and endorsed Wolfenden's report, "If it is wrong to treat as crimes those so widely practised 'aberrations' of pre- and extramarital unchastity (in the private sphere and between consenting adults), then it cannot be right to punish the far less frequent 'aberration' of sexual relations between men, especially when the same lapse among women has never been criminalized."[25]

Above all, then, and significantly, what Wolfenden stands for is the ascent of the legal concepts and moral values of *consent* and *privacy*. Wolfenden's committee, like so many other European legislators and commentators before it, was deeply concerned about the vulnerable status of sexual orientation not only in adolescence but also in young adulthood, and it is noteworthy that once decriminalization of adult homosexuality went into effect in 1967, prosecutions for homosexuality among men younger than 21 quintupled. Nonetheless, the achievement of Wolfenden was considerable – and was received that way at the time by homosexual rights activists in many lands.

Yet both British and international observers realized that winning decriminalization was only the first battle in a larger war. Police harassment, popular homophobia, and a hypocritical notion of sexual morality remained pervasive in many nations. New arguments and strategies would be needed, and sex rights activists experimented with a variety of possible approaches. In the commentary on the Wolfenden Report, some of these new arguments were already in evidence. Thus, for instance, an author in the *New Statesman* applauded the report but also warned of the upsurge of petty and ugly moralizing that it might provoke and, despite the recent conversion to ideas of tolerance among their leaders, went on to criticize above all the Christian churches for having spent centuries narrowing discussions of morality solely to matters of sexuality. Her comments were a harbinger of arguments that would shortly, in the liberalizing – and then also rapidly radicalizing – climate of the 1960s, become far more widely advanced:

In 1938 the Archbishop of Canterbury forced a king [Edward VIII] to abdicate his throne in the name of sexual morality [because Edward insisted on marrying the twice-divorced American socialite Wallis Simpson], but the archbishop could find not one word to speak against the Nazi regime. Today the Archbishop of Canterbury has clear strong words about divorce, but in his opinions on "apartheid" he is quite more reticent... In our huge, overpopulated, modern civilization the church wants to force us to follow a set of prescriptions that was developed for little nomadic tribes whose continued existence was dependent

[25] Quoted in Rudolf Burkhardt, *Der Sturm bricht los: Der Streit um den Wolfenden Report in England* (Zurich: Verlag Der Kreis, 1957), 13.

on a goodly supply of children and an absence of internal conflicts. This is, by the way, the original source of the damnation of adultery as also homosexuality. Now these days we are obsessed with the problems of sexual life. A divergence from the norm in the sexual behavior of a man can ruin his career and blacken his name. But if a man is honorable: then what in the heavens difference does it make, if he is homo- or heterosexual, whether he has one wife or six lovers? As long as he makes those with whom he has bonds happy, no person has the right to condemn him, for happiness is the sole measuring gauge in sexual matters.[26]

In addition to the insistence here on seeing homo- and heterosexuality as comparable, at least two other rhetorical tactics are especially notable. One is the effort to expand what counts as moral discussion away from a limited fixation on sex and toward issues of anti-Semitism, anti-black racism, barbarism, and cruelty. The other is the rise of the idea of *happiness* as a measure of moral value.

Also in West Germany, new rhetorical tactics were needed, and as it turned out, nothing would be more important in helping liberals and leftists redirect the moral terms of conversation about sex than the return with full force to public discussion of the Holocaust as its details were made public in the postwar trials of perpetrators. Preeminent among these was the trial, held in Frankfurt am Main from 1963 to 1965, of twenty-two SS men and one prisoner *Kapo* – all perpetrators in Auschwitz. This trial soon provided a major focal point for rewriting the memory and lessons of the Third Reich for liberal-left purposes. Yet even before the Auschwitz trial began, the political mobilization against the culture of sexual conservatism had already gained considerable momentum.

A proposed reform of the Federal Republic's criminal code with respect to sexual matters served as an early occasion for the coordinated emergence of critical liberal voices. As in Britain with Wolfenden, so also in West Germany, the development of a new criminal code had been underway since 1954, when a commission comprised of jurists and politicians had been established for this purpose. Medical and legal experts were consulted at various stages, and in 1960 a first draft was published, with a revised version of the draft appearing in 1962. This revised draft rapidly won approval from the cabinet of the Christian Democratic government and thereafter the Federal Council. By 1963, discussion of the draft was imminent also in the Bundestag.

The 1962 draft was profoundly conservative. It retained the criminalization of adultery, and of pornography and mechanical sex aids. It

[26] Diana M. Chapman quoted in Burkhardt, *Der Sturm bricht los*, 11.

constrained the advertising and marketing of contraceptives and maintained the criminalization of abortion. Throughout, the draft was suffused with the notion that the purpose of the law was to guard citizens' morality, and it frequently invoked the idea of "the healthy sensibility of the people" – i.e. popular prejudices – as a legitimate reference point for legal rulings. The draft also continued to criminalize male homosexuality, averring that homosexuals did not act from an "inborn disposition," but rather were "overwhelmingly persons who . . . through seduction, habituation or sexual supersatiation have become addicted to vice or who have turned to same-sex intercourse for purely profit-seeking motives."[27] And the commission expressed the view that homosexuals should in most instances be capable, if they made enough of an effort, of suppressing their desires and hence living lives in accordance with the law. The commission reiterated key notions about youthful fluidity in sexual orientation and about homosexuality as a deficit of heterosexuality that had been developed under Nazism, and promoted into the postwar years by the Christian churches as well as prominent experts like Helmut Schelsky. But unlike in the climate of the 1950s, by the early 1960s critics of such notions were less easily cowed. The commission's recommendation that male homosexuality continue to be criminalized was found ultimately both to be the single most offensive aspect of the draft and as symptomatic of the commission's broader anti-sexual attitude.

A pathbreaking interdisciplinary anthology entitled *Sexualität und Verbrechen* (Sexuality and Crime, 1963) contributed more than any other text to reframing the terms of debate about sexuality in postwar West Germany. The anthology brought together Jewish re-émigrés like Frankfurt School philosopher and sociologist Theodor Adorno and the jurist Fritz Bauer (soon to be the main prosecutor at the Frankfurt Auschwitz trial) with former collaborators with Nazism like the head of the family planning association Pro Familia, Hans Harmsen. (Harmsen had been more appealing to US Planned Parenthood experts than the more radical sex rights activists from the Weimar era, tainted as they supposedly were by association with communism.) The volume also included the formerly NSDAP-affiliated sexologists Hans Giese (himself homosexual) and Hans Bürger-Prinz (who had made his career under Nazism by promoting anti-homosexual theories), as well as such gentile non-Nazis as the liberal jurist Herbert Jäger. With its more than twenty

27 See "Anhang: Auszüge aus der Bundestagsdrucksache IV/650 vom 4. Oktober 1962 (Regierungsentwurf eines Strafgesetzbuches–E 1962)" in Fritz Bauer, Hans Bürger-Prinz, Hans Giese, and Herbert Jäger (eds.), *Sexualität und Verbrechen* (Frankfurt am Main: Fischer Verlag, 1963), 406–7, 409–11.

contributors, the book provided a key instantiation of the intense cultural energy produced in postwar West Germany precisely by the mix of Jewish and ex-Nazi and non-Jewish liberal intellectuals. All three constituencies would prove to be necessary for the liberalization of the sexual culture.

Sexualität und Verbrechen vigorously challenged the 1962 conservative draft of the criminal code. Overall, and in this way modeled on the concepts developed by the Wolfenden Report, the book strongly advanced the legal ideals of consent and privacy and called for separating the realm of morality (the business of religion) from the realm of crime (the business of the law). The book also called attention to the fact that adult homosexuality was not criminalized in numerous nations, including France, Italy, Spain, Belgium, Sweden, Denmark, and Switzerland. What is most notable, however, both in this book and in its reception, is how extraordinarily important specifically the invocation of the Holocaust would be for pushing the case for sexual tolerance.

Two essays from the collection would be cited more than any others: one by the liberal Berlin education professor and psychotherapist Wolfgang Hochheimer, the other by Theodor Adorno. Hochheimer offered the most outraged condemnation of the commission's draft. He pointed out that empirical reality in no way lined up with the commission's conservative ideals. Again, as with Wolfenden, the key was the changed climate of heterosexual behaviors and beliefs. The vast majority of West Germans – perhaps 90 percent – were not virgins when they married; 40 percent of sexually mature individuals were not married at all; nor did sexual behavior within marriage match normative expectations. Hochheimer forcefully contended that homosexuality was simply a natural variant of human sexuality; he also did not hesitate to ascribe twisted impulses to the homophobic members of the commission. But his punchline invoked the Third Reich. Hochheimer above all made plain how offensive it was for the commission to justify its conservative opinions with repeated references to such concepts as "the moral sensibility of the people [*sittliches Volksempfinden*]," and he observed acerbically that "just yesterday" (i.e. during the Third Reich), "the 'sensibility of the people' was addressed and unleashed quite differently... in order cruelly to annihilate 'those of a different nature' as though they were 'insects,' 'lice,' 'devils,' 'animals,' 'subhumans.' Also the sexually 'abnormal' were expressly included here."[28]

Adorno too invoked Nazism and its legacies to promote the liberalization of 1960s West German sexual mores. Disgusted by the lack

---

[28] Wolfgang Hochheimer, "Das Sexualstrafrecht in psychologisch-anthropologischer Sicht," in Bauer *et al.* (eds.), *Sexualität und Verbrechen*, 90, 97–98.

of courage evinced by so many otherwise progressive postwar German intellectuals whenever the subject turned to sex, Adorno decisively defended sexual freedom. "Precisely when it is not warped or repressed, sex harms no one," he wrote. Adorno found it especially disturbing that even as taboos against premarital heterosexuality had become obviously outdated, sexually conservative, even aggressively punitive, messages against sexual minorities still reached a wide audience. And like Hochheimer, he concluded caustically that the sexual taboos still prevailing in his contemporary moment were a piece of the very same "ideological and psychological syndrome of prejudice, that helped to create the mass basis for National Socialism and whose manifest content lives on in a depoliticized form."[29]

The book did not singlehandedly defeat the commission's proposal for a revised criminal code. But it had a huge impact on the younger generation. Youth magazines frequently cited the book's arguments in their own attacks on the commission's draft. Progressive youth magazines not only documented the concrete damages done by laws which criminalized consensual sexual activity and its consequences, but also, and with increasing fervor, challenged what they saw as the hypocrisy of sexual conservatives and religious leaders the moment moral discussion turned to questions of racism and murder, and skewered with outrage the ways conservatives apparently found nudity more offensive than anti-Semitism. Liberals and leftists began to contend that the right to sexual activity was a fundamental human right, and that the desire for sex was something for which no one needed ever again to apologize. They started to assert forcefully that sexual pleasure was itself a moral good. Rather than placing their emphasis on Nazism's incitements to sexual activity also outside of marriage, as for example conservative Christians had done in the more immediate aftermath of the war, liberals and leftists began ever more frequently to stress Nazism's sexually repressive aspects. This collective move would deal a staggering blow to the commission's draft for the new criminal code, and would finally cause the Bundestag first to set the matter aside – and then fail eventually ever to return to it.

In retrospect, the 1950s and early 1960s in Western Europe can definitely be interpreted as an era of transition toward greater liberality. This was not least because the security and future-orientation made possible by steady economic growth, full employment, new consumer opportunities, the proliferation of private housing away from the prying eyes of neighbors and extended family alike, and a belief that one's children would

---

[29] Theodor W. Adorno, "Sexualtabus und Recht heute," in Bauer *et al.* (eds.), *Sexualität und Verbrechen*, 301–3, 305, 310.

have better chances than oneself facilitated more expansive notions of the pursuit of pleasures as not only a possibility but also a right. By contrast, in the Soviet Union and in many of the Eastern Bloc states, people certainly found ways to live their emotional and erotic lives in the interstices of the surveillance and privation (although in view of the utterly overcrowded housing, the biggest question for young lovers hoping to have sex was often: "Where?"). But there was no opportunity to push for a more liberalized sexual politics.

Yet what also must be acknowledged are the darker sides of the Cold War-era sexual politics in the West. These include the variously cruelly punitive or simply dismissive treatments of sexual minorities – homosexual men and lesbians as well as prostitutes; especially in Austria, the postwar prosecution of both homosexual men and lesbians remained intense, as Austrians continued to present themselves to the world as victims of Nazism rather than participants in it, and felt no pressure to change their laws. They also include the extraordinary aggressions unleashed at European women who were drawn to men of color, and at those men – whether they were African American GIs or immigrants or former colonials. In West Germany, the first "guestworkers" were from the "Mediterranean" countries of Italy, Spain, Greece, eventually also Turkey; in Britain the newly arrived came from the Caribbean or South Asia or other parts of the former British Empire. "We are here because you were there," as a subsequent slogan put it, about the presence of numerous people of color in the British Isles in the postwar era of decolonization.

Debates about the countless ensuing "interracial" relationships were a major site for expressions of both banal stereotyping and more vicious racism. There was less worry about European men's relationships with immigrant women, but a great deal of concern with the reverse. West Indian men in Britain, for instance, who were in romantic relationships with white women were a focus of continual negative obsession. But so too were the men who supposedly controlled the London prostitution scene; during a debate in parliament over a reform in prostitution law it was said that "the great majority of ponces and pimps in this country are not Englishmen. They are principally Maltese, Ghanaians and Jamaicans . . . they are a pest to this country, and the crime of poncing is a singularly un-English crime," and one MP went so far as to speak of "these stinking people who come to this country and earn money from the bodies of women."[30] In many countries, moreover, debates over women

---

[30] Quoted in Helen J. Self, *Prostitution, Women and Misuse of the Law: The Fallen Daughters of Eve* (London: Routledge, 2003), 189.

who were involved with GIs, immigrants, or former colonials also provided the occasion for the expression of hostility and confusion over the unmistakable loosening especially of female sexual mores. Widespread popular ambivalence about sexual freedoms – particularly freedoms for women and homosexuals – kept reformers in all Western European countries embattled and isolated. It would take a much wider revolution in popular values for the ideas the reformers advanced to come to seem like common sense.

Further reading

Bauer, Ingrid, and Renate Huber, "Sexual Encounters across (Former) Enemy Lines" in Günter Bischof, Anton Pelinka, and Dagmar Herzog (eds.), *Sexuality in Austria*. Contemporary Austrian Studies 15 (New Brunswick, NJ: Transaction Publishers, 2007), 65–101.

Coffin, Judith G., "Between Opinion and Desire: *Elle* Magazine's Survey Research in 1950s France" in Kerstin Brückweh (ed.), *The Voice of the Citizen Consumer: A History of Market Research, Consumer Movements, and the Political Public Sphere* (Oxford University Press, 2011), 51–73.

Collins, Marcus, "Pride and Prejudice: West Indian Men in Mid Twentieth-Century Britain," *Journal of British Studies* 40 (2001), 391–418.

Modern Love: An Intimate History of Men and Women in Twentieth-Century Britain (London: Atlantic Books, 2003).

Connelly, Matthew, *Fatal Misconception: The Struggle to Control World Population* (Cambridge, MA: Harvard University Press, 2008).

Francis, Martin, "A Flight from Commitment? Domesticity, Adventure and the Masculine Imaginary in Postwar Britain," *Gender and History* 19 (April 2007), 163–85.

Heineman, Elizabeth D., *What Difference Does a Husband Make? Women and Marital Status in Nazi and Postwar Germany* (Berkeley: University of California Press, 1999).

"The Economic Miracle in the Bedroom: Big Business and Sexual Consumption in Reconstruction West Germany," *Journal of Modern History* 78 (December 2006), 846–77.

Hoffmann, David L., "Mothers in the Motherland: Stalinist Pronatalism in its Pan-European Context," *Journal of Social History* 34 (Fall 2000), 35–54.

Höhn, Maria, *GIs and Fräuleins: The German American Encounter in 1950s West Germany* (Chapel Hill: University of North Carolina Press, 2002).

Jackson, Julian, *Living in Arcadia: Homosexuality, Politics, and Morality in France from the Liberation to AIDS* (University of Chicago Press, 2009).

Kon, Igor S., *The Sexual Revolution in Russia: From the Age of the Czars to Today* (New York: Free Press, 1995).

Laciak, Beata, "Sex, Gender and Body in Polish Democracy in the Making," *International Journal of Law, Policy and the Family* 10 (April 1996), 37–51.

Langhamer, Clare, "The Meanings of Home in Postwar Britain," *Journal of Contemporary History* 40 (2005), 341–62.

Laubier, Claire (ed.), *The Condition of Women in France, 1945 to the Present: A Documentary Anthology* (London: Routledge, 1990).

Martel, Frédéric, *The Pink and the Black: Homosexuals in France since 1968*, trans. Jane Marie Todd (Stanford University Press, 1995).

Merridale, Catherine, *Ivan's War: Life and Death in the Red Army, 1939–1945* (New York: Metropolitan Books, 2006).

Moeller, Robert, "The Homosexual Man is a 'Man,' the Homosexual Woman is a 'Woman': Sex, Society, and the Law in Postwar West Germany," *Journal of the History of Sexuality* 4 (1994), 395–429.

Nash, Mary, "Pronatalism and Motherhood in Franco's Spain" in Gisela Bock and Pat Thane (eds.), *Maternity and Gender Policies: Women and the Rise of the European Welfare States, 1880s–1950s* (London: Routledge, 1994), 160–95.

Pittaway, Mark, *Eastern Europe 1939–2000* (Oxford University Press, 2004).

Schumann, Dirk, and Richard Bessel (eds.), *Life after Death: Approaches to a Cultural and Social History of Europe* (Cambridge University Press, 2003).

Self, Helen J., *Prostitution, Women and Misuse of the Law: The Fallen Daughters of Eve* (London: Routledge, 2003).

Sohn, Anne-Marie, "French Catholics between Abstinence and 'Appeasement of Lust', 1930–1950" in Franz Eder, Gert Hekma, and Lesley A. Hall (eds.), *Sexual Cultures in Europe: Themes in Sexuality*, 2 vols. (Manchester University Press, 1999), vol. I, 233–54.

Somers, Angelo, and Frans van Poppel, "Catholic Priests and the Fertility Transition among Dutch Catholics," *Annales de Démographie Historique* 2 (2003), 57–88.

Vickers, Emma, "'The Good Fellow': Negotiation, Remembrance, and Recollection – Homosexuality in the British Armed Forces, 1939–1945" in Dagmar Herzog (ed.), *Brutality and Desire: War and Sexuality in Europe's Twentieth Century* (New York: Palgrave Macmillan, 2009), 109–34.

Virgili, Fabrice, *Shorn Women: Gender and Punishment in Liberation France*, trans. John Flower (New York: Berg, 2002).

Wanrooij, Bruno P. F., "Carnal Knowledge: The Social Politics and Experience of Sex Education in Italy, 1940–80" in Lutz Sauerteig and Roger Davidson (eds.), *Sex Education of the Young in the Twentieth Century: A Cultural History* (London and New York: Taylor & Francis, 2008), 113–33.

4   Pleasure and rebellion 1965–1980

"The more I make love, the more I make revolution." So went the popular slogan in France at the height of the student revolts in 1968, when radicals also plastered the walls of Paris with signs demanding "Orgasm without Limits." Or as a West German saying from the era had it, "Pleasure, sex and politics belong together." It felt as though a new era had dawned. In British feminist Angela Carter's words, looking back on the later 1960s, "Truly it felt like Year One."[1] In Italy there was a slight time lag. As one commentator put it retrospectively, remembering the year 1975 (in not quite grammatical English): "In my (religious) country we saw sexual revolution only in TV, from U.S.; hippy generation was end in America but was just arrived in Italy!"[2]

Yet the relationship between radical activism and the massive transformation of the sexual landscape of Europe in the 1960s–1970s remains unclear. What caused "the sexual revolution"? For too long, commentators writing about sexual developments in the second half of the twentieth century operated within a paradigm that simply assumed steady liberalization and the gradual overcoming of obstacles to sexual freedom. Scholars tended to oscillate between presuming either that the growth of a culture of consumerism and the medical-technological invention of the birth control pill in the early 1960s sparked the sexual revolution or that this revolution was the logical result of courageous social movement activism on behalf of sexual liberties, legalization of abortion, and gay and lesbian rights. Neither of these versions is wrong, but they leave questions about the interactions between market forces and activism unresolved. More problematically, both approaches tend to assume that the sheer overwhelming attractiveness of sexual freedom can explain the

---

[1] Quoted in Paul Barker, "Angela Carter: Clever, Sexy, Funny, Scary," *The Independent*, January 22, 2006.
[2] Tweet about Renato Zero (Italian pop star) and Italian Sexual Revolution, Canzoni Italiane – Italian Songs, http://canzoniitaliane.blogspot.com/2007/10/renato-zero-and-italian-sexual.html, accessed October 25, 2009.

revolution's success. Liberalization, however, was not a straightforward (and also not an unambiguous) process.

The market of desire

Certainly, the rise of consumer capitalism played its part in making the revolution happen. So too did the media and the advertising industry. The supersaturation of the visual landscape with ever more risqué images, along with the increasing space taken up in mainstream periodicals by sensationalist reportage on sex-related matters (an especially good way for magazines and newspapers to increase sales among all age groups but also and especially to reach that new lucrative market of postwar youth, a generation with more spending money than any that had gone before) certainly helped to wash away the old culture of hypocrisy and taboo. The gap between what people were doing in private and what they were willing to declare in public narrowed dramatically. What had been *covert* became *overt*. The change between 1964 and 1968 was profound. Public nudity, premarital sex, marital infidelity, strip clubs, specific sexual techniques that intensified pleasure: all were suddenly fodder for media and public discussion, indeed for obsessive preoccupation. Sex was endlessly and everywhere promoted as the most desirable thing on the planet. And there is no question that this new glaringly conspicuous ubiquity of sexual imagery and inundation of all media with talk about sex exposed the gap between the loosening popular behaviors and the inherited official norms still enshrined in legislation – and thereby also created an opening for liberal and radical public intellectuals, politicians, artists, and activists to press for changed laws as well.

Yet it is absolutely crucial to recall how extraordinarily difficult it would be – despite all this – to transform each country's legal system. It would ultimately take a complex combination of pressure from below, in the form of daring and creative – often deliberately and defiantly outrageous – social movements, and strategizing from above, as individual activists and politicians worked within and across party-political lines, to rewrite the laws of every land. In addition, it was often the example of developments in other countries that helped activists and pro-liberalization government leaders to persuade more reluctant politicians that legal change was necessary. Thus, for instance, Italians seeking to decriminalize contraception contended that it was "embarrassing" that in this matter Italy was so behind and backwards in comparison with more progressive nations like the United Kingdom or the Netherlands. Or to take another example: Swiss and Austrian feminists and politicians working to legalize abortion (efforts that failed in Switzerland but succeeded in Austria) followed closely the debates and changes taking place in the early 1970s in the neighboring nations of West Germany and France. And in many nations, activists invoked the supposedly so sex-liberal Scandinavian countries, especially Sweden, as models for enlightened sex education. Yet although international trends mattered, each country's story was distinctive, and it remains notable just how diverse were the moral arguments and political strategies that ended up being most effective in each country for changing the laws in more tolerant directions.

It is no less vital to recall how many ambivalences and confusions the sexual revolution caused. Some of those ambivalences had to do with the discomfort among radical activists that, of all things, it was apparently the loathsome system of capitalism that was advancing new sexual possibilities. The hopes that making love would also make revolution were rather quickly dashed. Perhaps pleasure, sex, and politics did not really belong together after all, since evidently encouragements to ever new sexual experimentation could coexist quite comfortably with support for militarism in Vietnam and a profit-oriented market economy. In fact, perhaps incitement to sexual activity was a way of keeping the lower classes politically quiescent. Many radicals were drawn to philosopher Herbert Marcuse's theory that the sexual revolution fostered by consumer capitalism had wrought only "repressive desublimation": seeming freedom and constant encouragement to pursue sexual activity, but only in order to distract attention from political struggle and to make the daily anxieties caused by life in a competitive and unjust society moderately more bearable. Or as John Lennon put it with caustic cynicism in his song "Working Class Hero": After having been pummeled into insecurity for "twenty-odd years" ("they make you feel small"), while being kept "doped with religion and sex and TV," a young working-class man was told there was still "room at the top," but he must first learn "to smile as you kill."[3] In short, rather than being the path to revolution, maybe sex was an antidote to revolution.

A second source of ambivalences had to do with the puzzle over what it actually *meant* to liberate desire – and also what the limits of liberation might be. What about coercion, harassment, and violence against women? What about the vulnerabilities of children? Where did one person's right to sexual self-expression end and another's begin, and how could self-determination for everyone be secured? The feminist movement that emerged in tandem with the sexual revolution ultimately

---

[3] John Lennon, "Working Class Hero," lyrics *John Lennon/Plastic Ono Band* (Apple/EMI, 1970).

advocated not just for laws decriminalizing divorce, contraception, and abortion, but also for laws that prosecuted rape more effectively while protecting rape victims' rights to privacy, and for laws and awareness campaigns against child sexual abuse. Feminists also vehemently criticized the self-involved and often misogynist pretensions evident among too many New Left male activists and politically mainstream men alike. Meanwhile, lesbian and gay liberation activists exposed the heteronormative assumptions evident not just in conservative quarters but among self-styled progressives as well. And eventually, despite initial defensiveness around lesbianism, the wider and predominantly heterosexual women's movement by the early 1970s took lesbian challenges seriously and made the call to "end compulsory heterosexuality!" its own.

Yet disconcerting conflicts persisted. What exactly was sex for? There was, for instance, enormous controversy and perplexity over how to feel about sex in exchange for money. Feminists argued about whether prostitutes were sisters in the struggle for female sexual self-determination, victims of male turpitude, or (at least for straight women) rivals for men's interests. They also puzzled over other forms of depersonalized sex, like peep shows. What exactly *was* the appeal of depersonalized sex and why did so many men seem drawn to it? Many women – and some men – began to wonder and worry over whether the idea of emotional connection during sex was just an illusion. Similarly, gay male activists calling for homosexuals to come "Out of the toilets and into the streets" struggled mightily over whether transactional sex was something to be defended or to be overcome.

More broadly, many of the ambivalences and confusions that swirled through the sexual revolution, as it quickly grew far beyond the counterculture to take over mainstream culture as well, had to do with the emotional complexities inevitably unleashed both by the new freedoms and by the new pressures those freedoms brought with them. Was sexual fidelity an antiquated petty bourgeois ideal or a legitimate progressive practice – now that the formerly respectable, staid masses were enthusiastically and openly exploring their own adulterous impulses? What if someone wanted you to sleep with them but you weren't interested and they declared you frigid or uptight? And all through: What if you were having sex but you weren't as happy with it as you thought you should be, now that everyone was talking about how absolutely great it was?

The pill

Indisputably, an important factor in changing mores was the invention of the birth control pill in the early 1960s and its ever wider distribution

in the following years, in most countries first only to married women
and then by the late 1960s and early 1970s accessible, with a doctor's
prescription, also to single women. Although premarital intercourse had
been on the rise in all nations after World War II, albeit at widely varying rates (depending on nation and regional differences within nations,
but also especially class differences), the pill's reliability contributed substantially to taking the fear out of coitus, and for the first time ever freed
women to experiment sexually as only men had been able to before.

Initially it was hoped – indeed expected – that the pill, as a "natural"
rather than mechanical method of birth control, would meet with Vatican
approval and relieve the pangs of conscience of millions of Catholics. As
of 1964, optimistic protesters in St. Peter's Square in Rome carried banners proclaiming "Yes to the Pill!" and "No to the Population Bomb."
In 1965, eighty-one Nobel laureates petitioned the Pope to accept birth
control on the grounds of a demographic crisis, the difficulties faced by
an "unwanted child", and the argument that parents had the right to
bear "that number of children which can be cared for and cherished."[4]
Ultimately, however, and despite strong support for the pill from prominent Catholic clergy, Pope Paul VI in 1968 in *Humanae Vitae* reiterated
the Catholic church's rejection of all contraception other than periodic
abstinence. Nonetheless, conservative politicians were not necessarily
hostile. In Britain, in 1961, the Conservative (and famously racist and
anti-immigrant) Minister of Health Enoch Powell announced that the pill
Conovid (equivalent to the US version called Enovid) would be available
by prescription through the National Health Service at a government-
subsidized price. For medical doctors, prescribing the pill was certainly
less awkward than fitting a diaphragm.

And the expansion in use was exponential. The pill had been on sale in
Italy since 1964, but only for treating menstrual disorders; the promotion
of contraceptives by doctors would be illegal until 1971. Nonetheless,
by 1969, the Italian Ministry of Health estimated that one in ten Italian
women was using oral contraceptives. Also in Francoist Spain, from 1965
on, gynecologists were permitted to prescribe contraceptives for health
purposes (even though contraceptives would not be formally legalized
until 1978, several years after Franco's death).

In France, too, the pill was initially only made available by prescription
for the purpose of "regulating menstruation." Yet already by 1966, the
French Movement for Family Planning (*Mouvement français pour le planning familial*, MFPF), founded in 1956, had managed to establish 200
centers across the nation and was so openly flouting the 1920 law against

[4] John Cogley, "Nobel Laureates Petition the Pope," *New York Times*, June 22, 1965.

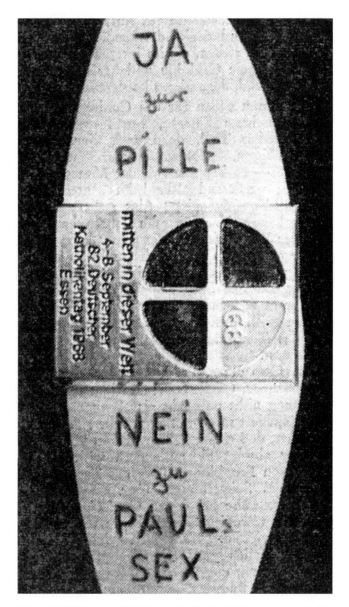

Fig. 4.1 "Yes to the Pill, No to Paul's Sex." Button worn in September 1968 at the *Katholikentag*, a major biannual gathering of West German Catholics. The slogan is a protest against Pope Paul's anti-pill encyclical *Humanae Vitae*, promulgated in July of that year. Many believing Catholics were astonished and dismayed that the Pope had decided against the recommendations of his advisers, many of whom had urged that the pill be endorsed.

the promotion of contraception, including by promoting the pill (the trick for circumventing the law was for interested individuals to become "members" of the organization), that this very contrast between practice and legislation prompted the Gaullist deputy Lucien Neuwirth to propose legislation decriminalizing contraception in France. It passed in 1967; among other things, politicians were persuaded that by promoting contraception, the rate of illegal abortions could be reduced. Although, by 1970, only 6 percent of French women had used the pill, by 1975, once the national health insurance covered the costs and restrictions against its use by minors had been removed, fully a quarter of all French women had tried it.

In West Germany, the shift was even more dramatic. As of 1964, only 2,000 West German women had tried the pill and the majority of doctors refused to prescribe to the unmarried. Furious at the refusal, radical activists turned the pill into a cause célèbre, auctioning pills as a form of guerilla theatre, circulating addresses of doctors willing to prescribe to singles, and demanding that universities provide pill access. And soon many women simply made up their own minds. By 1968, the number of West German women using the pill had jumped to 1.4 million and would climb even more thereafter. By 1975–77, one third of all fertile women in West Germany were relying on the pill; among younger women, the rates were even higher – close to 80 percent of young women under age 20.

Porn

Yet the desire for sexual connection with another flesh-and-blood human being that the pill so facilitated was quite apparently not the only contributory impulse in the transformation of European sexual cultures, for porn too played its part in setting the sexual revolution in motion. In Britain in 1964, the first recognizably modern (glossy *and* affordable rather than solely either elite or scuzzy) porn magazine, *King*, hit the stands. A year later Bob Guccione's *Penthouse* was launched, and a year after that *Mayfair*, followed in 1968 by *Penthouse* spin-offs *Forum* and *Lords*. As British scholar Marcus Collins observed acerbically, the new climate of permissiveness in the 1960s was not just based in "a series of liberalizing laws but also a popular movement supported by the legions of male masturbators who bought soft-core porn."[5]

The apparent ocean of popular demand for stimulating images demonstrably made the obscenity laws unenforceable. In laws passed in 1959

[5] Marcus Collins, *Modern Love: An Intimate History of Men and Women in Twentieth-Century Britain* (London: Atlantic Books, 2003), 134.

and 1964, Britain decriminalized arousing material if it could be proven to have artistic or scholarly merit. Although clearly neither was the case with these magazines, nonetheless the marketers simply were no longer prosecuted. In 1966, it was said of the American magazine *Playboy* that "half a million of the four million copies of the monthly" were sold in Europe; also "in Italy, *Playboy* can be received through the mail if the mail is not censored. And we must also consider all the good Italian husbands who drive to the Swiss border just to buy *Playboy*."[6] In France as well, although official decriminalization would not occur until 1994, as of 1969 one commentator remarked that "the pornographic press, foreign and French alike, is virtually sold openly at every newspaper kiosk."[7]

The tiny nation of Denmark took the lead in formal decriminalization (literary and other narrative porn was decriminalized in 1967, sexually explicit visuals in 1969), and for several years Denmark became the world's largest exporter of pornography. Tens of millions of dollars were made in these first years. Denmark also became home to a hundred sex shops, for which a quarter of the visitors were tourists from other countries. The first pornography trade fair was held there in October 1969. Sweden and then West Germany followed suit in officially decriminalizing pornography a few years later. Perhaps not incidentally, these two countries were as of 1969 considered the top European producers of erotic films. But even while it was still illegal, already, as of 1968, West Germany was said to have the highest rate of porn consumption on the planet. By 1971, West Germans spent 50 million Deutschmarks annually on imported pornography (mostly hard-core magazines from Denmark and other Scandinavian nations), and more than twice that (approximately 125 million) on domestically produced print pornography. And although this was not well known at the time, quite a few respectable publishers and organizations (including trade unions and the Social Democratic Party on the Left, the Axel Springer and Bauer publishing companies on the Right, and even some Catholic presses) did double duty printing legitimate and illegitimate wares. Publishers in danger of being caught simply closed down one magazine and launched a new one. At the same time, soft-core imagery went completely mainstream. Voluptuous naked breasts were suddenly everywhere, gracing the covers of family magazines available at every neighborhood newsstand and filling huge billboards on city streets.

[6] Oriana Fallaci, *The Egotists: Sixteen Surprising Interviews* (Chicago: H. Regnery Co., 1966), 115.
[7] Jacques Natanson, "Education sexuelle et maturité sociale," *Revue Française de Pédagogie* 9 (Oct./ Nov./Dec., 1969), 15.

Meanwhile, the well-regarded West German journalist and soon-to-be sex education specialist Oswalt Kolle turned an article series he was writing into a sequence of wildly successful movies in which naked couples haltingly and awkwardly discussed their sexual problems (from female difficulty reaching orgasm due to male inattentiveness or hapless technique to men's problems with premature ejaculation) while expert voice-overs assured people that marriages could be mended through open communication and extolled the benefits of such practices as cunnilingus and fellatio. Kolle films like *Das Wunder der Liebe* (The Miracle of Love, 1967), *Deine Frau, das unbekannte Wesen* (Your Wife, that Unknown Creature, 1969), and *Dein Mann, das unbekannte Wesen* (Your Husband, that Unknown Creature, 1970) became smash hits, shown in cinemas and also schoolrooms in even the smallest towns. Deeply moved and motivated by the thousands of readers' letters he had received for his article series (90 percent of the women who wrote in said that their first sexual experiences had included absolutely no pleasure), Kolle was able to prevent censorship by pleading that the films strengthened marriages and encouraged a healthier, happier citizenry. These movies, like the West German government-sponsored *Helga* (1969) which imitated Kolle's style – here too the entire family went nude and, in addition, a real childbirth was for the first time ever shown on screen – would eventually be seen by tens of millions of people, not just in West Germany but also in the Netherlands, France, Switzerland, Spain, and Turkey – and as far away as Australia. As the Australian posters for *Helga* raved, this "frank!" and "fascinating!" movie was "a sex education film for ALL."[8] In France, 5 million citizens saw it (among them 50,000 of the 160,000 inhabitants of Grenoble); in Paris, a special private viewing was organized for 1,500 Catholic clergy. In Spain, hundreds of thousands read translations of Kolle's books and his promoters there produced a three-volume videocassette of his films that became a popular wedding gift.

While in hindsight it might seem that women would have more worries about the rampant commercial exploitation of their bodies and also would have reason to fear that the new liberties might above all be liberties for men – even more opportunities for men to multiply the number of their sexual partners, while giving their promiscuity the enhanced moral justification that they were bravely bucking repression and inherited prohibitions – in fact many men had a variety of hesitations as well. In Britain a poll showed that in the 1970s almost half of the young British

[8] Poster for the Australian version of *Helga*, available at: www.wrongsideoftheart.com/wp-content/gallery/posters-h/helga_poster_01.jpg.

Fig. 4.2 *Your Husband, that Unknown Creature*. In English the title was "The Sensual Male." Oswalt Kolle's hit sex advice film of 1970.

Fig. 4.3 *Helga*. Sex education film sponsored by the West German government in 1969 and seen by tens of millions of Europeans. Poster for the French version of the film.

Fig. 4.4 Paola Pitagora in "The Secret: A Love Story." First page of one of the *fotoromanzi* created in 1974 by the Italian social psychologist and sex rights activist Luigi De Marchi to encourage the use of contraception by playing on men's desires to be considered good lovers.

men polled in one survey objected to the birth control pill – specifically because it gave *women* sexual freedom. In Italy, the social psychologist and sex rights activist Luigi De Marchi in 1974 developed a brilliant strategy for promoting contraceptive use which also implicitly revealed men's discomfort. In De Marchi's view, the main challenge in encouraging the use of birth control was not availability of contraceptives but rather *motivation* to use them. And he strongly suspected that it was *men* who were reluctant precisely because contraception afforded wives more freedom to do what they wanted – including the pursuit of infidelity. With the help of prominent actors and actresses, he developed *fotoromanzi* (little stories using photos that looked like film stills), in which people talked about the pill. In one of the most effective ones, a beautiful woman (the actress Paola Pitagora) is miserable and does not enjoy sex. Her husband is given the advice that she should take the pill – not, however, to encourage her freedom, but rather – because, so this *fotoromanzi*'s argument went, if she stopped being afraid of pregnancy, then she would climax more easily with her husband. And *then* she would stop looking around. As Pitagora says to her husband: "And you want to know something else? Now other men don't interest me anymore because you give me everything."[9]

Numerous other commentators were concerned that while sex was being "talked to death," it was unclear whether people were truly happier. It was no minor matter, a West German Protestant church spokesman noted astutely, that "the newly won freedom can also be experienced as burdensome and insecurity-inducing." Quite apparently, moreover, there was not only such a thing as frustrated desire due to prudery and repression, but "also a frustration that is the result of fulfillment that is experienced as disappointing."[10] The Rolling Stones' 1965 hit "(I Can't Get No) Satisfaction" turned out to have a totally different possible meaning. Even if people were having a lot of sex, that did not necessarily mean they were genuinely satisfied. "Are the constant sex-, love-, and enlightenment-series in the mass media really meeting a need of the reading public or is the frenzy being whipped up artificially?" a critical journalist writing in a church newspaper asked as early as 1968. "Is everyone everywhere loudly demanding a revolution that has already long since occurred? Are wishes and lusts being awakened only for commercial purposes?"[11] Moreover, this author went on to note, it was not that shame had disappeared; it had simply been displaced from the realm of sex

---

[9] *Paola Pitagora in Il Segreto* (Rome: IRIDE, 1975), 3.

[10] Wilhelm Quenzer, "Sexuelle Befreiung und Aggressivität," *Evangelische Zentralstelle für Weltanschauungsfragen: Information* 47 (1971), 3.

[11] Geno Hartlaub, "Leben für den Sex (II)," *Deutsches Allgemeines Sonntagsblatt* 47 (November 24, 1968), 17.

(where all taboos had long since been ruptured to the point that nothing new could be said) to the realm of deeper feelings like love and suffering, longing and passion. Intensity of emotion and specificity of desire for a particular unique individual: *that* was what had become difficult to talk about.

Revolutionary theories

Young New Left activists had their own qualms about the commercial exploitation of sexual desires, but they certainly did not think the problem was that there was too much sexual freedom. Instead, they strove to theorize, in numerous variations, just how *politically* significant sexual liberation would be. "Make Love Not War": The most popular slogan of the era was not solely a recommendation for a more decent and pleasurable activity than slaughtering other human beings while risking one's own life – in Vietnam or elsewhere. It was also a theory of human nature, an earnest and deeply held conviction that those who made a lot of love simply would not be interested in hurting or killing others.

The rediscovery of the at once anti-capitalist and sex-radical tradition of the interwar era, and especially the 1920s–1930s work of the Austrian Freudian Marxist Wilhelm Reich, was an enormously important factor in lending moral authority to this worldview. From London to Copenhagen, Paris, Amsterdam, and Berlin, and in many smaller university towns as well, Reich's titles (*The Sexual Revolution, The Function of the Orgasm*, and *The Mass Psychology of Fascism*) were reissued in various languages in mimeograph and subsequently in paperback. Excerpts of Reich's texts and a plethora of Reich quotes were published in early guidebooks and "bibles" of the student movement, including, in French, the special issue of *Partisans* entitled *Sexualité et répression* (Sexuality and Repression, 1966), as well as *Le petit livre rouge de la révolution sexuelle* (The Little Red Book of the Sexual Revolution, 1969); quite a few books of the era provided not much more than an enthusiastic endorsement and cut-and-paste pastiche of Reich's main tenets. Above all, his ideas captured the imaginations of those who urgently hoped that the struggle for social justice and the pursuit of pleasure were mutually enhancing projects. This had a great deal to do with Reich's central argument that (as he phrased it) "cruel character traits" were evident among those "in a condition of chronic sexual dissatisfaction," while "genitally satisfied people" were notable for their "gentleness and goodness."[12]

---

[12] Wilhelm Reich, *Die Funktion des Orgasmus: Sexualökonomische Grundprobleme der biologischen Energie* (1927; reprinted Cologne: Kiepenheuer und Witsch, 1969), 139.

Sexual emancipation was no trivial matter; to be sexually liberated was already to be a better, kinder person – and potentially even a courageous anti-fascist.

Reichian ideas were taken up in Eastern Europe as well. In 1971, the Yugoslav filmmaker Dušan Makavejev produced the movie *W.R.: Mysteries of the Organism* (W.R. being a reference to Wilhelm Reich), an eccentric mixture of fiction film and documentary footage which followed the story of a working-class Yugoslav woman, Milena, who seduces a Russian ice skater named Vladimir Illyich and – because he is unable fully to experience pleasure – is ultimately killed by him. Intercut with this story is a montage of interviews with individuals who personally knew Reich and others like the masturbation guru Betty Dodson who provide encouragement for the pursuit of intensified orgasms. Not least because Vladimir Illyich was the real name of V. I. Lenin and thus the unsatisfied Russian man represented repressive and uptight forms of socialism, the film was indisputably also a strong political critique of the Soviet system as not an improvement over or adequate alternative to Western capitalism. With dialogue in Serbo-Croat and English, and although it was never released in Makavejev's native Yugoslavia, the film quickly developed a cult following and was much discussed in the USA and Western Europe.

In West Germany, the preoccupation with Reich was particularly passionate because of the urgency for young radicals to grapple with the lessons and legacies of the Nazi past. The hope was that in Reich they had found the key to the participation of their parents' generation in the persecution and murder of European Jewry – and simultaneously, that taking Reich's cue to treat their own young children's sexuality as normal and healthy rather than dangerous and deserving of repression could help prevent the formation of fascistic personalities in the future. How could the student radicals' so profoundly propriety- and respectability-obsessed elders have become such enthusiastic supporters of Adolf Hitler or even participants in genocide? As the feminist journalist Ulrike Heider summarized the evolving Reich-inspired consensus in hindsight, "harmless, so-called well-behaved people had . . . been able to become sadistic SA henchmen and concentration camp guards because they had been tormented and sexually repressed by their parents."[13] Or as the New Left sociologist Dietrich Haensch put it in 1969, capitalist class relations, fascism, and brutality in warfare were all three products of the "genital weakness"

---

[13] Ulrike Heider, "Freie Liebe und Liebesreligion: Zum Sexualitätsbegriff der 60er und 80er Jahre" in Ulrike Heider (ed.), *Sado-masochisten, Keusche, und Romantiker: Vom Mythos neuer Sinnlichkeit* (Reinbek: Rowohlt, 1986), 94.

induced in those whose natural drives had been coercively distorted and
repressed and who had been forced to develop "cramped-up" concepts of
honor, duty, and self-control. "The tendency to sadism is maintained,"
Haensch informed his readers, "by diverting the libidinal energies away
from the sexual drive and toward the drive for destruction and aggression; the necessary fixation on the enemy occurs by diverting the hatred
produced by the ambivalent hate–love fixation on the sexual oppressor
onto the military opponent."[14]

The lessons for childrearing also seemed clear. Children should certainly never be beaten. But they should also be given free rein to choose
their own games and to run around naked and to enjoy touching their
own and each other's bodies. In a combination of impulses taken from
both Reich and the Scottish educator A. S. Neill (founder of Summer-
hill School), West German radicals developed their own version of anti-
authoritarian education. Neill put the child's happiness at the center of
the educational enterprise. Rather than obedient workers and soldiers,
children raised in a non-repressive environment would develop strong
capacities for self-determination and critical thinking. West Germans
took this a step further, actively promoting disobedience in their children and also encouraging them to develop a curious and relaxed attitude about sexual matters. As Reich had taught, the prohibition against
childhood masturbation was the beginning of the production of under-
lings, of human beings susceptible to authoritarianism and unsuited to
democracy.

In France, Reich was popular especially for his criticisms of premarital abstinence and of the ideal of lifelong marital monogamy. A group
of radical French high school students, in a much-discussed manifesto,
"Fifteen Theses on the Sexual Revolution," argued both that "sex is
a necessary activity" and that institutionalized durable coupledom was
"alienating": "Ownership relations thus introduced between two partners are a theft of the same sort as is capitalist property."[15] And also
in France, it was apparent that radicals believed in Reich's theory that
there was an inverse relationship between cruelty and enjoyment. "*La
puissance ou la jouissance?*" (Power or pleasure?) was the rhetorical and
rhyming question posed by French sex radicals in an elaborate and hilar-
iously pointed cartoon in the special issue of Jean-Paul Sartre's journal
Tout! published April 23, 1971 on sex and the "free disposition of our

[14] Dietrich Haensch, *Repressive Familienpolitik: Sexualunterdrückung als Mittel der Politik* (Reinbek: Rowohlt, 1969), 12, 14, 66–7.
[15] Comités d'Action Lycéens, "Quinze thèses sur la révolution sexuelle" (1968), quoted in Natanson, "Education sexuelle," 15.

bodies." The authors' own choice between the posed alternatives was clear, as they juxtaposed images of people who were calling for "order and obedience" and exercising inappropriate power over others (policemen aggressively beating, clergymen and politicians hectoring) with alternative images in which those same people actually got to indulge in what they *really* wanted – or so the cartoon authors fantasized: being penetrated (homosexually as well as heterosexually), kissing with passionate abandon, experiencing fabulous sexual delight. Significantly, radicals did not think that conservatives were irredeemable. On the contrary, even the American president Richard M. Nixon secretly wished to be buggered by Superman. The message was that sex could cure even the worst case of right-wing attitudes.

Not every radical was an instant fan of Reich. In already long-liberal Sweden, for instance, Wilhelm Reich was barely invoked, and inspiration was instead drawn from the researches of the American Alfred Kinsey. Especially appealing was Kinsey's idea that a wide variation in sexual behaviors was normal and thus traditional norms were outdated and unnatural. The argument was that if erotic minorities like homosexuals could be more fully accepted, it would greatly benefit the heterosexual majority as well, for then heterosexuals too could embrace perversions and would be able to expand their own "spectrum of desire and pleasure."[16]

There were, however, also other ways that sex and politics could be theorized together. In some instances, the argument was that sex itself was a political activity. "Our assholes are revolutionary," argued gay activists. Or the point was made that sex enhanced politics: Makavejev's film heroine Milena declared forthrightly: "Socialism without fucking is dull and lifeless." At some moments, sexual activity and political activity were conceived as nicely parallel. As the West German New Left advice suggested, the best way to be was: "Tough on cops, tender in bed." Alternatively, the police themselves could shift their purpose. The anarchist *Provos* in the Netherlands, for instance, called for "the policeman to become the disarmed social worker of the future," distributing chicken drumsticks and oranges to the hungry and contraceptives to all.[17] Sometimes the passionate defense of the *moral* value of sexual pleasure was made by analogy: "Chastity is no more a virtue than malnutrition." And sometimes the argument was more a pedantic reminder to care about politics

[16] Lars Ullerstam, *De erotiska minoriteterna* (Stockholm: Zindermans Förlag, 1964), 84.
[17] *Provos* quoted in Richard Neville, "Carry On Motherfuckers" in Neville, *Play Power: Exploring the International Underground* (New York: Random House, 1970), 28.

Fig. 4.5 "Power or Pleasure?" Cartoon published in the special issue of the French journal *Tout!* (April 23, 1971) on sex and the "free disposition of our bodies."

as much as about sex: "Brothers and sisters / whether queer or not / combating capitalism / is a duty we've got."

Sometimes leftists admitted that they were just looking for a good lay, instead of (what they saw as) the humiliatingly paltry satisfactions of adult masturbation. "Away with the wank-devil!" announced two "red" workers in an underground West German newspaper in 1969 as they placed a personal ad pleading their case: "Two comrades require the immediate restoration of their sexual equilibrium. Help them, female comrades."[18] Or: "Just look at the sexually inhibited faces in the subway, on the construction site, at the office. Almost all pleasure themselves or masturbate instead of asking one another if they'd like to fuck," lamented a letter to the editor of the same paper in 1970.[19] But in yet other cases, there was the sincere idea that sexual expression would trigger political change. As medical doctor and member of the British counterculture Matthew Russell remembered with self-critical bemusement:

With hindsight it was fantastically naïve and innocent. At the time one generally believed that this was changing the world, that if you fucked the girl that you rather fancied with the big tits next door in Kathmandu Valley on Buddha's birthday then that actually was going to make nuclear bombs disintegrate. You really thought that. It was naïve but it was an innocent and quite healthy exploration of sexuality . . . There was a lot of this belief that if you took your knickers off you'd smash the state.[20]

There is no question that everywhere conservatives were put on the defensive with these new moral arguments that combined sexual with other kinds of politics, but conservatives were no less put on the defensive by the growing chorus of voices insisting that the pursuit of sexual pleasure was simply "natural" and "healthy." As the first Australian and then British countercultural satirical *Oz* magazine editor Richard Neville put it in 1970 in *Play Power: Exploring the International Underground*: "Thousands of young people all over the world are quietly accomplishing an authentic sexual revolution without even knowing they are part of it." He elaborated: "When boy meets girl, within minutes of drifting off to a comfortable location, boy can be happily splashing about in girl's cunt, both of them up each other's arses, sucking and fucking with compassionate enthusiasm." This, he argued, was "a total tactile information exchange . . . If the attraction is only biological, nothing is lost except a few million spermatozoa and both parties continue their separate ways. If there is a deeper involvement, the relationship becomes richer, and

---

[18] *Agit 883* 41 (November 20, 1969), 3.   [19] *Agit 883* 73 (December 24, 1970), 12.
[20] Matthew Russell quoted in Jonathon Green, *It: Sex since the Sixties* (London: Martin Secker & Warburg Ltd, 1993), 11.

so does the sexual experience. One way to a girl's mind is through her cunt."[21]

Young people were not only choosing to defy the inherited rules, but also challenging their elders and arguing that it was the conservative traditions that were truly immoral. As early as 1964–65, a survey conducted among Italian teen girls in and around Milan, Turin, Rome, and Palermo turned up some quite sassy and self-determined statements about sex: 22 percent of the thousand girls questioned (ages 13 to 19) had already had intercourse; not one said that premarital sex was wrong. In response to the question, "Is it moral to have premarital sex?" 17-year-old Laura had declared "Yes" in no uncertain terms: "I've done it, perhaps because everybody does it and perhaps because I believe it's something one ought to do. Also, nature wants you to do it, waiting is contrary to nature." But she also contended:

It is our elders who behave scandalously . . . Previously women were kept under lock and key and had no hope of sexual relations until after marriage but the boys, even the very youngest, had total freedom and so queued up at the brothels . . . Now when girls no longer marry old men and boys no longer go to brothels, society says that is scandalous and accuses us of immorality. I don't consider myself immoral.[22]

(Laura was not so far off the mark in her scathing summary of the misogynist hypocrisy structuring pre-sexual revolution values. Another survey conducted in 1965 with over 1,000 Italian men aged 20–50 found 81 percent of the men nostalgically missing the houses of prostitution that had just been shut down in 1959 due to the combined activism of feminists and conservatives; 71 percent had themselves had sex with prostitutes; meanwhile, 75 percent opposed premarital sex for women and 66 percent thought it was "more or less important" to marry a virgin.)

Changing the law

Yet neither the revolutionary theories nor the fact that young people were simply voting with their bodies in and of themselves made changes in European nations' legal systems. Those changes were quite evidently the result of extraordinary hard work on the part of activists both in the streets and in the courts and halls of governments. It remains something

---

[21] Neville, *Play Power*, 92.
[22] Quoted in Arthur Marwick, *The Sixties: Cultural Transformation in Britain, France, Italy and the United States, c. 1958 – c. 1974* (Oxford University Press, 2000), 388.

of a mystery to historians how the tide of public opinion turned enough for judges and politicians to believe that they were so out of step with the populace in their own countries and with international developments that laws could, indeed should, be changed. After all, in nation after nation, the 1950s had witnessed the consolidation of a culture of intensified sexual conservatism, with very few individuals willing or able to protest openly against the trends of the time. It was not at all self-evident which arguments eventually would succeed in expanding what could be thought or said with respect to sex. How people actually *lived* in the first two postwar decades was at great variance with what was openly, publicly *defensible*.

In imagining the stultifying postwar climate, it bears remembering as well that many of the leading sex rights activists of the interwar years had been either forced into exile or murdered by the Nazis – for being either Jewish and/or leftist – and not just in Germany itself. Among the most prominent interwar Dutch sex rights activists were Leo Polak (killed by the Nazis at Sachsenhausen) and Charlotte Polak-Rosenberg and Bernard Premsela (murdered at Auschwitz); in France, the militant contraceptive rights activist and member of the resistance Berty Albrecht had committed suicide after being captured and imprisoned at Fresnes by the Gestapo. In general, across Western and Eastern Europe, the leaders of sex rights activism had been disproportionately Jewish and politically left-leaning. But in the anti-communist climate of the postwar era in Western Europe also those prominent interwar progressives who survived the Nazi onslaught were not welcomed back into positions of leadership in government-approved public health initiatives. The entire project of progressive sex rights activism had come to be portrayed – first by National Socialists and fascists and their collaborators and then again by postwar Christian conservatives – as somehow dirty and dangerous to touch. Moreover, and strikingly, the western Communist political parties in the postwar era also tried to keep their distance from sex-related issues, either because they feared being tainted by a subject that was perceived as unclean, or on the grounds that campaigns for contraception were a bourgeois distraction which undermined the class struggle against capitalism.

As a result, the postwar efforts to liberalize sex-related laws were initially carried by only a handful of contrarians – and it took them quite some time to find legal and moral arguments that would be persuasive as well as politicians and further activists willing to support their aims. Italy provides an interesting case. There, deputies from the small Socialist Party – especially Giancarlo Matteotti, who later worked together with

Fig. 4.6 Maria Luisa De Marchi (now Zardini) visiting women in the *borgate* – working-class neighborhoods on the outskirts of Rome – to offer urgently sought basic information on birth control as well as contraceptive products. She had begun these visits in 1958, initially providing vaginal suppository contraceptives that had been supplied free of charge by a British manufacturer. She continued this work for two decades, visiting hundreds of clients each year.

the sex rights activist Luigi De Marchi – repeatedly advocated for the right to contraception specifically as a postfascist imperative; but these efforts were recurrently blocked by Christian Democrats in cooperation with an Italian Communist Party uncomfortable with challenging the Catholic church. Repeated efforts to liberalize the law on contraception were made in the course of the 1950s, but all to no avail – and this despite the fact that in a 1958 attempt Matteotti pointed out that 800,000 abortions were being performed in Italy every year and that access to contraception could bring this number down. De Marchi, an enthusiastic Reichian, was convinced that sexual reform and a freer sexuality were the foundation for both individual happiness and an improved society. He frequently diagnosed Italian culture as suffering from "sex-phobia" (*sessuofobia*). In 1956, De Marchi and his then wife Maria Luisa De Marchi (later Zardini) opened a center for sexual and contraceptive counseling in Rome. From 1958 on, with the support of American contraceptive rights activists, she brought diaphragms and contraceptive gels and basic information about fertility control directly to the poorest households in the tenements surrounding Rome – even as the Vatican called for Luigi's arrest and priests circulated photos of Maria Luisa to their parishioners declaring that whatever products this woman gave them could give them cancer. Although the authorities initially refrained from prosecuting the De Marchis for fear that this would give undesirable publicity to the pro-contraception cause, Luigi was eventually arrested for "violating public morals" – in this instance for giving a public lecture in Florence in which he provided information about birth control – and the De Marchis spent years fighting the charge, as well as instigating additional cases.

As of 1965, in a case that made it to the Constitutional Court, Matteotti and Luigi De Marchi together contended that retaining the 1931 law passed under fascism (that punished "whoever publicly incites practices or engages in propaganda against procreation") was a violation of citizens' fundamental right – secured in the postfascist Constitution – to freedom of speech. In addition, they argued that the Catholic church's moral opposition to contraception could not be used as justification for the formulation of a secular state's policies. In their rejection of Matteotti and De Marchi's arguments, the fifteen judges of the Constitutional Court went out of their way to note that just because something was associated with fascism did not automatically discredit it. And they opined further that "good custom" (*buon costume*) and public morality demanded the ongoing retention of the law; to change the law on contraception would be to undermine "sexual decency."

Nonetheless, as of 1971, the Court (composed in this round of fourteen judges, six of whom had sat on the 1965 case as well) abruptly repealed the articles criminalizing discussion of contraception, declaring them "illegitimate." The transformation of public values not only in surrounding nations but also within Italy had become unmistakable. Now it was the judges themselves who argued that the anti-contraception law was indeed a violation of freedom of speech; that it had been, moreover, "a product of its era" (i.e. fascism), that surely contraception was preferable to abortion, and that having too many children – or not spacing children sufficiently – was in itself a serious health risk for women. Nonetheless, it would not be until 1976 that the Ministry of Health finally authorized pharmacies to carry contraceptives.

Abortion rights

In Britain and in France, the laws against abortion changed for related as well as different reasons; in those nations, the key shifts were made in the parliament, by politicians, rather than in the courts. In the UK, in 1967, Member of Parliament David Steel introduced a bill to legalize both first- and second-trimester abortions (and provide them free of charge through the National Health Service); after strong debate, the measure passed. As with the decriminalization of contraceptives in France that same year, where the hope had been that legalizing birth control would bring down the rate of illegal abortion, Steel's main concern too was that the provision of legal abortion would significantly reduce the health damage and deaths caused by illegal abortion. However, the early 1960s scandal surrounding thalidomide, an anti-morning sickness drug that caused 2,000 children in Britain (and more than 10,000 worldwide) to be born with truncated limbs, together with a concurrent scandal of birth defects caused by rubella, was also a key factor in making Britain the first Western European country outside of Scandinavia fully to decriminalize abortion. Because the drug also caused malformation of internal organs, only half of the 2,000 British children survived beyond a few months of life; many of the women carrying them had been denied abortions. One immediate effect of the dramatic liberalization of the abortion law in Britain was that while in the past British women had gone to France, now French women who could afford it started to travel to Britain to procure safe abortions.

In France, abortion remained illegal, although widely practiced. By some estimates between 300,000 and 400,000 clandestine abortions were taking place within France every year; others believed that there were more than twice that many annually. In protest against the illegality, hundreds of women signed a public declaration in the magazine *Nouvel Observateur* in April 1971, among them such celebrities as Simone de Beauvoir, Catherine Deneuve, Françoise Sagan, and Marguerite Duras. The women knew that by confessing to having aborted they were courting criminal prosecution. The statement became known as the "Manifesto of the 343" (in some later renditions, with deliberate insolence, the "Manifesto of the 343 sluts [*salopes*]") and its opening paragraph announced:

A million women have abortions in France each year. They do it in dangerous conditions because they are condemned to secrecy, even though, if done under medical control, this operation is extremely simple. No one talks about these millions of women. I declare that I am one of them. I declare that I have had an abortion. Just as we demand free access to birth-control methods, so we demand freedom to have abortions.

The manifesto went on to make powerful points about the contempt for women's lives evident in the inability of the society to deal directly with such a massive open secret as the prevalence of illegal abortion:

Abortion. That's a matter that concerns broads, like cooking, like diapers, like something foul. Fighting to obtain the right to free abortion, that has the air of the pathetic and trivial. There's always that smell of hospital or food around women, that scent of baby poop . . . The complexity of emotions that surrounds the fight for abortion shows with great precision our very difficulty in simply being, the difficulty we have convincing ourselves that it's even worth it to fight for ourselves. It goes without saying that, unlike other human beings, we do not have the right to dispose of our own bodies. Yet our bellies are part of us. Freely accessible abortion is not the ultimate aim of women's struggle. On the contrary, it is nothing but the most elementary demand, that without which the struggle cannot even begin.[23]

Abortion soon became the single biggest mobilizing issue for the Movement for the Liberation of Women (*Mouvement pour la libération des femmes*). In the summer of 1971, a march in the streets of Paris (from the Bastille to Nation) demanded free abortion. And another new organization, To Choose (*Choisir*) anticipated the possibility that the signers of the declaration would be prosecuted. Its main organizer, the French-Tunisian lawyer Gisèle Halimi (previously famous for her defense of the Algerian nationalist Djamila Boupacha, tortured by the French army), took on the defense of the mother of a young girl raped by a schoolmate whose abortion (procured by her mother and friends) had been denounced to the authorities by the rapist. The ensuing "Bobigny trial" in October–November 1972, and another march in November 1972, provided important occasions for shifting public consciousness toward sympathy with the idea of decriminalization. Then, in February 1973, 331 medical doctors went public with a declaration that they had broken the law by performing abortions. And yet another new organization, the Movement for the Liberation of Abortion and Contraception (*Mouvement de libération de l'avortement et de la contraception*) announced it would openly provide abortions. The family planning organization MFPF followed suit in the summer of 1973, announcing it too would provide abortions.

Faced with such massive civil disobedience, the government of President Georges Pompidou was caught off guard. Pompidou's death and the subsequent election in May 1974 of Valéry Giscard d'Estaing to the

---

[23] The original text is reprinted at "Le 'Manifeste des 343 salopes' paru dans le *Nouvel Obs* en 1971," *Le Nouvel Obs.com*, June 23, 2008, http://tempsreel.nouvelobs.com/actualites/20071127.OBS7018/?xtmc=343&xtcr=1.

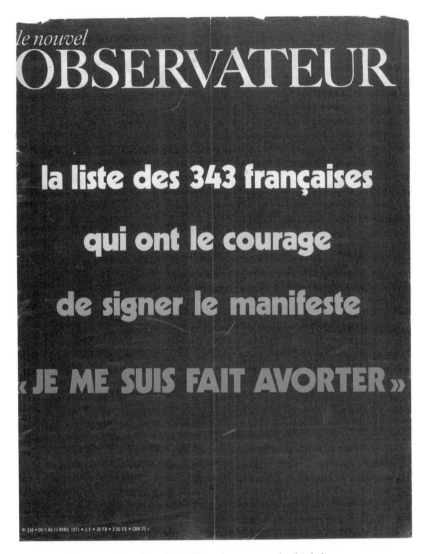

le nouvel
OBSERVATEUR

la liste des 343 françaises

qui ont le courage

de signer le manifeste

« JE ME SUIS FAIT AVORTER »

N°334 • DU 5 AU 11 AVRIL 1971 • 3 F • 30 FB • 2.50 FS • CAN 75 c

Fig. 4.7 "The list of 343 French women who had the courage to sign the manifesto 'I have had an abortion.'" Cover of *Le Nouvel Observateur*, April 5, 1971.

presidency created a new opportunity. Giscard D'Estaing wanted to be seen as a modernizer and a friend to women, and he charged his Minister of Health, Simone Veil, to take the lead in presenting to the French parliament a law decriminalizing abortion. Her personal moral authority

was as indispensable to the success of the campaign as was the movement in the streets. A survivor of Auschwitz-Birkenau who lost part of her
family in the camp, Veil walked out of the parliamentary debates when
a conservative delegate compared abortions to Nazi crematoria. Even
more significant was Veil's core argument in favor of decriminalization
(which had not so much to do with women's self-ownership but instead
emphasized that the law itself was being disrespected and losing value
because it was so routinely flaunted).

Certainly not everyone was convinced. Delegates opposed to decriminalization argued fervently that to liberalize abortion law was only a first
step on the slippery slope toward permitting euthanasia of the handicapped – and they gestured to the ways the Nazis had tried to justify
the killing of "useless eaters" (*les bouches inutiles*). They also contended
that sexual morality would be destroyed. Nonetheless, enough centrist
and right-wing delegates supported the measure that the vote ended up
at 284 to 189. What bears emphasis, in short, is what a complex mix
of eloquent activist rage, courage to put oneself at risk (on the part
of both celebrity and ordinary women and medical doctors), lawyers'
strategic use of scandal, politicians' appeals to pragmatism, and, not
least, growing splits among conservatives over sexual politics, all needed
to come together in order for widely disobeyed laws to change. The law
was a provisional one; five years and many further activist campaigns
later, in 1979, after another debate, it was finally reaffirmed in its lasting
form.

It would not be until 1978 and against fierce Vatican opposition that
abortion would be decriminalized in Italy as well. In 1971, the Italian Movement for Women's Liberation (*Movimento di Liberazione della
Donna*) organized a self-denunciation campaign, imitating the strategies
that had been used in France (and subsequently also in West Germany):
"We declare to have willingly and knowingly aborted or helped others to
abort, rendering them accomplices." Their statement also emphasized
the specifically fascist origins of the anti-abortion law, as well as the
hypocrisy of the Catholic church in supporting such a law, even though,
for countless women each year, it resulted in "murder according to class
membership." Women with means could find skilled doctors; working-
class women were subjected to sterility, severe health problems, and death
at the hands of "midwives and criminal butchers."[24] In 1973, the feminist
Gigliola Pierobon in Padua, together with the group Feminist Struggle
(*Lotta Feminista*), had turned her own case (she had had an abortion at

---

[24] "Anche in Italia 'autodenunce' per l'aborto." *Liberazione Notizie*, August 4, 1971,
http://old.radicali.it/search_view.php?id=44852&lang=&cms=.

age 17) into a political one – just as lawyer Gisèle Halimi had done in the Bobigny trial in France. Equally significant was the outpouring of support, in 1974, when the government charged 263 women in the city of Trento with having had illegal abortions and – in yet another self-denunciation campaign – more than 2,500 women publicly declared that they too had undergone abortions. In the years that followed, activists mobilized tens of thousands of marchers in Florence and Rome and hundreds of thousands of petition signatures – not only with arguments by women that "My Body Belongs to Me!" and "My Womb Is My Own" but also with reference to the powerful claim that surely the health of half of the population was itself a *moral good*, the preservation of which was fully in keeping with Italy's Catholic traditions. Increasingly, as is apparent, the feminist movement was becoming a transnational phenomenon, and models for action developed in one nation were put to use in others. Similar campaigns succeeded in Spain after the end of the Franco dictatorship, and abortion was legalized there in 1985.

Meanwhile, the legal trajectory in Belgium, instructively, diverged sharply from what occurred in the other predominantly Catholic nations of France, Italy, and Spain – even as there too the issues of contraceptive rights and abortion rights were complexly intertwined. Like those other nations, each of which promulgated laws restricting contraception and abortion in the 1920s–1940s due to concerns about promoting higher birthrates, Belgium had instituted a ban on the dissemination of information on contraception and abortion in 1923, on the grounds that promoting reproduction was an act of "ardent and clairvoyant patriotism."[25] In 1973, a bill was before the Belgian parliament which would have reversed the ban, yet no activist groups mobilized on behalf of this bill. Instead, public outrage and protest were focused on the arrest of a popular leftist physician who had purportedly performed an abortion. The Christian Democratic government was resolutely opposed to liberalizing the law on abortion. But in view of the ongoing street demonstrations on behalf of the physician, and to appease public opinion, the government rushed to reverse the ban on contraceptive information and then actively promoted contraception through an information campaign in the months that followed – thereby managing to put off any national conversation about abortion for another decade.

---

[25] Contraception Act, Belgium, 1923, quoted in Liesbet Stevens and Marc Hooghe, "The Swing of the Pendulum: The Detraditionalisation of the Regulation of Sexuality and Intimacy in Belgium (1973–2003)," *International Journal of the Sociology of Law* 31 (2003), 156.

Heterosexual disillusionment

While campaigns for contraception and abortion rights had won broad
support from men across Western European nations, the feminist movements that evolved in and around those campaigns were met with far
greater skepticism and outright resistance. Men and women found themselves all too often at odds – not just at street demonstrations and political
meetings but also in the kitchen and the bedroom. As numbers of British
feminists complained, what exactly was the difference from a 1950s-style
marriage when in the 1960s–1970s the woman was still expected to be on
hand "cooking, answering the phone and rolling her master's joints"?[26]
Similarly, a French woman writing in a leftist journal in 1969 observed as
she pondered the many slogans being propounded about the "liberation
of peoples": "My liberation consists of serving him after my work while
he reads or 'thinks.' While I peel [*épluche*] the vegetables, he can read
[*éplucher*] at leisure – either *Le Monde* or works on Marxist economy."[27]
Or as West German feminists in the town of Münster, tired of the self-
important pontificating about Marxist theories so common at New Left
gatherings, put it in a so-called "Jenny-Flyer" circulated in 1972:

Jenny von Westphalen – that is the wife of [Karl] Marx. Put better: his cleaning
lady, cook, washerwoman, prostitute, birthing machine – and all that without any
labor law regulation, without agreed-upon work hours, without wages. Karl did
not lift a finger in the household, with the exception that he screwed the maid, got
her with child and then on top of that was too cowardly to admit it. But to sit at
the desk and write big books, blather on about the liberation of humanity . . . We
are all Jennys! For we live in a system of male supremacy.[28]

Many men were furious and confused when women started to demand
rights for themselves – such as intellectual respect, equal pay, or
government-funded childcare – and to assert that justice for women was
just as important as the proletariat and the class struggle. The trou-
ble, as women in the Italian feminist group Demystification of Authority
(*Demistificazione Autoritaria*) put it in 1969, was that their male comrades
remained "involved in the same masculinist logic of the old culture that
they say they want to combat."[29] Over and over, women tried to put into

---

26 Complaints summarized by David Widgery in Nigel Fountain, *Underground: The London
    Alternative Press, 1966–74* (London and New York: Routledge, 1988), 106.
27 Quoted in Bonnie S. Anderson and Judith P. Zinsser, *A History of their Own: Women in
    Europe from Prehistory to the Present* (Oxford University Press, 1989), vol. II, 406.
28 Quoted in Alice Schwarzer, *So fing es an! 10 Jahre Frauenbewegung* (Cologne: Emma-
    Frauenverlag, 1981), 34.
29 Quoted in R. Spagnoletti, *I movimenti femministi in Italia* (Rome: Giulio Savelli, 1974),
    49.

words the seriousness of their demands in language that would make sense to leftist men, arguing variously that "women are the Negroes of all peoples" (as Karin Schrader-Klebert put it in 1969) or that "the process of decolonization of woman" needed to begin (as Simone de Beauvoir announced in 1976).[30]

Many men were also perplexed at the assault on male sexual privilege just at the moment when they themselves were starting to enjoy new opportunities. Occasionally, feminist protest could take funny as well as outraged forms. In France in 1970, feminists broke up a conference on "Woman" convened by *Elle* magazine and replaced the questionnaire about female happiness the conference organizers had circulated with mock questions like these: "Do you wear make-up (a) out of self-loathing? (b) to look less like yourself and more like what you are expected to look like?" and "When a man talks to a woman, should he address (a) her tits and her legs? (b) her arse and her tits? (c) just her arse?"[31] And in the Netherlands, the feminist group *Dolle Minas* undertook what the American *Time* magazine in 1970 not without admiration referred to as "mass sensitivity training for Amsterdam males": "In broad daylight, they wolf-whistle at men, visually undress them with dare-me eyes, and call out suggestive remarks. Some have even pinched the guys in a sort of derrière-guard action."[32] Yet growing numbers of women saw little compromise possible. In Oxford, England, at a Women's Lib conference, feminists strung up banners declaring that "Phalluses are Fascist" and "End Penile Servitude." In West Germany, feminists in Frankfurt am Main circulated a flyer which showed the image of an old hag with a hatchet, while above her on the wall like trophies hung chopped-off penises, captioned with the names of well-known male New Left leaders. The slogan read: "Liberate the socialist pricks from their bourgeois dicks."

It seemed that the sexual revolution, in both its countercultural and its mainstream market-driven manifestations (and these were hardly separable), had fairly quickly turned out to be not quite as lovely as hoped for many women. Some women enjoyed the freedom and lack of emotional entanglement just as much as the men did and experimented just as widely. But a great many women just felt confused both about men's newfound ability to "screw women around the clock" and their own

---

[30] Karin Schrader-Klebert, "Die kulturelle Revolution der Frau," *Kursbuch* 17 (1969), 1–45; Simone de Beauvoir, "Quand toutes les femmes du monde . . . ," *Le Nouvel Observateur*, March 1, 1976, 52.

[31] *Mouvement de libération des femmes* (MLF) questionnaire circulated at *Elle* conference, quoted in Clare Duchen, *Feminism in France: From May '68 to Mitterand* (London and Boston: Routledge and Kegan Paul, 1986), 10.

[32] "Europe: Women's Lib, Continental Style," *Time*, August 17, 1970.

all-too-frequent sense of emptiness and lack of enjoyment of sex.[33] In short, it was not only the non-monogamy that could be as distressing as it was potentially exciting. It was that all the opportunities for copulation were turning out to be not necessarily all that pleasurable for the women. "There was lots of promiscuity," one Italian New Left-affiliated woman remarked retrospectively – as she also ruefully recalled, "we were *all* unhappy."[34] The men were trying to see themselves as pro-feminist, she noted. But nonetheless the sex remained, for many women, unsatisfying.

One of the major debates in the 1970s concerned what American Anne Koedt called – in a much translated and much mimeographed and cir- culated pamphlet – "The Myth of the Vaginal Orgasm." Freud-inspired doctors and therapists routinely informed women that they were abnor- mal and dysfunctional, and met the official definition for "frigidity," if they could only orgasm when they were clitorally stimulated. A mature woman, it was asserted, should be able to leave behind the "infantile" focus on clitoral stimulation and consistently have orgasms during het- erosexual penetration. Astonishingly but tellingly, despite the criticisms leveled against this theory first by Alfred Kinsey (already in 1953) in his report on *Sexual Behavior in the Human Female,* as well as in the studies conducted by sexologists William Masters and Virginia Johnson in the 1960s and 1970s, the pervasively disseminated idea that women should be able to come from penetration alone left countless women internally conflicted and countless couples in a state of dissatisfaction and mutual misery. For decades the factually false consensus had not been effectively disrupted – with depressing consequences. Women faked orgasms. Men had no idea that this was what was happening, and hence were quite taken aback when in the 1970s women went embarrassingly public with their complaints.

In 1968, Danish feminist Mette Ejlersen, in her widely discussed best- seller *Jeg Anklager* (published in Britain in 1969 as *I Accuse!*), was already writing about what she called the woman's "tragic little comedy during intercourse," which she actually did not think was very amusing at all.[35] As Anne Koedt summarized Ejlersen's findings, in this ugly game played by far too many women and men, women recurrently pretended to have orgasms even when they didn't. As Koedt put it, "Perhaps one of the most infuriating and damaging results of this whole charade has been that women who were perfectly healthy sexually were taught that they were not. So in addition to being sexually deprived, these women were

[33] Michelene Wandor quoted in Collins, *Modern Love,* 176.
[34] Conversation with D.R., 2010.
[35] Mette Ejlersen, *I Accuse!,* trans. Marianne Kold Madsen (London: Tandem, 1969), 16.

Fig. 4.8 "What's an orgasm, Mum? I dunno love, ask yer father."
Cartoon by Liz Mackie. Copyright Liz Mackie 1971.

told to blame themselves when they deserved no blame. Looking for a
cure to a problem that has none can lead a woman on an endless path of
self-hatred and insecurity."[36]

Other critical voices soon chimed in. The Australian-born (and subsequently part-time British) writer Germaine Greer worried, also in 1970,
in *The Female Eunuch* (the book sold millions of copies and was widely
translated) that while women could have as much sex as they wanted –
and Greer herself admitted to having rather a lot – women nonetheless remained for all practical purposes castrated, cut off from their own
sexuality and from themselves. Verena Stefan's popular and influential
1975 novel *Häutungen* (Shedding), one of the key texts of the West German women's movement, apparently spoke to many women with such
descriptions of heterosexual encounters as this one: "I make an effort,
move everything properly, until *he* has an orgasm."[37] One study published
in 1975 found that despite the pill and the constant detailed sex-chatter
in the media many women felt "just as frigid as before."[38]

Yet as through the 1970s the evidence accumulated that women could
come far more easily through masturbating by themselves than through
sex with a man – with American bestsellers like Shere Hite's *The Hite*

---

[36] Anne Koedt, "The Myth of the Vaginal Orgasm" (1970) www.uic.edu/orgs/
cwluherstory/CWLUArchive/vaginalmyth.html.
[37] Verena Stefan, *Häutungen* (Munich: Verlag Frauenoffensive, 1975), 25.
[38] Leona Siebenschön, "Noch genauso frigide," *Die Zeit*, July 18, 1975, 37.

Report, Betty Dodson's *Sex for One*, and Lonnie Barbach's *For Yourself*
immediately translated and discussed in the media across Europe – and
as women were expressly encouraged to experiment with masturbation
in order to discover what they liked, the backlash from men was not far
behind. Rather than finding it erotic that women were finally learning
to enjoy themselves, men threatened to lose desire for women entirely if
they became too demanding. The West German media ran endless articles declaring that feminism was bad for heterosexual sex, that "militant
masturbation . . . means man-hatred," that "performance expectations"
blocked men's sexual capacities (because "fear is the enemy of erection"), and – eventually – that "the women's movement has reduced our
horniness to zero."[39] In Britain, porn impresario Paul Raymond, whose
relaunched *Men Only* became *the* best-selling men's magazine of the
1970s, advanced his own "manifesto for the restoration of male dom-
inance." In Raymond's view, "As woman's public sensuality blossoms
and spreads, so man's correspondingly withers and shrivels." Women's
greater interest in vibrators than in penises, Raymond opined, had left
men "redundant" and removed men's masculinity "as neatly as a vet
castrating a sheep."[40]

Domestic violence and rape

Many men were also stunned when feminists affiliated with the New Left
started to raise questions about issues like domestic violence or rape. Far
from distancing themselves from the phenomena of abusers or rapists
(as one might expect in hindsight), countless men apparently identified
strongly with men accused of anti-female violence. When in March 1976
over 2,000 women from forty nations gathered in Brussels, Belgium,
for an International Tribunal of Crimes against Women (modeled on
Bertrand Russell's tribunal against the crimes against humanity being
committed in the context of the Vietnam War), the aim was above all –
as Simone de Beauvoir summarized it – "to talk, to talk, to bring into the
light of day the scandalous truths that the other half of humanity tries
hard to conceal." Subjects for discussion ranged from clitoridectomy to
violent porn to psychiatric abuse to the routineity of domestic violence
and the near-impossibility of bringing its perpetrators to justice. De Beauvoir noted that in the immense majority of domestic violence cases, "it

---

[39] "Jüngstes Gerücht," *Der Spiegel*, February 28, 1977, 191; "Mild bis wild," *Der Spiegel*,
March 7, 1977, 207; "Stunde der Wahrheit," *Der Spiegel*, April 18, 1977, 231; and
Conrad Zander, "Die Männer werden keusch: Schluss mit dem Sex," *Stern* 51 (1982),
50.
[40] Paul Raymond, *Men Only* 36 (1971), 23–5, quoted in Collins, *Modern Love*, 159.

seems that the fate of the woman is to submit and be quiet." Yet many men seemed more invested in maintaining the status quo than in being concerned. For, as she noted acerbically, "despite the inferior status to which they are reduced, women are for men the privileged object of their aggression."[41] In a study conducted by Italian feminists in preparation for an international conference to be held in Rome in 1978, 51 percent of the 1,000 women surveyed had been on the receiving end of violence by their husbands. In country after country, feminists pushed city and state governments to open women's shelters; soon there were a considerable number of these in the UK, West Germany, and the Netherlands, as well as Belgium, France, and Luxembourg.

A few men did strive to make sense of the attraction of domestic violence and the difficulty for its perpetrators not to be in denial. French philosophers Pascal Brückner and Alain Finkielkraut, in their 1977 book *Le nouveau désordre amoureux* (The New Disorder of the Passions), worried openly that the emancipation of women was triggering hateful resentment and thus even more uninhibited misogynist animosity from men. Among other things, Brückner and Finkielkraut observed that domestic violence was "by no means the result of an unrestrainable wild primate impulse, but rather the reaction of a property-owner when he finds out that slavery is to be abolished. Recourse to violence is sought by those who miss the power that is no longer theirs."[42]

One major achievement especially of French feminists in the later 1970s was the campaign to revise the rape laws. Preexisting law was problematic both because it focused primarily on the damage done to the "honor" of a woman's family – rather than damage done to a woman as an individual – and because, unless a woman had been able to prove fierce physical resistance, lawyers and judges often found plausible the claims of defendants that they had *interpreted* the woman's behavior as consent. Feminist activism to sensitize the public grew especially in response to the much-discussed rapes in 1974 of two young Belgian women, Anne Tonglet and Aracelli Castellano, who had been camping near Marseilles, by three local French men. In the first round, the perpetrators had been charged only with assault, and in September 1975 the trial began in (the French equivalent of) a civil court in Marseilles. The attorneys for Tonglet and Castellano argued that the court lacked jurisdiction for the very reason that the crime of rape had not been acknowledged as what was legally at

---

[41] De Beauvoir, "Quand toutes . . . ," 52.
[42] Pascal Brückner and Alain Finkielkraut, *Le nouveau désordre amoureux* (Paris: Éditions du Seuil, 1977), 293.

stake, while the defense attorneys for the men tried to play down what had occurred by remarking suggestively that "resistance has its whims and the will has its mysteries." One of the lawyers said: "The two girls enjoyed it." The two young women were lesbians and – far from reading this as evidence that they were not likely to have "consented" to have sex with the men – the lawyers for the defendants tried to make the case that the lesbianism and the outdoor camping were both signs of a "liberated" attitude and that what happened to the women simply showed that liberation was not without its risks. Thankfully, the court decided it did lack jurisdiction and the matter was turned over to a criminal court (*Cour d'Assises*) in Aix-en-Provence. Gisèle Halimi was the lawyer for the victims, hoping to use the case to make a larger statement about rape, just as the 1972 Bobigny trial served as an occasion for raising public awareness around abortion. The three men were convicted, one for six years, the others for four years in prison (even as the lawyers for the three perpetrators continued to plead that the future of the young men should not be ruined "for what was after all just a holiday joke").[43]

French feminist organizations, having just achieved a law change guaranteeing the right to legal abortion, now increasingly turned their attention to the topic of rape – even though they were also acutely conscious of, and worried about, the problematic potential outcome of exacerbating the punitive powers of the state. Simultaneously, feminist activists struggled to find the words to explain the gravity of the crime of rape, while many men, also on the Left, continued either to treat rape as a triviality or to pretend that rapists were driven by "sexual need." Halimi remembered overhearing a policeman during the Aix-en-Provence trial warning a colleague joshingly: "Watch out, Matteo, you'll make love and you'll end up in prison." Or as sociologist Alice Braitberg put it in *Le Monde* in 1978: "For men, the line is so thin between sexual extortion through persuasion (which is part of their conception of amorous conquest) and through violence that they have difficulty comprehending what rape is." In this context, feminist journals reached for the strongest language possible. Arguing that rape was motivated above all by men's hatred of women, not by desire, *Les Pétroleuses* declared in 1975: "The rapist wants to destroy." *Choisir* argued that rape is "an act aiming at humiliation, the destruction of the personality, the negation of the woman aggressed upon." And for *Le Quotidien des Femmes*, rape "is a murder, truly a murder, the worst kind of murder, really the destruction of the interior of the individual . . . It is killing the woman within the woman." Even if the

---

[43] Quoted in Janine Mossuz-Lavau, *Les lois de l'amour: les politiques de la sexualité en France de 1950 à nos jours* (Paris: Éditions Payot, 1991), 194, 198, 200.

woman kept walking around afterwards with the air of someone who was still living, "inside herself she has a cadaver."[44] In 1980, the French parliament passed a new law against rape.

Homosexual liberation

Just as heterosexual conflicts – over everything from banal unhappiness to brutal violence – were being aired ever more in public, homosexuals were coming out of the closet to demand recognition and an end to discrimination. Lesbian and gay liberation movements emerged in the early 1970s in many Western European nations, as they did in the USA, often spontaneously and without initially knowing about each other's existence. And they emerged in quite different legal climates. In Sweden, where homosexuality had been decriminalized since 1944, an organization calling itself the National Organization for Equality of Sexual Rights (*Riksförbundet för Sexuellt Likaberättigande*) was formed in 1970 to press for a reduction of discrimination against homosexuals in daily life. In France, the occasion for mobilization was provided by a radio show hosted by the popular celebrity Ménie Grégoire, who decided in March 1971 to broadcast on the theme of "That Painful Problem, Homosexuality." Grégoire believed that homosexuals were inevitably "suffering," but as a self-defined liberal she thought it important to be "doing something for them." She also took the view – in response to a question from a woman in the audience about male domination – that "You know very well that the happy women are those who have met men who have satisfied them; that's obvious." Suddenly militant lesbian women disrupted the show, shouting: "It's not true, we're not suffering!" and "Down with the heterocops!" Later the group, which called itself the Homosexual Front for Revolutionary Action (*Front homosexuel d'action révolutionnaire*, FHAR), provided an additional press release: "Homosexuals are sick of being a painful problem." Although eventually the men predominated, the group initially brought together lesbians and gay men, and lesbian feminists were prominent in the early leadership. One was Françoise d'Eaubonne, who perfectly encapsulated the group's radical aims when she noted: "You say society ought to integrate homosexuals. I say homosexuals ought to disintegrate society."[45]

In a subsequent statement in the special issue of *Tout!*, male members of FHAR also at once parodied and emulated the "Manifesto of

[44] Quoted in Mossuz-Lavau, *Les lois de l'amour*, 195–98.
[45] Quoted in Frédéric Martel, *The Pink and the Black: Homosexuals in France since 1968*, trans. Jane Marie Todd (Stanford University Press, 1995), 18–19.

the 343" women that declared they had had an abortion. Reversing the
at once racist and homophobic assumptions prevalent in French culture
that Arabs were especially interested in homosexuality, FHAR members
defiantly announced: "We are more than 343 sluts. We have been buggered by Arabs. We're proud of it and we'll do it again. Sign and circulate
this petition."[46] The *Tout!* issue brought FHAR great publicity and the
membership rose tenfold.

In Britain and West Germany, where in contrast to Sweden and France
decriminalization was extremely recent, protest movements took other
forms. In Britain, where decriminalization had occurred in 1967, the Gay
Liberation Front (GLF) was launched in 1971, directly modeled on the
organization of the same name in the USA. The British GLF's first major
action in 1971 was to disrupt that year's Christian conservative "Festival
of Light" (annual gatherings organized since the late 1960s by television-
cleanup campaigner Mary Whitehouse and the former agnostic convert
to Christian piety author Malcolm Muggeridge in reaction against the
growth of what they called "the permissive society"). For the 1971 event,
GLF members showed up in drag, kissed each other openly, released
mice among the visitors, and managed – dressed up as workmen – to
enter the basement and shut off the lights.

In West Germany, where consensual adult male homosexuality for
those 21 and older had been decriminalized in 1969, the first result
of decriminalization was a proliferation of publications directed at the
gay male market niche and the expansion of a gay nightclub scene. But
decriminalization was also the crucial precondition for the emergence of
a publicly visible gay rights movement. Here the impetus was provided
by a 1971 movie by the sociologist Martin Dannecker and the filmmaker
Holger Mischwitzsky (better known by his pseudonym Rosa von Praun-
heim) entitled *It's Not the Homosexual Who Is Perverse, but Rather the
Situation in Which He Lives* (*Nicht der Homosexuelle ist Pervers, sondern
die Situation in der er lebt*). This movie was no plea for tolerance. Rather,
it was a movie by homosexuals for homosexuals, urging them to leave
behind a life of furtive cruising and come out. The filmmakers took the
movie to towns all across the nation, and in the discussions after each
showing local gay rights groups were formed – often affiliated with the
New Left student movement.

The relationships between homosexual liberation and the wider
sexual revolution proved to be complex and paradoxical. The wider sexual revolution created an important opening for homosexual liberation
efforts. Quite concretely, the differences between heterosexuality and

[46] "Nous nous sommes faits enculer par des arabes," *Tout!* 12 (April 23, 1971).

homosexuality were eroding – and for multiple reasons. For one thing, with increasing availability of contraceptives and legal abortion, the possibility of reproduction no longer defined most heterosexual encounters. At the same time, moreover, practices long associated with lesbianism or male homosexuality, such as oral or anal sex, were becoming eagerly adopted by heterosexuals. And more generally, for heterosexuals, sexual desire and experience outside of marriage were being promoted not just as acceptable, but as moral goods unto themselves. Marriage was no longer understood as the most important framework for sexual expression. It was no coincidence that decriminalization of homosexuality could occur in the context of broader transformations in legal systems and reorientations of sex-related laws toward the foundational concepts of privacy and consent. For instance, the official decriminalization of male homosexuality that occurred in West Germany on May 9, 1969 was passed in conjunction with the decriminalization not only of heterosexual adultery but also of the anachronistic transgression of "seduction through false promises." In short, rapidly changing attitudes about heterosexuality had created the grounds for a rethinking of attitudes about homosexuality. And yet, and however counterintuitive this may seem, it was just as the differences between heterosexuality and homosexuality were in so many ways eroding that homosexual men and lesbian women began to assert their distinctive "sexual identities" and to claim their "right to difference."

What exactly this difference from heterosexuals meant remained a matter of great contention, and divided homosexual activists from each other as much as it engendered conflict between them and heterosexuals involved in various progressive causes. At the root of the conflicts, and despite all the inventive theories put forward in the 1960s and 1970s about the relationships between sex and social justice activism – between making love and making revolution – there was no consensus about whether one could in fact make politics out of desire and, if so, how. Some Swedish lesbian activists, for instance, were hostile to the idea that gays or lesbians should fight for civil unions or same-sex marriage because they did not like the idea of "forcing lesbians to accept the outmoded institution of the family."[47] Some lesbians in every country argued that lesbianism was a political choice, and a necessary one for *all* feminists.

---

[47] Kristina Orfali, "The Rise and Fall of the Swedish Model" in Antoine Prost and Gérard Vincent (eds.), *A History of Private Life: Riddles of Identity in Modern Times* (Cambridge, MA: Harvard University Press, 1991), 432.

Italian lesbians involved in the organization Female Revolt (*Rivolta Fem-minile*), for example, argued that lesbianism was the necessary first step for any feminist searching for a truly free sexuality. In nation after nation, lesbian activists were often torn between working together with straight feminist women in campaigns for contraception and abortion rights or working together with gay men to combat homophobia. What, if any-thing, did straight and lesbian feminists or (in an alternative pairing) lesbians and gay men really have in common, or were the differences in their experiences too profound to advance shared causes? And what about differences *within* each group? Did those who desired individuals of the same sex *have* to declare their solidarity with other same-sex-desiring individuals, or was it acceptable to prefer the pursuit of pleasure and be uninterested in politics? One of the major conflicts that ended up driving lesbians out of the *Front homosexuel d'action révolutionnaire* was the fact that political meetings had primarily turned into cruising opportunities for the men. And, of course, countless homosexual men and lesbian women never got involved in activism of any sort. One of the wonderful things about the sexual revolution, after all, was that it was no longer necessary to justify the pursuit of pleasure – no matter how anonymous or how promiscuous – as an end in itself.

On the other hand, there were certainly moments of strong identifi-cation *across* the boundaries of sexual orientation. In West Germany, in a case that riveted the nation's attention in 1974, two women who were lovers, Marion Ihns and Judy Andersen, stood accused of having hired a man to murder Ihns' violently abusive husband (he tried to kill Ihns with poison and raped her repeatedly). Many heterosexual women identified strongly with the accused. They protested vocally against the humiliation of all women that was expressed by (what turned out to be) a viciously lesbophobic outpouring in the courtroom and the press. Because of the very different legal history of lesbianism – which had never been crimi-nalized in Germany – lesbians, unlike gay men, were mostly pitied for not having been able to find the "right" man, or contemptuously patholo-gized, or simply treated as invisible. The Ihns–Andersen case rallied also heterosexual feminists to compare the persecution of lesbians to the per-secution of witches in medieval days and to argue that female sexuality as a whole was on trial. "By the way: being a lesbian is beautiful," read a sign carried by two women at a demonstration supporting Ihns and Andersen. And heterosexual women also avidly followed debates among lesbians and bisexual women over sexual practices, not least hoping to learn from them as they sought to repair what they felt were damaged relationships to their own bodies.

The turn inward

Yet just as gay and lesbian rights movements emerged as recognizable forces to be reckoned with and even as the feminist women's movement became one of the largest and most influential – and impressively transnationally networked – social movements Western Europe had ever seen, doubts about the idea that sexual emancipation would inevitably contribute to the advancement of social justice more generally continued to mount. As British feminist Linda Grant once summarized the problem retrospectively:

> What had characterized the sixties was optimism. Men and women were confident that they could do anything they liked: go to the moon, solve the population crisis, end hunger and inequality. They thought they could make a sexual revolution because they believed in the future. When they stopped believing, they continued to fuck. But removed from the context of history, of a sense of past, present, and future in which sexual freedom was the most personal expression of revolutionary change, sex became an isolated event, turned inward.[48]

Rather than feeling unburdened by the depoliticization of sex, however, numerous contemporaries felt even more unmoored and disoriented about their bodies, desires, emotions, and relationships than before.

Simultaneously, hesitations about whether the sexual revolution itself was really bringing greater sexual happiness to more people were also building. An especially important summary critique of the sexual revolution was offered in 1977 by Brückner and Finkielkraut in *Le nouveau désordre amoureux*, which was published also in German translation in 1979 and widely debated in the press. Brückner and Finkielkraut were hardly puritanical moralists – in fact, *Playboy* published the German translation. But they nonetheless found the revolution problematic. They pointed out that instead of *forbidding* sex, as traditionalist conservatives had, sexual revolutionaries were establishing new *norms* of sexuality, but those norms were nothing but another way of constraining the freedom of individuals. They particularly mocked the mixture of New Age and Wilhelm Reich-inspired sexological technique tips (massage, deep breathing, nipple stimulation, the woman's hands on the man's buttocks, one of the man's fingers in the woman's anus, coupled with first slow and then rapid-fire penetration) that so many people had tried to introduce into their own lives to expedite the achievement of the supposedly so holy grail of spectacular mutual orgasm. Their central

---

[48] Linda Grant, *Sexing the Millennium: A Political History of the Sexual Revolution* (New York: HarperCollins, 1993), 6.

point was that all the instructions for how to intensify pleasure were actually ruining people's enjoyment of sex – and ruining it *especially for men*. The mechanized streamlining and functionalization of every activity, all designed to lead teleologically to the endpoint of orgasm, had an unexpected opposite effect from the one hoped for. The effect was that for men a deep sense of betrayal all too soon set in. "The so-called climax, the magic around which everything circles, and for which all the efforts are expended," as Austrian journalist Christa Karas – in a review of the book indicatively headlined "Rejecting the Dictatorship of the Orgasm" – noted, turned out to be fairly boring for most men. "That was all?" they asked themselves. "What a lot of effort for a little bit of sperm."[49] Whether or not Brückner and Finkielkraut were correct or just eccentric in their analysis, they clearly had identified an ever-widening popular sense of discomfort and disappointment that the sexual revolution was not all it had been touted to be.

Qualms about anomie and alienation even showed up in *Playboy*. A cartoon from the German version of *Playboy* spoofed the mechanization and depersonalization of sexuality that had been one aspect of the sexual revolution. In the cartoon, all physical and emotional connection between the partners was gone. A man and a woman were lying in bed, but they were staring into space and not even touching each other. The woman's body was covered with electrodes and the man – ready to flip the switch – said, "If you'd like, Fräulein Geiger, we can now come to the climax."[50] In the German news magazine *Der Spiegel*, another reprinted cartoon showed a woman comparing a man's lack of energy in bed with nicotine-free cigarettes. Not only love had disappeared, lust itself seemed to be in short supply.

Karas outlined what she too saw as the accumulating problems, for both men and women: "There is much evidence that pleasure has become a burden for us . . . The sexual revolution has produced rules (love must be made in all positions, genitally, orally, anally, in twosomes, threesomes, foursomes and frequently – and yet, as extensive as this list might seem, so narrow nonetheless are its boundaries." For, "in place of the freedom of one's own sexual imagination, there are the purchasable pleasure-options, the prefabricated fantasies of purportedly exciting transgressions. These promised much but have mostly left behind insecurity as the celebrated miracle techniques failed pathetically, and the advertised

[49] Christa Karas, "Absage an die Orgasmusdiktatur," *Arbeiter-Zeitung* (Vienna), April 12, 1980, 17.

[50] Cartoon from German *Playboy* 2 (1980), reprinted to accompany Karas, "Absage an die Orgasmusdiktatur," 17.

ecstasies were not forthcoming." And Karas concurred with the authors that the only hope for the future was to bring more "disorder" into the passions, to let emotions back in, to let individual fantasy back in, and for heterosexual men to learn from the rebelling women and homosexuals and transvestites and prostitutes and all those still marginalized from the world of hygienic streamlined interactions. In Karas' own statement of hopes: "One should once again be able to caress someone, without this having to have a particular purpose, one should – without neurotic expectations – be able to do whatever feels fun . . . to invent one's own adventures."[51]

At the turn from the 1970s to the 1980s, it was uncertain whether this new dissident romanticism might yet win out over the discomfort building around the commercialization of sex that had also been such an important factor in making the sexual revolution possible in the first place. What was clear was that discomfort was growing, not so much in the form of conservative attacks on sexual freedoms, but rather more in a vague sense of dissatisfaction and loss of conviction that sex was an unruly and exciting force rather than a site of difficulty. As the West German magazine *Stern* asked in 1980, could it be that "after the rush of freedom comes the hangover?"[52] In short, and although the forms in which disappointments were expressed were still rather inchoate, a backlash against the sexual revolution was already building before anyone had ever even heard of the disease that would eventually be called HIV/AIDS.

Further reading

Bourg, Julian, "'Your Sexual Revolution Is Not Ours': French Feminist 'Moralism' and the Limits of Desire" in Lessie Jo Frazier and Deborah Cohen (eds.), *Gender and Sexuality in 1968: Transformative Politics in the Cultural Imagination* (New York: Palgrave Macmillan, 2009).
Bourke, Joanna, *Rape: Sex, Violence, History* (London: Virago, 2007).
Chaplin, Tamara, "Orgasm without Limits: May '68 and the History of Sex Education in Modern France" in Julian Jackson *et al.* (eds.), *May '68, Forty Years On* (London: Palgrave, 2011).
Escoffier, Jeffrey (ed.), *Sexual Revolution* (New York: Thunder's Mouth Press, 2003).
Grant, Linda, *Sexing the Millennium: A Political History of the Sexual Revolution* (New York: HarperCollins, 1993).
Green, Jonathon, *It: Sex since the Sixties* (London: Martin Secker & Warburg, 1993).

[51] Karas, "Absage an die Orgasmusdiktatur," 17.
[52] Headline accompanying Ingrid Kolb, "Zwischen Lust und Frust," *Stern* 21 (1980), 120.

Hekma, Gert (ed.), *A Cultural History of Sexuality in the Modern Age* (Oxford and New York: Berg, 2011).

Herzog, Dagmar, "'Pleasure, Sex, and Politics Belong Together': Post-Holocaust Memory and the Sexual Revolution in West Germany," *Critical Inquiry* 24, no. 2 (Winter 1998), 393–444.

"Christianity, Disability, Abortion: Western Europe, 1960s–1970s," *Archiv für Sozialgeschichte* 51 (2011): forthcoming.

Lennerhed, Lena, "The Pursuit of Pleasure: Sex Liberalism in Sweden in the 1960's" in Gert Hekma (ed.), *Past and Present of Radical Sexual Politics* (Amsterdam: Mosse Foundation, 2004).

McLellan, Joise, *Love in the Time of Communism: Sexuality and Intimacy in the GDR* (Cambridge University Press, forthcoming 2011).

Perinelli, Massimo, "Sex and the Radical Left, 1969–1972" in Scott Spector, Dagmar Herzog, and Helmut Puff (eds.), *After the History of Sexuality: German Interventions* (New York and Oxford: Berghahn Books, 2011).

Shepard, Todd, "Sexual Revolution in France and the Algerian Man, 1967–1974," *Journal of Modern History* (forthcoming 2011).

5   Partnerships and practices 1980–2010

The unexpected and devastating emergence of HIV/AIDS in the early 1980s was to have considerable consequences for how the sexual revolutions of the prior decades would be remembered. The initial media responses to the disease were largely horrific. The ultimate result, however, was more complex. Eventually, the collective public and governmental response brought many positive changes as Europeans developed greater comfort both with negotiating sexual practices and with appreciating human sexual diversity. The trend toward broad commitment to individual sexual rights would be even further consolidated by developments in the wake of the fall of communism as well as Europeans' efforts to grapple with the challenges wrought by the rise of Islam – a striking and important counterpoint to the more disturbing reactions to Islam evident in the ascent of far-right, explicitly anti-immigrant and anti-Muslim political parties. Most notably, the consensus in favor of the value of individual sexual self-determination came to incorporate also the traditionally conservative parties. The pressure to promote tolerance became strong. The results were evident in both law and culture.

Yet around the turn of the millennium, new sexually conservative countermovements began gaining greater visibility and influence within Europe, both East and West. Some were backed by the Catholic church, others by secular initiatives. Liberals found themselves caught off-guard by the new conservatives' rhetorical and organizational tactics. It became apparent that older strategies for defending sexual rights would require revision. This was not least because of unprecedented transformations in the very nature of what counted as sex under the impact of the invention of Viagra and the growth of Internet porn and chat rooms. For these new developments raised unexpectedly difficult questions about the relationships between bodies and emotions, lust and love, the capacity to perform and the experience of intimacy.

HIV/AIDS

"It would be difficult to exaggerate the impact of media sensational-
ism, stupidity, and malicious inhumanity, in drawing gay men together
in those early years of the epidemic," observed British cultural studies
scholar and gay rights activist Simon Watney in 1994, looking back on
the first years of the 1980s. Gay men, he continued, were "the targets
of repeated insult and vilification . . . We saw the sick pilloried, and the
worst abuse reserved for the most severely devastated communities."[1]
Kaye Wellings – preeminent British specialist on sexual and reproductive health issues – made a related point in 1993. "We use deviants to
reinforce the moral order. You always need deviancy to ensure a ninety-
nine per cent regular society . . . This is where the need for moral panic
comes in." During the heyday of the sexual revolution, antibiotics and
the birth control pill removed the time-honored deterrent to unorthodox
and precocious sexual behavior: fear of disease and pregnancy. "With
the advent of AIDS," she reflected, "I think there was a pent-up moral
repression that needed expression. The AIDS scare was almost deliberately fanned. Every social institution was involved – the press, the Law,
even the Church."[2]

These comments capture crucial points about the momentous impact
of the disease that would subsequently be abbreviated as HIV/AIDS, but
was first, in June 1981, described as an unusual form of pneumonia found
in five homosexual men in Los Angeles. HIV/AIDS did *not* cause a return
to sexual conservatism – the effect was eventually far more convoluted
and contradictory. But it did certainly provide an opportunity for an
aggressive outpouring of homophobia and of animus against what were
perceived as the "excesses" of the sexual revolution more generally.

Across European nations, the media published breathless exposés that
were as frightening as they were factually false. Among other things, the
reports suggested: that AIDS could be acquired by casual contact, by
breathing shared air at stores, school, or work; that those infected – in
the early days primarily homosexual and bisexual men, prostitutes, and
injection drug users – should be quarantined; or that the best way to
prevent infection was to avoid sex altogether. Conservatives – politicians
and pundits alike – could scarcely contain their glee that homosexuals,
drug users, and prostitutes were apparently to be punished, whether by
God or nature did not matter. And even moralists who steered clear of the

---

[1] Simon Watney, *Practices of Freedom: Selected Writings on HIV/AIDS* (Durham, NC: Duke
University Press, 1994), xiii.
[2] Kaye Wellings quoted in Jonathon Green, *It: Sex since the Sixties* (London: Secker and
Warburg, 1993), 240.

178 Partnerships and practices 1980–2010

most egregious contempt for socially marginalized groups nonetheless preached that the emergence of the disease was a sign that surely it was time to end the sexual revolution. Finally, sex could once again be associated with gruesome death.

In France, homosexuality had just finally been fully decriminalized in 1981, but the window for celebrating the new freedoms closed abruptly. In the early months of 1982, "not a week has gone by when the mainstream press has not reveled in sensational headlines about a disease that is preying on the sorry queers. More virulent than the plague and gangrene combined."[3] In Spain, gay rights activists noted a "new Puritanism" and overt homophobia, because of AIDS, in the mass media. In West Germany, journalists were pleased to pontificate that "'sexual liberation' is at an end" and that intercourse was meant to be solely "between man and woman." Further, "the bowels and anus are made for excretion. Security can only be provided by abstinence and lifelong monogamy."[4] It was left to the prominent London rabbi Julia Neuberger (the second female rabbi ever in the UK) to make the pertinent point, several years into the crisis, that "it is a strange God who chooses to punish male homosexuals and not female, and who is angry with drug-takers who inject intravenously but not with those who sniff."[5] And it would be among others the American historian of medicine Allan Brandt who movingly warned against draconian but unhelpful public health measures and argued succinctly that "we must recognize that behavioral change does not mean encouraging celibacy, heterosexuality, or morality; rather, it means developing means to avoid coming into contact with a pathogen."[6] Despite such voices, the ongoing cacophonous misinformation of the public had devastating consequences. One poll published in Britain in March 1986 found more than half the readers favoring a "total recriminalisation" of homosexuality and an even higher percentage affirming that "AIDS carriers" should be "sterilised and given treatment to curb their sexual appetite."[7]

By 1982, the term Acquired Immune Deficiency Syndrome had been coined. Technically, AIDS is the actual disease; it involves the progressive breakdown of the body's immune defenses while opportunistic infections

---

[3] *Gai Pied*, April 1982, quoted in Frédéric Martel, *Le rose et le noir: les homosexuels en France depuis 1968* (Paris: Seuil, 1996), 324.

[4] Volkmar Sigusch, "Aids für alle, alle für Aids" (1986), reprinted in Volkmar Sigusch, *Kritik der disziplinierten Sexualität* (Frankfurt am Main: Campus, 1989), 117–18.

[5] Julia Neuberger, "Aids and the Cruelty of Panic," *The Guardian*, December 9, 1985.

[6] Allan M. Brandt, *No Magic Bullet: A Social History of Venereal Disease in the United States since 1880* (Oxford University Press, 1985), 203.

[7] *News of the World*, March 1, 1986, quoted in Simon Watney, *Policing Desire: Pornography, AIDS and the Media* (Minneapolis: University of Minnesota Press, 1987), 141.

and tumors disrupt the functioning of the pulmonary, gastrointestinal, and neurological systems, as well as the spread of cancer on the skin. HIV – isolated in 1983 by French researchers Luc Montagnier and Françoise Barré-Sinoussi – is the Human Immunodeficiency Virus that triggers the damage to the immune system's ability to ward off the various infections caused by bacteria, viruses, fungi, and parasites. Until effective antiretrovirals were made available in 1995, an HIV infection generally progressed to AIDS.

Initially, those involved in caring for the ill and in reacting against the onslaught of aggression knew just as little about how the disease worked as those who were fulminating against them, but gradually they began to formulate an informed counterdiscourse to the outpouring of contemptuous ugliness, as well as a set of counterpractices. By November 1982, even before HIV had been isolated as the infectious agent (at first, it was thought that perhaps the source of the infections among gay men was poppers or hot tubs), and then gathering in intensity through the year 1983, gay men began to devise and promulgate safer sex strategies, especially promoting the use of condoms. Once HIV had been identified, activists learned also to make the point that HIV/AIDS was better understood as a *blood* disease, not a "sexually transmitted disease." (Wellings among others noted that if everything that could be transmitted via sexual contact was considered a sexually transmitted disease, then the common cold would qualify as well.) In addition, activists demanded that governments stop investing in punitive projects such as mandatory HIV testing and instead put money into researching a cure. Above all, and with growing anger and clarity, activists pointed out that calls for "partner reduction" and the shutting down of gay clubs and bathhouses (two favorite recommendations from ill-informed public health authorities) were both dangerously misconceived. After all, it was not the number of *partners* but rather the *practices* one engaged in with those partners that determined the risk of infection.

Step by step, country by country, activists succeeded in moving government public health authorities also to spread the news: Condoms were an absolutely essential line of defense for anal as for vaginal sex; generous amounts of lube were helpful as well for preventing rips and discomfort alike. Fellatio without swallowing semen carried some risk. But stimulation by hand, as long as there were no cuts on the skin, was safe; so, certainly, were voyeurism and exhibitionism.

Launched in 1985, the Swiss campaign was one of the earliest and most innovative in Europe. (Other notably proactive governments were those of Norway, Finland, and the Netherlands.) The emphasis from the start was on eroticizing condom use, reimagining condoms as an exciting part of sex-play rather than an inhibiting annoyance. For instance, as part of the campaign, condoms began to be marketed in Swiss grocery stores under the English-language brandname "Hot Rubber." *Ohne Dings kein Bums* (which might loosely be translated as "No glove, no love") and *Sortez couvert!* (Use protection!), the Swiss government informed its citizens bilingually. In addition, the government worked to develop campaigns addressed to the specific needs of diverse vulnerable groups, including the establishment of clean needle programs for injection drug users.

West Germany soon followed suit with an equally impressive campaign. In 1987, the influential right-wing Bavarian politician Peter Gauweiler and others called for quarantining HIV-positive individuals, forced testing, and contact-tracing. It was not least because of the inescapable echoes with the Third Reich that Gauweiler was forcefully rebuked (critics accused him of wanting to open an "AIDS-concentration camp" and to prepare "a kind of Final Solution" for the infected). In reaction, Gauweiler's colleague Rita Süssmuth, the Christian Democratic Minister for Youth, Family, Women, and Health, became one of the foremost spokespeople in the West German government advocating for Safe Sex/Save Sex campaigns coupled with the protection of individual rights. Her concept from the start was: "We are battling the disease, not those infected."[8] And to promote the cause, she permitted the news magazine *Der Spiegel* to place an image of her covered with a full-body condom on its cover.

In many nations, however, mixed messaging remained. The awareness growing as of the mid-1980s that heterosexuals were in danger as well was recurrently met with a thoroughly confused response, in which helpful and misleading, pointedly specific and hopelessly vague information existed side by side. The British government, when finally – in 1987 – induced to mount a television and flyer campaign that reached every household in the nation, began its television ad with the threatening image of dynamite exploding a mountain like a volcano erupting, followed by footage of miners drilling, as the voice-over intoned ominously: "There is now a danger that has become a threat to us all . . . So far it's been confined to small groups, but it's spreading . . . If you ignore AIDS, it could be the death of you. So don't die of ignorance."[9] And as the flyers elaborated on that plea, the text declared: "Gay or straight,

---

[8] Quoted in "Ehrenvorsitzende der Deutschen AIDS-Stiftung Rita Süssmuth vollendet das 70. Lebensjahr," *presseportal*, February 15, 2007, www.presseportal.de/pm/42803/941990/deutsche_aids_stiftung.

[9] Central Office of Information for Department of Health, "AIDS: Don't Die of Ignorance" (1987), www.nationalarchives.gov.uk/films/1979to2006/filmpage_aids.htm.

Risk Factor Love

Benny Henriksson

This study focuses on homo- and bisexual men's sexuality, love relations and families, as a background to understand the men's reactions, interpretations and responses to the HIV crisis in Sweden. The findings confirm those of other social researchers (e.g., Bolton, 1992a), who believe that we have to *re-think HIV prevention*.

Homosexuality, sexual interaction and HIV preventation

Fig. 5.1 "Risk Factor Love." Advertisement for an event on the work of the Swedish sociologist Benny Henriksson (1947–95).

male or female, anyone can get AIDS from sexual intercourse. And the more partners, the greater the risk. Protect yourself. Use a condom." It was left to activist groups, like the Terrence Higgins Trust, to provide alternative imagery that promoted condom use as something sensual and sex-enhancing.

As activists and experts acquired more understanding of how individuals negotiated sexual practices, they discovered what initially seemed counterintuitive but upon deeper consideration made complete sense. It was precisely in the context of sex with strangers in non-domestic spaces like public toilets or clubs or bathhouses that safer sex strategies were increasingly being effectively employed. By contrast, it was specifically within the most emotionally intimate relations, as the Swedish scholar Benny Henriksson noted in his eloquent and indicatively titled study *Risk Factor Love*, that it was difficult to negotiate safer sex, not least because the riskiest practice – unprotected anal sex – was precisely the one associated with showing trust and care.

In time, the emergence of the disease had yet other paradoxical effects. Far from generating an overall return to conservatism, the epidemic

spawned ever greater public frankness and directness about sexual practices and the intricacies of behavior and desire. The attempt to reduce
new infections prompted a surge in far more explicit public health messaging across European nations. In Spain, where the rate of infections
was especially high while media coverage remained woefully uninforma-
tive, Matilde Fernandez, the socialist Minister of Social Affairs, in 1988
released a clever television ad which clarified that exchanging saliva via
a shared soda bottle was safe but that sharing a razor, by which blood-
based transmission could occur, was not; in addition, the ad showed
two smiling little male symbols cheerfully engaged in rollicking condom-
ized anal intercourse. In 1990, Fernandez stirred further controversy
but eventually great acclaim with her unambiguous billboard campaign
directing also heterosexual women to take charge and insist on condoms:
"Put it on. Put it on him." (*Póntelo. Pónselo.*) It was not only because this
had been an era in which public opinion still assumed that AIDS solely
affected homosexuals and drug users that the new campaign caused much
public debate. And it was not only the casual explicitness that offended
(even as the Council of Spanish Bishops denounced the campaign as
"irresponsible" and declared that it could "lead boys and girls to possibly
irreparable psychological and physical traumas").[10] It was also that the
slogan inevitably conjured the image of a woman confidently handling a
man's penis and "taking the initiative in a terrain in which the man was
accustomed to controlling."[11]

In general, then, a major effect of the public awareness efforts was
to transform the condom from a reluctantly used object with a still
slightly tawdry aura into something commonly accepted and no longer
controversial. But another huge consequence of the ongoing garrulous
babble swirling in the media was the new legitimacy with which the
details of sexual fantasies and activities – among homo- and heterosexuals alike – were engaged directly in the public sphere. No part of the
body, no invention of the desiring imagination, escaped scrutiny. Dildos
and rimming, latex dental guards and golden showers, masturbation
aids and staged scenarios: Everyone became newly knowledgeable, if
not through their own practices then by learning about the practices of
others. And, however ironically nonetheless decisively, the effect was to
erode ever further simplistic assumptions about the differences between
homosexuals and heterosexuals. The lines between daring and dull,

---

[10] "Condom Ads Get Hit in Spain," *Advertising Age*, November 26, 1990, 44.
[11] Lola Fernández, "'Póntelo. Pónselo': 20 años después," *El Mundo*, January 31, 2010,
www.elmundo.es/suplementos/magazine/2010/540/1264678195.html.

Fig. 5.2 Spanish TV ad still from HIV prevention campaign, 1988.

kinky and vanilla, promiscuous and monogamous, quite apparently ran
through, not between, each group.

The catastrophe provided the basis first for an efflorescence of homophobia but eventually for its dramatic reduction. The initial responses
to the disease had been filled with venom, cruelty, and disdain and, as
a result, desire itself became inescapably repoliticized. In time, however,
and although against tremendous odds, the battle against both the disease and the disdain spurred enormously creative and courageous gay
and lesbian rights activism as well as, after many setbacks, much greater
social acceptance of gays and lesbians – and more comfort with reporting
bisexual life histories. In general, the public health initiatives led to more
ease among both sexes in talking about sex and in using contraception
and strategies of disease prevention. Far from marking an end to the
sexual revolution, then, the emergence of the disease and the fight to
contain it were accompanied by ongoing sexual liberalization.

The fall of communism

Communism's first gradual and then complete disintegration had multiple contradictory effects on sexual politics, and not only the persistence
but also the export and expansion of Western forms of sexual liberalization were strongly evident. The process which eventually led to the
rending of the Iron Curtain in the course of 1989 had already been underway from the mid-1980s on with the rise of the trade union Solidarity

in Poland, with pressure for reform building within the highest levels of Hungary's government, and with Soviet leader Mikhail Gorbachev's encouragement of *glasnost* (freedom of information and transparency of government) and *perestroika* (political and economic reforms). Once the Iron Curtain was gone, "the West" and all it stood for quickly flooded into "the East." Trucks trundled across the borders almost immediately, proffering pornographic magazines and sex toys (and somewhat later also contraceptives). Video stores opened. Sexualized advertising filled public space. And talk about sexual matters saturated the previously so typically prim and robotically propagandistic media. From Slovakia to Russia, everywhere pornography began conspicuously to be displayed.

Yet not only the West's capitalist economic system was exported; efforts to demand from the formerly Eastern Bloc nations commitments to democratic values were made as well – and within this wider project sexual matters accrued surprisingly high symbolic importance. For instance, within a few years, after the European Union was established in 1993, discussions about Eastern European countries' entry into the EU sometimes turned on whether or not these nations had developed proper sensitivity to homosexual rights. This led to interesting disjunctions between the level of gay and lesbian self-organization within a particular country (often not high), average popular opinion in those countries toward homosexuality (frequently quite hostile), and legal innovations made to please the Western decision-makers gathered in Brussels. As the international gay rights activist Scott Long helpfully albeit sarcastically summarized the ensuing dynamic:

East European governments more or less look on European structures as a nephew might look on a rich eccentric uncle who is forever rewriting his will. The uncle's every crotchet must be humored if the nephew wants to get his hands on the inheritance, and if the uncle suddenly takes an interest in the shine on the nephew's shoes, or the cut of his hair, or the way he treats homosexuals or other nonexistent creatures, the nephew must put up a quick and busy show of improvement.[12]

A striking example was the case of Romania. As of 1995, it was one of only three countries in Europe that still criminalized homosexuality – including lesbianism – with the punishment set at one to five years imprisonment. (Hungary and Czechoslovakia, by contrast, had decriminalized same-sex sex for consenting adults in 1961. In Poland, homosexuality

[12] Scott Long, "Gay and Lesbian Movements in Eastern Europe: Romania, Hungary, and the Czech Republic," in Barry D. Adam, Jan Willem Duyvendak, and Andre Krouwel, eds., *The Global Emergence of Gay and Lesbian Politics: National Imprints of a Worldwide Movement* (Philadelphia: Temple University Press, 1999).

had never been illegal.) Under the cruel reign of Nicolae Ceauşescu, Article 200 of the criminal code above all served as a trouble-free way to jail political dissidents. Small homosexual subcultures existed in the larger cities, but below the surface of public awareness. As of 1993, a survey found that 85 percent of Romanian citizens believed that homosexuality was unacceptable. EU access for Romania was made contingent on changing the law on homosexuality, but the Romanian government dragged its feet. The Romanian Orthodox church fanned homophobia further as part of its efforts to regain moral authority and deflect attention from its extensive complicity with the Ceauşescu regime; homosexuality became a flashpoint in resistance to the West. In this context, gay rights groups modeled their cause on that of disenfranchised ethnic minorities, both the Roma and the minority of Hungarians within Romania. Ultimately, however, it was the pressure from Brussels that proved decisive. Decriminalization was finally enacted in 1996, anti-discrimination laws were put in place in 2000, and the age of consent for hetero- and homosexual activity was equalized – to 15 – in 2002. In 2006, Romania was named by Human Rights Watch as one of five countries in the world that had made "exemplary progress in combating rights abuses based on sexual orientation or gender identity."[13] In 2007, the country joined the EU. Along related lines, as of 2009, the government of the (predominantly secular Muslim) nation of Albania was announcing that it would push its parliament to recognize same-sex marriage in hopes of hastening EU accession.

Further developments also involved importation of Western ways into the former East. A key example was HIV/AIDS prevention work. Although homosexuality had been legal in the former Czechoslovakia, for instance, awareness of safe-sex practices remained low into the beginning of the 1990s; 90 percent of AIDS cases in the Czech Republic as of 1991 were among homo- and bisexual men. (Meanwhile, popular homophobia remained high.) It was the Dutch Ministry of Health that provided the funds for a condom promotion initiative directed specifically at men seeking same-sex sex in the Czech Republic; 14,000 brochures were handed out in gay and lesbian clubs and gay male saunas, as well as to male prostitutes who serviced men. The campaign was a great success. It provided not only the opportunity for greater discussion of safe sex practices within gay subcultures, but also an increase in condom sales, and – in a nice example of the possibilities for synergy between

---

[13] "'Hall of Shame' Shows Reach of Homophobia: On International Day against Homophobia, Violations Mixed with Victories," Human Rights Watch, May 17, 2006, www.hrw.org/english/docs/2006/05/17/global13393.htm.

capitalism and public health – the Czech condom industry approached a Czech gay and lesbian rights organization to ask to be involved in further safe-sex promotion projects. (Similar transnational cooperation evolved between a major Austrian HIV prevention organization and Hungarian, Czech, and Slovak groups.)

Within a few years, condoms began to be sent in the opposite direction, from East to West. The Polish company UNIMIL Cracow stepped up production and exported its product to Sweden and Germany. But also within Poland, condom use rose – not just among homosexuals, but primarily among heterosexuals as, in a complicated irony, precisely the rise of anti-abortion forces in post-Communist Poland prompted heterosexuals to seek to prevent pregnancies more assiduously than they had in the Communist era. (Previously, a survey had shown that the estimated 11 million sexually active couples in Poland used on average at most 4.5 condoms each per year; a prior survey had found an average of 2 condoms used per year.) In yet another new East–West partnership venture, UNIMIL Cracow joined with a Swiss division of UNIMIL to operate condom vending machines in Warsaw.

On a more subtle and complex level, the emergence within Eastern European countries of politically active gay and lesbian rights organizations based on Western models confronted both the wider public *and* same-sex-desiring individuals themselves with new paradigms of same-sex desire. There was nothing necessarily more "true" about Western ideas that same-sex desire is innate in a certain subset of individuals and that those individuals should declare their preferences publicly. And also in the West, many people continued to seek same-sex encounters without ever self-defining as gay or lesbian. But by the early 1990s groups had been formed all across the former East – from Albania, Bulgaria, Croatia, and Estonia to Slovakia, Slovenia, and the Ukraine – and, even if in some cases these organizations had at best twenty members, the meeting between cultures indisputably brought novel notions about both desire and rights into the discourse of Eastern countries. As Leszek Bolewski, editor of *Lesbian and Gay Express*, the newsletter for the newly formed Central and East European Gay and Lesbian Network (based in Poznań, Poland) put it in 1994 in the first issue, "East–West," in evocative halting English, "Democracy has just been born in our countries, gay movement is like a baby."[14] Another item in the newsletter emphasized how "invisible" lesbians and gays still were in Polish society since the Western-style practice of "coming out" was just beginning, as it also reported that the

---

[14] Leszek Bolewski, "Dear Friends," in *Lesbian and Gay Express* 1, "East–West" (1994), www.qrd.org/qrd/world/europe/eastern/central.and.eastern.european.lgb.network-01.

magazine *Twoj Styl* (Your Style) had surveyed more than a thousand Polish women and that more than 78 percent had declared that they would not like to have a homosexual as a neighbor (while former agents of SB, the Polish KGB, were apparently much less threatening). But that first issue also showed just how quickly the topics of legalization of gay and lesbian partnerships, adoption of children, and efforts to combat discrimination against individuals diagnosed as HIV-positive (as well as the need for greater "self-acceptance") were put on the agenda for discussion by the newly formed rights groups, and how rapidly the public debates began to resemble those within the West.

Crossing borders: prostitution and marriage

Beyond the shifts in product placements, legal systems, public health provisions, and new categories of self-understanding, the disappearance of the Iron Curtain was evident as well in the movements of peoples – and here the flows were by no means primarily from West to East, but rather went in several directions. A major development was the transformation and expansion of hetero- as well as homosexual sex tourism. Without question, both straight- and gay-servicing commercial scenes in numerous cities and beach towns across North Africa, the Middle East, Latin America, and Asia continued to attract visitors from Europe. But now heterosexual men from the formerly communist portion of Germany, for example, eager to use their newfound freedom to travel, emulated a longstanding practice among Western European heterosexual men and headed overseas to East Asia or Latin America with a view to "finally" being able to experience women of "other ethnicities."

Some of the borders crossed were within Europe. In prior decades, Amsterdam had been a favorite gay travel destination. But in the 1990s, gay Austrians, for instance, also increasingly traveled to the Czech Republic, especially the "golden city" of Prague – imagined, in indisputably neocolonial fashion, as a fabulous "boyopolis" (coinage of the Canadian journalist Stan Persky, who also described his mid-1990s exploits with hustlers in Warsaw, Budapest, and Zagreb). But heterosexual Austrian men too headed "East" (technically of course north) and took to picking up Czech women directly by the sides of the highway as soon as they crossed the border. Over time, opportunities for purchasing prostitutes' services were not just available in the immediate proximity of the borders but spread even further along the main highways crossing the lands of the former Eastern Bloc, including those in Hungary and Poland.

The problems that formerly Soviet-controlled economies soon confronted in adapting to an ever more globally interconnected capitalism – one that was itself increasingly in dysfunction and crisis – also triggered a substantial movement of (mostly female, but also some male) prostitutes in the other direction, away from the nations of the former East and into the West. There they joined prostitutes whose countries of origin were Asian or African. Of the several hundred thousand women working as prostitutes in Germany at the end of the 1990s, for example, over 60 percent were foreigners, and of those, two-thirds were from the countries of the former Eastern Bloc. Several hundred were suspected of being the victims of trafficking. No less striking was the prevalence of women from countries of the former Soviet Union (Russia, Georgia, Ukraine, Uzbekistan, Kyrgyzstan, Azerbaijan, and Belarus), but also from Bulgaria and Romania, among the high number of trafficking victims estimated to be among the approximately 100,000 prostitutes in Turkey. In the early twenty-first century, a survey found that Eastern European women (with Romania, Bulgaria, Russia and the Ukraine highest on the list) accounted for approximately 70 percent of *all* migrant sex workers within the 27-nation EU. By contrast, 12 percent came from African nations and 11 percent from Latin America and the Caribbean. In short, one of the extraordinary ironies of the accession of Romania and Bulgaria to the EU was precisely that sex workers from those nations could now more easily move into Western nations.

Nonetheless, the distribution of ethnic origins of prostitutes continued to vary widely by country and was often a matter of historical contingency. Thus, for instance, in the 1990s a disproportionate number of Nigerian women worked as prostitutes in Italy, Spain, and Greece – many of them trafficked. In the early twenty-first century, Nigerian women predominated in street prostitution in Norway. In Belgium, however, as of the early twenty-first century, 70 percent of foreign prostitutes came from Bulgaria. Overall, within Europe, Belgium, Italy, the Netherlands, and Germany became major destinations for victims of trafficking – with endless debates ensuing among sex workers' rights groups, NGOs, and government policy-makers over the importance of distinguishing between voluntary sex work (including migration for sex work) on the one hand, and sexual slavery and trafficking on the other.

In addition, and crucially, there was a new market in marriage opportunities. In France, for example, at the end of the twentieth century, one in every eight or nine marriages involved a foreign citizen, and by the early twenty-first century it was close to one in three. In Switzerland, too, it was one in every three marriages. Although great, often hysterical, media attention in Germany and Austria focused on native-born women who chose to marry men from predominantly Muslim countries, whether from Turkey or from countries in the Middle East or northern

Africa, binational marriages in those countries at the turn of the millennium statistically involved a preponderance of *men* choosing to marry women from the former Eastern European nations. In both Germany and Austria, the proportion of men to women in binational marriages hovered around 60–40. In France, however, where the preponderance of binational marriages typically involved a match between someone from a former colony or department of France in Africa (Tunisia, Morocco, Algeria, and Senegal), more women than men married foreigners (and often married overseas and then returned to France). Here, attention in the media tended to fixate on worries about women "forced" into arranged marriages that France then considered suspicious, which allowed the government to track and even annul them in certain cases. The high proportions of binational marriages among the grand total of marriages may be largely explained by the fact that committed couples unconcerned about citizenship felt much less need to marry.

At the same time, many of the binational marriages were certainly motivated by love. Indicatively, there were advocacy organizations working for the rights of binational couples with such slogans as "Marriage Is Not a Crime" and with pamphlets with such titles as "What Color Is Your Toothbrush?" which helped couples navigate the aggressively suspicious immigration bureaucracies. Under the combined impact of rising rates of heterosexual cohabitation without marriage, high numbers of divorces, increasing legalization of both same-sex and different-sex civil partnerships and of gay and lesbian marriages, not to mention the self-evident reality of countless loveless marriages also between individuals of the same nationality, the notion that one could cleanly distinguish between "genuine" marriages, on the one side, and "sham" or "fictitious" marriages – that is, marriages entered into for the sole purpose of acquiring European citizenship – on the other, was indisputably based on shaky foundations. But it was nonetheless also an open secret in all European nations that many marriages were entered into for the sole purpose of acquiring citizenship. This was a state of affairs memorably captured by Serbian artist Tanja Ostojić's deliberately provocative photo project of 2000, "Looking for a Husband with a EU passport" (in which Ostojić herself appeared, nude and shaved all over).

Resisting Westernization

Other developments were yet more convoluted. Into the ideological vacuum created by communism's defeat, Western European notions of secularism, sexual liberality, and capitalist free enterprise were after all not the only new political arrivals; conservative Christian and ethnic nationalist

forces – sometimes separate, often conjoined – vied for cultural and political influence as well. Church attendance rose rapidly in the 1990s in the
countries transitioning out of communism. This was not least because the
transition into capitalism was often rocky, in many places accompanied
by extraordinary corruption in government and strong overlap between
criminal and business worlds – not to mention abrupt declines in living
standards and losses of social security for both men and women (even
more so for women, as there was a strong trend toward feminization of
poverty). In this context, church leaders claimed authority on a wide
variety of social issues – even if their views did not necessarily represent
those of the laity. Among other things, a newly revitalized and politicized
Catholicism (especially in Poland and Hungary), and a revived Orthodox
Christianity (especially in Romania and the Ukraine), became powerful
political forces and were particularly important in giving voice to feelings
of aggrieved hostility at what were perceived to be the West's gratingly
self-righteous demands for legal and cultural protection of sexual liberality and sexual minorities.

At the same time, and just as the forms of politicized religion that
arose in the 1990s might best be described as *neo*traditional – i.e. new
postcommunist creations – so too the various and often quite aggressively articulated ethnic nationalisms that emerged in the aftermath of
communism's demise may be understood not as timeless value systems
but rather as utterly modern, indeed postmodern, inventions. They were
complex formations that borrowed freely from (distorted) references to
the communist past and invocations of fantasized ethno-religious identity coherences that in fact never existed. But as unstable as the bases for
these new political forces were, their consequences for policy and public
attitudes were quite real.

Most extreme were neofascist movements gaining strength in Poland,
Romania, and the Ukraine. These groups were not simply irritated by EU
demands for greater sensitivity toward homosexuals; they rather believed
that the EU was run by "fags" and therefore had to be resisted. Their
homophobic imagery – along with the slogan "Faggotry Forbidden" –
was reproduced in the media without criticism by more moderate political
groupings, and slathered in multiples across the walls of buildings on city
streets. The imagery could also be integrated with religious symbols –
as it was for example in the counterdemonstration to a gay pride parade
held in Bucharest, Romania, in 2006. The rhetoric was often violent.
Youth affiliated with the ultra-nationalist League of Polish Families, for
instance, taunted feminist and gay rights demonstrators with chants such
as "pedophiles and pederasts – these are Euro-enthusiasts," "labor camps
for lesbians," and "faggots to the gas." And over and over, from Cracow,

Fig. 5.3 Romanian Orthodox icons and anti-homosexuality signs were held up at a counterdemonstration to a gay pride parade, in Bucharest, Romania, June 3, 2006. The Romanian Orthodox Church and conservative groups including the far-right Noua Drepta had declared the scheduled gay pride parade immoral and "abnormal" and issued a call for the counterdemonstration. The image on the placards is the same as the one used in Poland where the text reads "Faggotry forbidden." The Romanian signs declare "Against homosexuality – for normality."

Poland, to Riga, Latvia, gay pride parades met with – and sometimes were shut down in fear of or in response to – physical violence.

The emotional associations between the perceived need to resist Westernization and Western ideas about sexuality and gender ultimately worked in a wide variety of ways – and always in complicated intersection with and backlash against the gender egalitarianism that was strongly (and however inaccurately) associated with communism. One effect was on debates about abortion rights. With the exception of Romania, where abortion had been illegal and prosecuted with brutal rigor since 1966, most of the Eastern Bloc countries, after a period of severe restrictions in the Stalinist era of the 1940s to the early 1950s, had between 1955 and 1960 liberalized legal access to abortion (usually on the grounds of the evident damage to women's health caused by the widespread persistence of recourse to illegal abortion).

As of 1960, abortion upon request of the pregnant woman became available in the USSR, Bulgaria, and Hungary. In Czechoslovakia and Yugoslavia, women needed to demonstrate that carrying the pregnancy to term would cause a "difficult" or "serious personal, familial, or economic situation."[15] In Poland, women had only to claim poor living conditions. The liberality of abortion law under communism and – especially in view of the near-nonexistence of contraceptive products in most Eastern Bloc countries, with the exception of East Germany and Yugoslavia where the pill and condoms were available – the ensuing widespread reliance on abortion for fertility control made it easy for those postcommunist commentators hostile to abortion rights to associate abortion with communism.

More generally, in a major misrepresentation of historical reality, women were positioned as having been the "narcissistic" and "selfish" beneficiaries of the communist regimes. Yes, women had worked outside the home in Eastern Bloc countries, but generally in lesser-status jobs; they had additionally been burdened with the bulk of responsibility for home and childcare, tasks made more arduous by daily life in a constant condition of consumer scarcity. Nonetheless, this background helps to explain how a return to the ideal of a non-working wife and mother could seem like a reaction against the era of communism – an era in which, both male and female anti-feminists complained, women were becoming *too* liberated. As has so often been true, arguments about abortion were inseparable from notions of women's place.

Strikingly, however, and in contradistinction to contemporaneous debates about abortion within the West, intensive concern focused not so much on sexual immorality as on demographics. Here there were strong echoes with the demographic worries in Western European nations in the first half of the twentieth century. Within Hungary, both before and after 1989, anti-communist populists associated abortion with "the death of the nation." "Abortion is a national catastrophe," a right-wing headline declared, while another commentator gestured to Hungary's massive population and territorial losses in the post-World War I Treaty of Trianon when it lamented the "Biological Trianon" caused by the decades of liberal communist abortion policy.[16] As a consequence of the postcommunist mobilization of groups such as "Defenders of the Fetus," the

---

[15] Christoph Tietze and Hans Lehfeldt, "Legal Abortion in Eastern Europe," *Journal of the American Medical Association* 175, no. 13 (1961), 1149.
[16] Quoted in Susan Gal, "Gender in the Post-Socialist Transition: The Abortion Debate in Hungary," *East European Politics and Societies* 8, no. 2 (Spring 1994), 271–2, 278.

abortion law passed in 1992 in Hungary, while retaining legal abortion access, forced women to go before a commission of doctors to make a case for the hardship that carrying the pregnancy to term would cause. In Poland, although a law banning all abortions was defeated in 1989, a highly restrictive law was put in place in 1990, and Poles' vigorous (and successful) efforts to retain the restrictive law became a major issue in EU accession negotiations. Also, in other countries formerly under communist rule, including in Russia, the early years of the twenty-first century saw novel efforts to raise the birthrate – and one specific strategy, in addition to incentives for large families, was to place renewed restrictions on abortion.

In other ways as well, in many former nations of the Eastern Bloc in the course of the 1990s and early 2000s, nativist pride and antagonism toward Western culture manifested in the form of vociferous demands for a return to conservative notions of gender roles. Sometimes the arguments were about quite specific issues. Thus, for instance, when international women's organizations as well as locally emerging feminist groups began in the 1990s to call attention to issues such as domestic violence, they were initially met by fierce resistance from conservative religious groups which, far from being sympathetic, saw these campaigns against domestic violence as an attack on traditional family values. But sometimes the rhetoric worked primarily on a powerful metaphorical level.

In Poland, communism frequently had been imagined as an ineffectual matriarchy which castrated men. But the Western model was seen as no solution either. In the Polish press, in the run-up to EU accession in 2004, new metaphors were introduced. The EU was provocatively described as "effeminate" in its preoccupation with gender equality and the rights of sexual minorities or, in another variation, as pathetically achieving orgasms only via vibrators rather than in actual partnered sex. Over and over, then, against these two "others" (the communist matriarchy of the past and the Western effeminacy of the present), the Polish press ran stories expressing anxiety that Polish women had excessive power in society and calling for a return of "the real man." This intensification of "gender talk" appeared not least to be a way to manage anxieties about EU accession; neoliberal economics were considered acceptable, but sexual egalitarianism was not. Also, in the years after EU accession had been granted, unapologetic homophobia and hostility to abortion became markers of pride as Polish politicians frankly enjoyed Poland's role as the deliberately un-politically correct *enfant terrible* of the EU.

The return of war rapes

The most overwhelmingly cataclysmic event in the aftermath of the collapse of Communism was the war that raged in the former Yugoslavia from 1992 to 1995, a war that left 100,000 people dead and in the course of which an estimated 20,000 to 50,000 women were raped. Soldiers from all sides of the conflict engaged in sexual violence. Croatian (Catholic) and Bosnian Serb (Orthodox) women were raped as well as Bosniak (Bosnian Muslim) women. Men were raped, too – as well as subjected to genital beating and mutilation. The evidence suggests that the largest numbers of victims were Bosnian Muslim women and girls raped by Serb forces, many in rape camps (in schools, sports facilities, and other buildings) where they were violated repeatedly for weeks or even months on end by multiple men. The subsequent trials held at The Hague, Netherlands, at the International Criminal Tribunal for the Former Yugoslavia (ICTY) have documented that rapes were encouraged among the troops. Indeed the enslavement of women was organized systematically. Not only did Serbian officers know about the sexual slavery within camps; they also participated. Moreover, sexual violence was used deliberately as a tactic of warfare, both in the sense that by spreading terror it expedited "ethnic cleansing" – flight and displacement of civilian populations – and in the sense that it worked as a strategy of genocide via the forced impregnation of Muslim women. An oft-quoted remark by one Serbian soldier captured the point: "We'll make you have Serbian babies who will be Christians."[17]

For decades women's rights activists had fought to get rape in war taken seriously against an international community that treated rapes as an unavoidable boys-will-be-boys byproduct of war. In 1996, the ICTY for the first time in legal history indicted individuals for sexual assaults "under the rubric of torture and enslavement as a crime against humanity."[18] Indeed, as recently as 1985, the United Nations General Assembly had found itself unable to pass a resolution taking a stand against "violence against women." (The Vatican had been among those in vigorous opposition to such a resolution, but various Arab states as well as the USA had also raised objections.) A key turning point was a UN-affiliated World Conference on Human Rights held in Vienna, Austria in 1993 at which the (now seemingly self-evident but at the time

[17] "Abuse of Civilians In Detention Centers," Seventh Report on War Crimes in the Former Yugoslavia: Part II, www.ess.uwe.ac.uk/documents/sdrpt7b.htm.
[18] "Gang Rape, Torture and Enslavement," ICTY Press Release, June 27, 1996, www.icty.org/sid/7334.

really innovative and pointed) slogan was popularized, "Women's Rights are Human Rights."

And yet the growth of international preoccupation with women's rights turned out in many ways to be painfully ambiguous. This was not only, though also, because of a broader sense of unease among feminists that the new ascent of women's rights as an international desideratum had been accompanied by the abuse of that ideal for the purposes of military interventionism. (Key examples of this were the tales of rapes of Kuwaiti women that were used to spur support for the USA's first Gulf War in 1991, but subsequently also the claim to be saving Muslim women from their oppressors that was invoked to justify the USA's war against Afghanistan in 2001.) The unease was also due to the recognition that making rape in war prosecutable has neither led to a substantial number of rape cases brought to trial – since even when there is substantial evidence, rape continues to be considered both complicated and costly to prove – nor, even more devastatingly, prevented further raping. The escalating incidences of rape and brutal genital mutilations in civil wars and interstate wars in Africa (Sierra Leone, Liberia, the Sudan, and the Democratic Republic of the Congo), despite the increasingly strong spotlight shone on them by European activists in particular, continued to show up the helplessness of the international community. As in the former Yugoslavia, so also elsewhere at the turn of the millennium, mass rapes in war served as an intentional military-political tactic to terrorize and impregnate, and as a mobilizing and bonding reward for the soldiers.

Postfascist lessons in human rights

Western Europeans' commitments to sexual rights were the result of a long and hard-fought postfascist learning process. After all, it was only in the course of the 1980s that the European Court of Human Rights based in Strasburg had begun to interpret key articles of the European Declaration of Human Rights of 1949 as pertinent to the protection of sexual rights. The year 1981, when Jeffrey Dudgeon took Northern Ireland to court for its ongoing criminalization of male homosexuality – and won – marked an important turning point. But it would take another ten years for the Court to become a premier site for vigorous defense of sexual rights. By the 1990s, in the wake of the collapse of communism, the Court had come to see the task of sex-related legislation as not only one of protecting individuals from sexual harm, i.e. from non-consensual sexual acts and violations of their sexual self-determination, but also one of protection of individuals' rights *to* self-determined sexual encounters and the freely chosen formation of intimate relationships. This included the protection of custody and visitation rights also for those openly living as homosexuals.

As it turned out, not only Eastern but also Western European nations needed schooling in these matters. A 1994 case in Portugal offered a typical example: An openly gay divorced father sued for visitation rights to see his young daughter and won at first but then was denied when the mother appealed. The Portuguese appeals court decision was overtly hostile to same-sex sexuality, arguing in part that the child should live in a "traditional Portuguese family, which is certainly not the set-up her father has decided to enter into, since he is living with another man as if they were man and wife... It is an abnormality, and children should not grow up in the shadow of abnormal situations."[19] The father in turn appealed to the supranational authority of the European Court of Human Rights. In 1999 the Court ruled in the father's favor, noting that the appeals court had made an unacceptable distinction based on sexual orientation, and it ordered the Portuguese state to pay the father a large sum in damages.

Not only the Court, but also the supranational entity of the European Union itself continued in the course of the 1990s and into the early twenty-first century to demand of its member countries advances in legislation around sexual rights. Again, these demands were addressed not only to countries from the former Eastern Bloc, but also to Western European nations. The quintessential case was that of Austria, which had been unusual in both the Nazi and the postwar period for criminalizing not only male homosexuality but also lesbianism. It had not been until 1971 that homosexuality was officially decriminalized (until then, multi-year prison sentences had been standard), but at the same time new legal strictures explicitly limiting queer associational life and media visibility had been enacted. Only in 1995, and specifically in the context of debates over whether Austria was "modern" and "mature" enough to become part of the European Union, did the Austrian government about-face and abruptly embrace its queers as symbols of cosmopolitan trendiness.

On all kinds of levels, the EU recurrently made it clear in the first decade of the twenty-first century that official rejection of homophobia was on the agenda. Christian Democrat Rocco Buttiglione of Italy, for instance, was in 2004 rejected for the position of EU Commissioner for Justice, Freedom and Security on the grounds of his remarks that "homosexuality is a sin" (while an unapologetic Buttiglione declared

[19] European Court of Human Rights, Fourth Section, Case of Salgueiro da Silva Mouta v. Portugal Judgment (*Application no. 33290/96*), Strasburg, December 21, 1999, Final Judgment March 21, 2000, http://cmiskp.echr.coe.int/tkp197/view.asp?item=1&portal=hbkm&action=html&highlight=PORTUGAL%20|%20family&sessionid=54845157&skin=hudoc-en.

that he was the victim of a "new totalitarianism").[20] By the end of the
first decade of the twenty-first century, in short, while it was apparent
that the kinds of passionate declarations of commitments to sexual rights
that became so de rigueur among Western politicians were actually of
rather recent vintage, there was no question that anti-homophobia had
become the new watchword for Western statesmen. As the then-Prime
Minister of Britain Gordon Brown (Labour Party) declared in 2009 in
an interview given to the gay magazine *Attitude*:

I'm fighting to get all the countries in Europe to recognise civil partnerships
carried out in Britain ... We want countries where that hasn't been the case –
especially in Eastern Europe – to recognise them. We're negotiating agreements
with France and then with Spain. But I think we can actually go further than
that. And if we could show Eastern Europe as well as Western Europe, that this
respect for gay people is due, that would be really important. Of course it will be
tough, and will take many years, but that has never ever been a good reason not
to fight.[21]

But most striking was that the consensus in favor of sexual liberality
and the value of individual sexual self-determination now incorporated
also the traditionally conservative parties. After Brown was defeated and
replaced by David Cameron in the close-run Tory victory of 2010, for
example, Cameron's new choice for British Home Secretary, Theresa
May, not previously known for particularly pro-gay stances, upon her
appointment made a special point of announcing her support for the
International Day Against Homophobia and Transphobia. Meanwhile,
the Christian Democratic party in Germany, too, declared itself officially
gay-friendly.

Not just politicians but also many voters had clearly decided that homophobia was passé. Openly gay and lesbian politicians could be found
across European nations – as mayors in Paris and Berlin, as heads of parties in Germany and the Netherlands, and most recently, in Iceland, as
Prime Minister (as the Social Democrat Johanna Sigurdardottir became
the first openly lesbian head of state in the world in 2009). Their orientation was considered either utterly politically irrelevant or an interesting
plus.

Nonetheless, among the various hard-won lessons eventually learned
by Europeans from the horrors of European fascism are some that have

---

[20] Stephanie Holmes, "Profile: Rocco Buttiglione," *BBC News*, October 21, 2004,
http://news.bbc.co.uk/2/hi/europe/3718210.stm; Peter Popham, "Rocco Buttiglione,"
The Independent, November 8, 2004, www.independent.co.uk/news/people/profiles/
rocco-buttiglione-the-left-does-not-want-to-talk-it-prefers-to-marginalise-this-is-the-
new-totalitarianism-532438.html.
[21] "Brown Pushes for Gay Rights in Eastern Europe," *BBC News*, December 16, 2009,
http://news.bbc.co.uk/2/hi/uk_news/politics/8414108.stm.

turned out to be not easily compatible with each other. On the one side, there were the important commitments to the imperative of protecting the inviolability of individuals' bodies and individuals' rights to choose their intimate relationships. Indeed, and wonderfully – and this too was the result of an arduous postfascist learning process – by the early twenty-first century the physically and cognitively disabled also came to be understood as individuals deserving of sexual and reproductive self-determination. Although the shift in thinking about disability remained unevenly distributed across European countries, it was particularly in Germany, whose record in disability rights was generally not good in the postwar decades, that the first years of the twenty-first century saw energetic and impressive campaigns on the part of sexual health activists and municipal governments not only to reduce anti-disability prejudice but also to affirm and facilitate the rights of both the physically and the cognitively disabled to romantic and sexual self-expression and to partnership and parenthood. Similar projects were underway in neighboring Switzerland.

On the other side, however, there was the urgent need to unlearn racism and to learn to develop respect for ethnic and religious diversity and greater comfort with multiculturalism. From the start, the EU also made the combating of racism part of its self-declared agenda. In 1997, for instance, the EU established the European Monitoring Centre for Racism and Xenophobia, based in Vienna, and it was explicitly tasked with researching the extent and manifestations of "racism, xenophobia, and anti-Semitism" within member states, including their "causes, consequences and effects," so as to assist in the development of counterracist measures.[22]

As of the turn of the millennium, however, it appeared that these two lines of commitment – to individual sexual rights and to anti-racism – had become almost impossible to reconcile. At the same time it became apparent that they had become intricately interconnected. This became above all evident in the growing confusion over how best to deal with a whole range of issues raised by the rise of Islam – both globally and within Europe's own borders.

Islam and the sexual borders of Europe

From the late 1990s on, the entire complex of issues surrounding European identities and citizenships began to rest with remarkable

---

[22] "Summary," European Monitoring Centre for Racism and Xenophobia, June 8, 2007, http://europa.eu/legislation_summaries/other/c10411_en.htm.

Fig. 5.4 Down syndrome bridesmaid catching the bouquet. From the campaign "We will not let ourselves be disabled" by Pro Infirmis, Switzerland.

frequency on sex-related concerns. Europe increasingly defined itself as the defender of "sexual democracy" against what was taken to be a constitutively homophobic and misogynistic European Islam. The long history of Europe's both practical and fantasized involvement with the purported sexual peculiarities of Islam – the at once outraged and voyeuristic obsession with the harem and with polygamy (inextricable from the concomitant disavowal of European men's own predilections for multiple relationships), or the fascination with many Muslim cultures' comfort with male bisexuality, to name just the two most persistent examples – had taken a sharp new turn. While once Europeans associated Islam with an overindulgence in sensual pleasures (well captured also in such appreciative comments as Lord Byron's that the Turkish baths of the Ottoman Empire were "marble paradise[s] of sherbet and sodomy"), now Islam was most often associated with sexual *repression*.[23]

Especially remarkable is the paradoxical impact of the spiraling anxiety over Islam. For it is unmistakably evident that the growth of European Islam was one of the major factors in making traditionally conservative parties become the newly vigorous defenders of sexual freedom and individual self-determination they never had been before. In the Netherlands and in the German state of Baden-Württemberg, for instance, in the first years of the twenty-first century, politicians from parties that once were more likely to be known for their homophobia and their negativity about female sexual expression outside of marriage were suddenly at the forefront of formulating new tests to be taken by would-be citizens who came from predominantly Muslim countries. In these tests, immigrants desiring citizenship had not only to demonstrate their knowledge of Dutch or German language and history and laws, but also testify to their comfort with homosexuality and female sexual independence (an attitude test that quite a few of those parties' Christian or post-Christian adherents might not have passed as recently as ten years earlier). Along related lines, both conservative and liberal-left politicians and pundits not generally known for their feminist commitments – from Sweden, Britain, and France to Austria, Switzerland, and Italy – decided that they were ardent feminists who found the Muslim forms of modest women's clothing (headscarves, veils, hijabs, and burqas) an offense to women's rights to display their faces and bodies more openly. Or to take yet another instance of newfound enthusiasm for female sexual activity outside of marriage: In France, a 2008 case of annulment of a marriage between Muslims who were both French citizens (on the grounds that the bride had misrepresented herself as a virgin when in fact she was not) led to an eruption of pronouncements, across the ideological spectrum, in defense of the right to lose one's virginity before marriage – an eruption that not only missed the fact that the bride had also wanted the annulment but that missed as well the fact that the possibility of annulments had originally been built into French divorce law in order to accommodate believing *Catholics*.

In short, one consequence of the rise of Islam within Europe has been to generate wholly new political alignments and to solidify a novel cultural consensus in support of gender egalitarianism, the rights of sexual minorities, and the right to engage in non-marital sex. On the other hand,

---

[23] George Gordon Byron to John Murray (1819), in Leslie Marchand (ed.), *Byron's Letters and Journals* vol. vi, "The Flesh is Frail" (Cambridge, MA: Harvard University Press, 1976), 207.

however, these new commitments have all too often been expressed in the form of anti-Muslim racism rather than being articulated as values on their own terms. Among other things, putting blame on the supposed idiosyncracies of Islamic sexual customs became one of the major strategies European politicians used for avoiding confrontation with difficult economic problems facing their societies in an increasingly inegalitarian capitalist world. Thus, for instance, a leading French politician blamed the riots in the *banlieues* of Paris in 2005 on West African habits of "polygamy" (which purportedly left too many young men under inadequate paternal supervision) rather than admitting that the government needed to be addressing systemic problems of immigrant youth unemployment. Once communism was defeated, Islam became the new enemy of the West.

Neofundamentalist Muslims were by no means passive objects of the escalating controversies. In a classic instance, in the wake of the first same-sex marriage celebrated in Amsterdam City Hall in 2001 and in the midst of concern about rising anti-gay violence in the Netherlands (disproportionately engaged in by Turkish and Moroccan youth), the imam Khalid El-Moumni of Rotterdam declared that Europeans were "less than dogs and pigs" because they condoned same-sex marriage. In the ensuing uproar (the Prime Minister defended gays and lesbians for the first time in his seven-year tenure, the cabinet minister responsible for integration assembled imams and informed them of the importance of tolerance, numerous imams interviewed in the succeeding days affirmed that within Islam homosexuality is considered a sin, and the media was full of lurid stories of how much Moroccan men in particular purportedly enjoyed same-sex sex), the terms of discussion about sexuality and ethnicity were set for years to come. In other ways also, neofundamentalist Muslims have worked directly to put non-Muslim Europeans on the defensive. For instance, German courts have sometimes found themselves hamstrung trying to prosecute honor killings as murders when defense attorneys for the accused try to bring in Muslim codes of honor as mitigating circumstances that could explain the perpetrators' behavior. In a milder vein, countless conservative Muslims have emphasized that they have legitimate criticisms of what they see as European hypersexuality and pseudo-freedom.

But the debates have by now become thoroughly snarled. On the one side are those who see the extreme phenomena of forced marriages, honor killings, and female genital cutting, as well as the more general effort to exert familial control over female – especially daughters' – sexuality, as symptomatic of the inner truth of Islam and its purportedly backward-looking ethos. Many of these, whether themselves of

Muslim or non-Muslim background, express outrage at what they perceive to be the taboos against criticizing others' religious beliefs or practices and/or express concern that Europeans, after fascism, are so afraid of being labeled racist that they, out of a misunderstood "cultural sensitivity," refuse to take an adequately strong stand against human rights violations. In this context it is important that quite a number of Muslim Europeans have taken it upon themselves to be the "culture brokers" and spokespersons who challenge neofundamentalism within Islam and use their authority as Muslims to do so. But it is no less important that on the other side there are those who repeatedly insist – variously patiently or passionately – that the vast majority of both immigrant and native-born Muslims in Europe are hardly militant Islamists, are well integrated into the society, and favor the separation of state and religion. In many European nations there are also organized groups of Muslims explicitly challenging neofundamentalism within Islam. *Forum for Kritiske Muslimer* in Denmark and Progressive British Muslims in the UK are two of the most vocal.

Yet in the efflorescence of sensationalized media coverage, too often Islam in general has been held responsible for criminality and cruelty. Not just in cases of honor killings, for example, but also in cases of domestic violence or of gang rapes, when a sex-related crime was committed by a Muslim man, this was regularly attributed to Islam or, more vaguely, to "immigrant culture." When such crimes were committed by a non-Muslim man, however, they were attributed to his masculinity or to his personal psychological or social deviance. Or to take another phenomenon, one which as of 2010 affected more than 2,700 women in Belgium, 20,000 women in Germany, 53,000 in France, and an estimated 130 million worldwide: Rather than campaigning against female genital cutting as a practice that is a violent violation of bodily integrity that has no basis in the Koran – a case increasingly being pushed also by feminist activists working within Islam as well as by avowedly anti-racist sex rights activists who are calling for an end to "this barbaric practice" and "zero tolerance for genital mutilation" – Islamic tradition has routinely been held responsible.[24] At the same time, misplaced eagerness went into suppressing practices which were actually freely chosen by individual Muslim believers – like the wearing of modest clothing. In 2010, Britain, Belgium, Italy, and France considered legislation to ban

<hr>

[24] Didier Stiers, "'Il fallait montrer l'excision'" (interview with Sherry Hormann, director of the movie *Desert Flower/Fleur du Desert*), *Le Soir* (Belgium), March 17, 2010, 33; Terre des Femmes e.V., "Null Toleranz gegen Genitalverstümmelung," www.frauenrechte.de/tdf/index.php?option=com_content&task=view&id=965&Itemid=83.

the wearing of a burqa in public spaces – even though the practice was exceedingly rare. In France, the legislation passed.

What was not rare but rather growing was an ever more complex set of Muslim European communities that bore no resemblance to the cliché of backwardness. Already by the late 1990s, to take just one indicative example, male-to-female transsexuals were a major public phenomenon in Turkey, a huge focus of public preoccupation, participating in the international market for sex-change surgery, working in European clubs, and able to count on the solidarity of European gay and lesbian organizations. Also, within the narrower borders of the European Union, gay and lesbian Muslims were by the early 2000s increasingly out of the closet, partying openly in clubs, negotiating tolerance with their families, and formulating alternative visions of Islam – and working together with non-Muslims to reduce both homophobia and Islamophobia. In the Netherlands, a foundation named Yoesuf provided support for Muslim gays and lesbians under the slogan: "The world should always welcome lovers." In Germany, "Body-Check," "Turkish Delight," and "Gayhane" were regularly recurring major queer immigrant dance parties. In Britain, as of 2009, gay Muslim activists were happy that the popular British soap opera *EastEnders* was about to start featuring a gay Muslim character falling in love with a non-Muslim man (even as a spokesman for the Muslim Public Affairs Committee told the BBC that "There's a lack of understanding of Muslims already and I think *EastEnders* really lost an opportunity to present a normal friendly Muslim character to the British public").[25]

Developing their own independent views and lives were also countless Muslim women, both self-described Muslim feminists and the many Muslim women who simply navigated the conflicting social and cultural pressures in their own ways (sexual liberality and prayer, for instance, were not necessarily irreconcilable, but nor were modest dress and careerism, or faithful marriage and women's rights activism). And the host societies were clearly catching on. Sex and reproductive rights groups as well as numerous medical professionals involved in providing sex- and reproduction-related healthcare adapted themselves to the new multicultural Europe, offering a plethora of culturally attuned services for migrants from all backgrounds, including various forms of Islam. Doctors and social workers alike were sensitized to deal with a wide range of issues – ranging from hymen repair to genetic counseling and fertility treatments. What had gotten lost in all the self-righteous animus against

---

[25] Shabnam Mahmood, "Gay Muslim Story for *EastEnders*," *BBC News*, May 28, 2009, http://news.bbc.co.uk/2/hi/entertainment/8072720.stm.

(a)

(b)

Figs. 5.5a and 5.5b "Allah has made me the way I am."
Anti-homophobia campaign in Austria. The remainder of the text
reads: "You belong to us! Just as many rights for just as much love."

Islam, in short, was a potentially counterintuitive but therefore no less important point: how completely the purportedly premodern and the seemingly postmodern had come to intersect.

Romantic liberality versus new conservatisms

On both sides of the Iron Curtain, the tendency as early as the 1970s, and certainly by the 1980s, had been toward earlier onset of coitus as, also on both sides, serial monogamy became the social norm (and among the younger generations relationships became shorter). While Eastern Europe had a less noisy sexual revolution – one that might be better understood as a sexual *evolution* – and while the governments maintained a puritanical tone (restricting both serious research and media reportage), at the grassroots dramatic changes quietly occurred. By the 1980s, Western travelers to the Soviet Union could marvel not only at the encounters with acquaintances and anonymous strangers initiated with audacity in public pools, parks, and streets but also at the elaborate love triangles – and even durable quadrangles and pentangles (often in complex bisexual combinations) – worked out in the interstices of crowded apartments and country dachas. And Poles or Czechs or Croatians, asked about sexual mores in the communist years, noted without hesitation the uncomplicated acceptance in their societies of premarital sex also for women, as well as of infidelity after marriage (albeit with somewhat greater latitude for men than for women). Overall, then, the trends at the grassroots were increasingly toward not only an erosion of differences between homosexuals and heterosexuals, but also an erosion of differences between men and women, as egalitarian erotic relationships, inside and outside of marriage, became the new ideal for most Europeans.

Meanwhile, the period from the later 1980s to the early twenty-first century, sex researchers declared, saw major changes in the ways ordinary people thought about sex and how they experienced sex. Among the findings was what social scientists and journalists described as a dedramatization of sex. While, during the sexual revolution of the 1960s–1970s in the West, progressives had thought of sex as both ecstatically thrilling and politically significant while conservatives thought that dangerous forces had been unleashed and that disinhibition would cause the social fabric to unravel, by the 1980s–1990s, sex had lost its explosive importance for both camps. Radicals had tried to liberate sex; conservatives had tried to contain it. But both had believed in its power. Yet, beginning in the 1990s, increasing numbers of respondents to surveys no longer seemed to think of desire as an unruly force erupting either within or between individuals. Instead, what the triumph of postcommunist consumer capitalism had wrought was nothing but an endless circuit of stimulus and arousal, display and looking. A generalized weariness about the benefits of sexual liberality was noted by some observers who argued that the 1990s to early 2000s were marked by an increasing "onanization of sex," not least because of the incessant pressure of pornographic images swirling relentlessly in everyone's heads – so that even when two people were in bed with each other, they were really just having sex with themselves or with their own fantasies. Others claimed that growing numbers of people were apparently more concerned with the ego-trip of being a hot object of desire than with the physiological sensation of orgasm. And yet others thought that orgasms themselves were starting to function more as trophies of self-reassurance in a battle with another body, rather than as the pleasurable byproducts of interaction with another person passionately desired in his or her particularity.

The turn of the millennium did see some major reconfigurations in the very nature of what counted as sex: from the invention of Viagra in 1998 (along with the questions it inadvertently raised about the relationship between performance capacity and experience of desire) to the apotheosis of Internet porn and cybersex (with the accompanying curious mix of possibilities for bodily detachment *and* intensification) to the prosaic but genuine difficulties of squeezing time for sex into exhausted, multitasking lives. Sexologists from the former East Germany, deeply skeptical of what they saw as damage done to interhuman relations by capitalism's competitiveness and achievement orientation, worried about what they saw as the "Fast Food Fast Fuck" culture of the West. "Eroticism feels with its fingertips," one East German commentator wrote. "Elbows destroy that. The pressure to achieve makes human beings sick and has a negative impact on sexuality."[26] And in addition, by the mid-1990s sexologists were documenting abrupt declines in felt levels of libido among both women and men across Western cultures. As of 2008, a British study conducted by a firm selling plasma TVs found that 47 percent of the men among the 2,000 Britons surveyed would be willing to give up sex for six months for a free large television (compared with just over one-third for the women).

Yet the increasingly histrionic reportage on the purported demise of lust in the first decade of the twenty-first century had become exceedingly difficult to disentangle from the obvious interests of pharmaceutical companies in raising consumption of libido- and arousal-stimulating products. Pfizer, for example, in promoting Viagra in Switzerland in 2007,

---

[26] Katrin Rohnstock, *Erotik macht die Hässlichen schön* (Berlin: Elefanten, 1995), 9–10.

had simply extrapolated its research findings from the USA, warning the Swiss that hundreds of thousands of their men were suffering from erectile dysfunction and urgently should be seeking medical assistance. When Flibanserin was discovered as a libido-generating compound for women by a German company in 2010, the British and French press carried the news the next day.

However, it also appeared that love was in the process of making a major comeback. For while news reports in the 1990s carried such alarmist headlines as "The Disappearance of Desire," subsequent sexological studies identified a different trend. An ever greater sexual liberality and relaxed live-and-let-live attitude about the choices made by others was nonetheless accompanied by an ongoing interest in, and lived experience of, passionate romance – and this through the entire life-span. In study after study, nationally and cross-nationally, European youth were found to be infinitely less conflicted about their adolescent sexual experimentation than US youth – and there was no social movement calling for premarital abstinence in Europe – but they also tended to have fewer partners than US youth, far higher levels of contraceptive use, and substantially lower levels of unwanted pregnancies and sexually transmitted diseases. For those in the middle of their lives, marriage was increasingly irrelevant to people, whether or not they had children, while fidelity in partnerships remained highly valued. Aging and sex also became a big subject, as not only Viagra for men and hormone supplementation for women, but also general trends toward healthier aging, meant that a large cohort of individuals was continuing to seek – and enjoy – sensuality and sex into their 70s and 80s and even 90s. Liberality and romance, it appeared, were not only compatible, but mutually reinforcing. This was evident both in bedrooms and in politics.

Nonetheless, not only in the nations of the former Eastern Bloc, but also within the West, there were new backlashes and ambivalences. Notably, precisely as homosexuality became largely non-controversial, new concerns arose around trafficking and adolescent sex, and new movements emerged against abortion. Some of the innovations were wholly in keeping with the ideals of self-determination – as in the Belgian case, for instance, where many of the same individuals involved in advocating for liberalization in the 1970s subsequently worked to build protections against violations of children's self-determination into Belgian law. Some of the new initiatives, however, created new restrictions for adults and adolescents in the name of protections.

Sweden, for example, passed a law in 1999 which criminalized the customers of prostitutes, although not the prostitutes themselves – and the government under Social Democratic leadership as well as the media engaged in an energetic campaign to shame men who purchased sex as "Omnivorous Consumers" (*Allkonsumenten*), "Relationship Avoiders" (*Relationsundvikaren*), or "Rejected Types" (*Den Refuserade*), or in some way suffering from low self-esteem and needing therapy. In various other European nations, concerns about sex worker trafficking as well as the potential vulnerabilities of adolescents subsequently led to new legislation and efforts to raise the age of consent for the exchange of sex for money or goods; again Social Democrats and more traditionally liberal parties took the lead. In Germany, for instance, the Social Democratic Minister of Justice Brigitte Zypries, purportedly to accommodate new EU guidelines about combating trafficking though actually quite on her own initiative, in 2007 announced she wanted to raise the age of consent from 16 to 18 for exchanging sexual contact for money or goods (even the attempt would be considered an offense). Zypries declared that she had young people's best interests at heart; in order to experience "undisturbed sexual development," youth needed the state's protection from "experiencing sexuality as a purchasable commodity."[27] This was a somewhat hapless phrasing in view of other feminists' longstanding efforts to point out that the conservative ideal of marriage in which only the man earned money while the woman stayed at home could also be interpreted as that kind of exchange. As in the Swedish case, Zypries displayed a normative assumption that there was a standard of proper sex from which consensual but emotionally depersonalized sex was an unacceptable departure (not to mention one which was in denial about the extent to which also within long-term partnerships one might find plenty of emotionally dissociative or depersonalized sex). In 2008, over protests from Greens and the small Free Democratic party, the law went into effect. In 2010, the government of the Netherlands not only announced efforts to clean up Amsterdam's red light district despite its role as a major tourist attraction, but also moved to raise the age of consent for exchanging money for sex from 18 to 21.

In short, one of the noteworthy trends at the turn of the millennium was the appropriation and redirection of erstwhile feminist concerns for rather more conservative purposes. In the Swedish case, many (though not all) women's longstanding discomfort with many (though not all) men's fascination with depersonalized sex – whether with prostitutes

---

[27] Brigitte Zypries quoted in "Besserer Schutz vor sexuellem Missbrauch von Kindern und Jugendlichen," press release of the German Ministry of Justice, June 20, 2008, available at www.bmj.bund.de/enid/0,ce78b5636f6e5f6964092d0935323239093a095 f7472636964092d0934393330/Pressestelle/Pressemitteilungen_58.html.

or in strip clubs or, more mundanely, with porn – had been put to use to shore up a phantasmatic idea that emotions could be legislated. (Not incidentally, in practice the impact of the legislation was wholly negative above all for the female sex workers themselves; they were subject to more police harassment and because the law meant they had fewer clients to choose from, they were more vulnerable to the violent clients they would previously have avoided.) Meanwhile, in the German case, a wholly appropriate alarm over sexual trafficking had been twisted into a policing also of the sexual encounters freely and consensually sought by adolescents. Overall, the ironies of the transformation caused scholar and activist Gert Hekma caustically to describe the new situation in Europe as "Pro-Gay and Anti-Sex."[28]

Clergy abuse

With regard to the vulnerabilities of children (as opposed to teenagers), the situation was complicated in a very different way. The string of scandals erupting in the spring of 2010 over the hundreds of cases of child sexual abuse by Roman Catholic clergy that had occurred over the prior decades – and the additional scandals of bishoprics' as well as the Vatican's own involvement in the subsequent cover-ups and relocations rather than defrockings of priests – provided the occasion for massive education of the public about the damage done to an individual through sexual abuse in childhood. In country after country, from Germany, Austria, and France to Belgium and the Netherlands, the media gave broad coverage to the topic. What had changed, in contrast to earlier decades, was that victims now came forward who had managed to have outwardly successful lives, but who could no longer tolerate the hypocrisy of the church and who were determined to demand not only official apologies, but also changed policies that would permit any future children who might be harmed to have recourse to authorities outside of church structures. At the national levels, governments initiated long-delayed investigations. Although most cases had by then outlasted the statute of limitations, governments were able to demand that official representatives of religious orders responsible for running the schools in which the abuses had occurred meet with survivors and show public remorse.

The results with respect to the Catholic church's prestige were mixed. In the 1990s, a prior round of exposés of Catholic clergy malfeasance

[28] Gert Hekma, "Queer in the Netherlands: Pro-Gay and Anti-Sex – Sexual Politics at a Turning Point" in Lisa Downing and Robert Gillett (eds.), *Queer in Europe: Contemporary Case Studies* (Farnham: Ashgate, 2011, forthcoming).

(a)

Figs. 5.6a and 5.6b "Whoever breaks the silence, breaks the power of the perpetrators." Images from the German government-sponsored campaign of 2010 against clergy abuse of children, encouraging also those who were victims decades ago to come forward and testify to their experiences. The scandals have led to massive public and media debate in many European nations and to the provision of funds for therapy and recognition of suffering as well as the development of new structures to prevent future abuse.

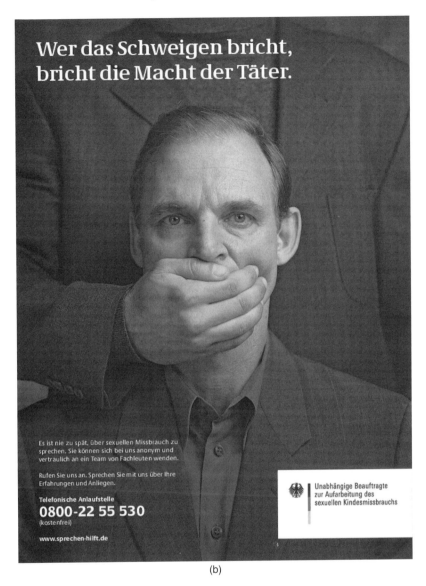

Wer das Schweigen bricht,
bricht die Macht der Täter.

Es ist nie zu spät, über sexuellen Missbrauch zu
sprechen. Sie können sich bei uns anonym und
vertraulich an ein Team von Fachleuten wenden.

Rufen Sie uns an. Sprechen Sie mit uns über Ihre
Erfahrungen und Anliegen.

Telefonische Anlaufstelle
0800-22 55 530
(kostenfrei)

www.sprechen-hilft.de

Unabhängige Beauftragte
zur Aufarbeitung des
sexuellen Kindesmissbrauchs

(b)

Fig. 5.6 (*cont.*).

in Ireland – including not only abuse cases but also cases of consensual sex with and impregnation of adult female lovers – had contributed
substantially to the dramatic loss of respect for Catholic church authority in Ireland and a shift to a far more tolerant and expansive attitude

about homosexuality and contraception alike. Public opinion in Ireland also shifted toward greater sympathy for women seeking abortions. In the debates around the cases coming to light in 2010, however, while progressive Catholic laity sought to use the occasion of the explosion of revelations about child abuse as an opportunity variously to recommend reconsideration of the Catholic church's insistence on celibacy, overt homophobia, and hostility to the ordination of women, and despite an additional public declaration by Italian women who had been secret lovers of priests that they no longer wanted to endure the church's duplicity, the Vatican remained, at least publicly, largely unmoved and its political authority hardly damaged. Even as the media across the globe gave extensive coverage to the child abuse revelations, Pope Benedict's public apology remained tepid and vague. Defenders of the Roman Catholic church developed a siege mentality and compared the criticisms to aggressive attacks on Jews in decades past.

Disability rights/women's rights

Among other things, notably, the Catholic church's moral authority in its opposition to abortion remained untouched – as it was also joined by newly emergent, deliberately secular movements against abortion rights not only in Eastern but also in Western Europe. An increasingly used tactic sought to divide progressives against each other by playing the hugely important and only recently consolidated (and in many ways still fragile) cause of disability rights off against women's reproductive rights. In Britain, for instance, the ProLife Alliance argued that antenatal testing for disability and the right to terminate a pregnancy on grounds of fetal disability was *in itself* prejudicial against the disabled. Already in 2001, anti-abortion activists had succeeded in getting the UK's Disability Rights Commission formally to declare that the abortion law of 1967, because it included the right to terminate a pregnancy on the grounds of fetal abnormality, by definition "reinforces negative stereotypes of disability," and in 2009, the prominent anti-abortion group LIFE called on Members of Parliament to introduce a bill that would ban all eugenic abortions under the headline: "LIFE calls for an end to the unfairness of eugenic abortion": "Women carrying disabled babies, special-needs children themselves and society as a whole deserve better than eugenic abortion. There is no need for it and there is a better way, more worthy of the civilized society we like to think we live in. Aborting some of the most vulnerable members of our community ultimately damages us all."[29]

---

[29] See Ann Furedi, "'Disability Cleansing' – or a Reasonable Choice?" Prochoice Forum, August 28, 2001, www.prochoiceforum.org.uk/comm78.php; and "LIFE

In Germany, the law had already been changed in 2009 (a change protested vehemently but unsuccessfully by reproductive rights activist groups like Pro Familia). Henceforth, pregnant women seeking later-term abortions in the wake of just having learned of a fetal disability would be subjected to a new three-day waiting and reflection period, and doctors who failed to counsel women appropriately on the matter would be subject to prosecution and high fines. Since the compromise law formulated in 1995 after the unification of West and East Germany, abortions on the grounds of fetal disability were already illegal. Instead, terminations of pregnancies due to fetal disability had been handled as a subset of the "maternal health" indication – in other words, a doctor could endorse a termination if carrying the pregnancy to term would seriously harm the physical or emotional health of the mother. This was an understandable postfascist stance, although still an agonizingly problematic one. It remained in deliberate ignorance of the ongoing inadequacy of social support structures for disabled individuals and their families and implied an expectation for a kind of moral machismo that few individuals or families could easily muster. Prior attempts led by Christian Democrats in 2001 and 2004 to introduce new restrictions on abortion access had failed; this time, however, a quarter of the Social Democratic legislators and a third of the Greens joined in voting for the new law. Key reasons for the broadened support were that this law criminalized the doctors rather than the pregnant women, but above all the fact that the law was strategically pitched as an important advance for disability rights – rather than, as it was immediately experienced in practice, as an additional traumatization of an already traumatized woman and in many cases also her partner – as couples would now worry even more than previously whether doctors would grant the maternal health indication. In the aftermath of the vote, the Vatican announced its delight at the change, and anti-choice groups within Germany moved quickly to use the new wedge of disability rights to push for further restrictions on access to terminations.

Different strategies have been used in Italy. The secular right-wing journalist and politician Giuliano Ferrara, editor of the conservative paper *Il Foglio*, in 2008 launched a new anti-abortion initiative when he compared abortion to "the Shoah" and sarcastically said that abortion clinics should be emblazoned with the (Auschwitz-echoing) banner "Abortion makes you free."[30] Ferrara also proposed to Catholic leaders

Calls for an End to the Unfairness of Eugenic Abortion," November 10, 2009, www.lifecharity.org.uk/node/557.
[30] "Dimenticare la 194 e combattere l'aborto," *Il Foglio*, May 20, 2008, www.ilfoglio.it/soloqui/337.

in Italy the idea that the United Nations' global campaign for a moratorium on the death penalty should be imitated with a campaign for a moratorium on abortions – an idea taken up enthusiastically by representatives of the church. Both religious and secular arguments against abortion have made an impact in Italy. As of 2008, 70 percent of Italian doctors and 50 percent of Italian anesthesiologists had already declared that they were conscientious objectors to abortion and would not participate in provision of the service (by 2003 only 58 percent of doctors had objected). New legal tactics have also been tried. Italy had become, in 2004, the first state to pass a law which, with the aim of preventing stem cell experimentation, could also be construed as deeming the fertilized cell to be a citizen in need of defense. This law too created grounds for further challenges to abortion rights. In short, the gains in sexual liberties and rights that were so long fought for – and which Western Europe had been pleased to demand of the countries both of the former Eastern Bloc and of the Muslim world – were not completely secure, not least because of new forms of sexual conservatism within Western Europe itself.

By 2008, activists from NGOs involved in public health had become so concerned about what they saw as "a growing opposition movement toward SRHR [sexual and reproductive health and rights]" that they convened a special international gathering in Uppsala, Sweden. The invitation headline asked: "Europe on the Brink: Who Will Decide over Your Body?" The major topics for discussion included: the growing role of religion in political life; the need for better integration of immigrants; the need for better sex education; and concern about the greater conservatism evinced by Eastern European politicians on the subjects of sexual and reproductive health. But as the discussions that ensued at the gathering made clear, participants were also above all concerned about the rise of anti-abortion movements within Western Europe.

Irene Donadio, the Italian representative of the International Planned Parenthood Federation, remained optimistic. She did note that in Brussels, where the politicians of the EU gather, new attacks on sexual and reproductive rights were increasingly heard especially from parliamentarians hailing from the nations of the former Eastern Bloc, and that this was different from "what we are used to in the Western countries of the European Union." She observed as well that, across Europe, new anti-abortion tactics were being deployed, often in the form of legal rather than religious arguments, and that these were presented in "moderate tones." These more "sophisticated" and "subtle" approaches she considered more dangerous than the older loud radicals. But Donadio also declared that whatever the politicians had to say, the sexual and reproductive rights advocates were the ones who were "attuned with the public opinion." And, she felt sure, "the public opinion in Europe is definitely pro-choice." Sexual happiness was not a party-political matter. As Donadio put it: "No matter if they are conservatives or if they are left-wing, people live their lives as they want – and people like to enjoy sex and to have the families that they wish." In sum, she concluded: "I am rather sure that we will win the battle."[31] Vigilance and creativity would certainly be called for. But the future, she proposed, might yet turn out just fine.

Further reading

Adam, Barry D., Jan Willem Duyvendak, and Andre Krouwel (eds.), *The Global Emergence of Gay and Lesbian Politics: National Imprints of a Worldwide Movement* (Philadelphia: Temple University Press, 1999).

Agustin, Laura María, *Sex at the Margins: Migration, Labour Markets and the Rescue Industry* (London: Zed Books, 2007).

Bos, Pascale R., "Feminists Interpreting the Politics of Wartime Rape: Berlin, 1945; Yugoslavia, 1992–1993," *Signs* 31, no. 4 (Summer 2006), 995–1025.

Brown, Jessica Autumn, and Myra Marx Ferree, "Close Your Eyes and Think of England: Pronatalism in the British Print Media," *Gender and Society* 19, no. 1 (2005), 5–24.

Bunzl, Matti, "The Prague Experience: Gay Male Sex Tourism and the Neo-Colonial Invention of an Embodied Border" in Daphne Berdahl, Matti Bunzl, and Martha Lampland (eds.), *Altering States: Ethnographies of the Transition in Eastern Europe and the Former Soviet Union* (Ann Arbor: University of Michigan Press, 2000), 70–95.

Drucker, Peter (ed.), *Different Rainbows* (London: Gay Men's Press, 2000).

Fiori, Matteo, "The Foča 'Rape Camps': A Dark Page Read through the ICTY's Jurisprudence," Commentaries, The Hague Justice Portal, December 19, 2007, www.haguejusticeportal.net/eCache/DEF/8/712.html.

Fuszara, Małgorzata, "Legal Regulation of Abortion in Poland," *Signs* 17, no. 1 (Autumn 1991), 117–28.

Gal, Susan, "Gender in the Post-Socialist Transition: The Abortion Debate in Hungary," *East European Politics and Societies* 8, no. 2 (Spring 1994), 256–86.

Georges, Eugenia, "Abortion Policy and Practice in Greece," *Social Science Medicine* 42, no. 4 (1996), 509–19.

Goven, Joanna, "Gender Politics in Hungary: Autonomy and Antifeminism" in Nanette Funk and Magda Mueller (eds.), *Gender Politics and Post-Communism: Reflections from Eastern Europe and the Former Soviet Union* (London: Routledge, 1993), 224–40.

[31] Irene Donadio video from "Europe on the Brink: Who Will Decide over Your Body?" Conference on political developments, trends and norms that affect sexual and reproductive health and rights in Europe, Uppsala, Sweden, April 28–30, 2008, www.iepfpd.org/images/files/i_donadio.mov.

Graff, Agnieszka, "We are (Not All) Homophobes: A Report from Poland," *Feminist Studies* 32, no. 2 (Summer 2006), 434–49.

Grigolo, Michele, "Sexualities and the ECHR: Introducing the Universal Sexual Legal Subject," *European Journal of International Law* 14, no. 5 (November 2003), 1023–44.

Gülcür, Leyla, and Pinar Ilkkaracan, "The 'Natasha' Experience: Migrant Sex Workers from the Former Soviet Union and Eastern Europe in Turkey," *Women's Studies International Forum* 25, no. 4 (2002), 411–21.

Healey, Dan, "Active, Passive, and Russian: The National Idea in Gay Men's Pornography," *Russian Review* 69 (April 2010), 210–30.

Hekma, Gert, "Queer in the Netherlands: Pro-Gay and Anti-Sex – Sexual Politics at a Turning Point" in Lisa Downing and Robert Gillett (eds.), *Queer in Europe: Contemporary Case Studies* (Farnham: Ashgate, 2011, forthcoming).

Herzog, Dagmar, "Post Coitum Triste Est? Sexual Politics and Cultures in Post-unification Germany," *German Politics and Society* 28, no. 1 (Spring 2010), 111–40.

Hubert, Michel, Theo Sandfort, and Natalie Bajos (eds.), *Sexual Behaviour and HIV/AIDS in Europe: Comparisons of National Surveys* (London: Taylor & Francis, 1998).

Hug, Crystel, *The Politics of Sexual Morality in Ireland* (New York: St. Martin's Press, 1999).

Kandiyoti, Deniz, "Transsexuals and the Urban Landscape in Istanbul," *MERIP Middle East Report* 206 (Spring 1998), 20–25.

Kontula, Osmo, *Between Sexual Desire and Reality: The Evolution of Sex in Finland* (Helsinki: Väestöliitto, 2009).

Kulick, Don, "Four Hundred Thousand Swedish Perverts," *GLQ* 11, no. 2 (2005), 205–35.

Maier, Sylvia, "Honour Killings and the Cultural Defense in Germany" in Marie-Claire Foblets and Alison Dundes Renteln (eds.), *Multicultural Jurisprudence: Comparative Perspectives on the Cultural Defense* (Portland, OR: Hart Publishing, 2009), 229–46.

Massad, Joseph A., *Desiring Arabs* (University of Chicago Press, 2007).

Occhipinti, Laurie, "Two Steps Back? Anti-feminism in Eastern Europe," *Anthropology Today* 12, no. 6 (December 1996), 13–18.

Oosterhoff, Pauline, Prisca Zwanikken, and Evert Ketting, "The Torture of Men in Croatia and Other Conflict Situations: An Open Secret," *Reproductive Health Matters* 12, no. 23 (May 2004), 68–77.

Pollak, Michael, *The Second Plague of Europe: AIDS Prevention and Sexual Transmission among Men in Western Europe* (London: Howarth Press, 1994).

Rotkirch, Anna, "'What Kind of Sex Can You Talk about?': Acquiring Sexual Knowledge in Three Soviet Generations" in Daniel Bertaux *et al.* (eds.), *Living through the Soviet System* (New Brunswick: Transaction, 2004), 93–119.

Scott, Joan Wallach, *The Politics of the Veil* (Princeton University Press, 2007).

Stevens, Liesbet, and Marc Hooghe, "The Swing of the Pendulum: The Detraditionalisation of the Regulation of Sexuality and Intimacy in Belgium

(1973–2003)," *International Journal of the Sociology of Law* 31 (2003), 131–51.

Štulhofer, Aleksandar, and Theo Sandfort (eds.), *Sexuality and Gender in Post-communist Eastern Europe and Russia* (New York: The Haworth Press, 2005).

Surkis, Judith, "Hymenal Politics: Marriage, Secularism, and French Sovereignty," *Public Culture* 22, no. 3 (2010), 531–56.

Watney, Simon, *Policing Desire: Pornography, AIDS and the Media* (Minneapolis: University of Minnesota Press, 1987).

Woesthoff, Julia, "Romancing the Foreigner" in Günter Bischof, Anton Pelinka, and Dagmar Herzog (eds.), *Sexuality in Austria (Contemporary Austrian Studies* 15 (2007)).

Epilogue

Looking backwards from the vantage-point of the early twenty-first century present, we can read the story of sexuality in twentieth-century Europe as eventually indeed a story of liberalization – but also one that was filled with tremendous conflicts. Without a doubt as well, the twentieth century witnessed a vastly intensified preoccupation with sexual matters. From the very beginning, there was heightened attention to issues pertaining to sex. In the midst of the emergence of the penny press, there was a powerful voyeuristic fascination with the doings of others; in the midst of worry about the spread of venereal disease, there was a useful opening for debating the sexual double standard and the prevalence of prostitution as a constant accompaniment to the institution of marriage; in the midst of growing efforts to separate sex from reproduction, there was intensified interest in contraceptive strategies and products. And in the midst of all this, there was increasing curiosity about the very nature of what sexual desire might be: Was it an internal drive seeking expression – or a pull toward another person? Did it involve love and affection or preferably not? Was the gender of the object choice significant or rather the particular practices that gave pleasure? Why did people do it? What exactly was *it*? Was sex a performance or a gift, a reassurance or a release, a process-oriented sensuous exploration or a goal-oriented endeavor, a means or an end? Was it a horror or a banality – or an absolute delight?

Yet at the same time, and also with the advantage of hindsight, we can see how truly complicated the many struggles over sexual freedom have remained. We need only note the recurrent violence with which gay pride parades are met in postcommunist Eastern European cities – most recently in Belgrade, Serbia, in late 2010 – to realize how contested a concept sexual freedom still is. And one need only consider the intensity of ongoing discussion around the long-delayed acknowledgment of the prevalence of sexual abuse of children among Roman Catholic clergy in numerous European countries in prior decades. The eagerness of church spokespeople to blame the sexual revolutionaries of the 1960s–1970s for creating an environment supposedly conducive to abuse (rather than acknowledging the dangers inherent in a closed and authoritarian institution more interested in protecting perpetrators than victims) reminds us once again how easy it is to reinterpret liberalization as a problem rather than a moral goal. And we need only consider the crescendo, in the early twenty-first century, of lamentation about the purported increase in emotionally dissociative sex due to the exponential explosion of Internet porn and chatrooms and other forms of sexual commercialization to recognize how people can become so quickly disoriented around these most intimate matters – and how rapidly they can forget how much emotionally dissociative sex there had been all through the twentieth century, if not already for centuries before – and that indeed we might ask if this is in fact infinitely more common a human experience than romantic mutuality.

A chief objective of this book has been to capture how people have expressed what they thought sex was and how they have felt about it – and how extraordinarily diverse those views have been and how much those views have changed over time. I was also especially interested in investigating what combination of factors pushed a national culture into either a more liberal or a more conservative direction – while also constantly keeping in mind that sex was (and remains) an issue (so private and often so vulnerable-making, so deeply interwoven with other aspects of culture and politics, so infinitely *usable* for seemingly unrelated other purposes) that studying it perpetually challenges our assumptions about what counts as liberatory or repressive.

This book opened with the presumption that there was and is no one definition of *it*, but that *it* certainly came to be interpreted as increasingly significant over the course of the twentieth century. *It* quite apparently mattered tremendously to human beings. And by the 1920s, state governments across the continent, West to East, had got themselves deeply involved in trying to manage *it*. Increasingly, moreover, *it* marketed all manner of consumer products as well. But *it* was also used to market political ideologies. This was apparent most dramatically and hideously in the case of Nazism, in which venomous sexual innuendo against Jews and vicious homophobia and contempt for the disabled, coupled with promises of fabulous guilt-free pleasure for healthy, heterosexual "Aryans," shored up widespread popular support for a genocidal regime. Notably as well, the initial round of daring sex rights activism that marked the 1920s across the continent was crushed by the Nazi behemoth. Across Europe, it would take another two decades of postwar struggle by all too often utterly isolated individuals to reinterpret the lessons of Nazism as a mandate to protect individual self-determination in the realms of sex and relationships.

In short, it has been because people bring such tangled and opposing emotions to sex – their own and other people's – that sex became such a widely used economic and political instrument in twentieth-century Europe. The French philosopher Michel Foucault once commented at the height of the sexual revolution (and in the context of a critique of the naiveté and overweening pretensions of too many self-styled sexual liberationists) that sex was "an especially dense transfer point for relations of power."[1] And yet sex has been even more than a relay system for relations of power. As elusive as *it* was, there was *something* else there as well. British gay rights activist Simon Watney observed, a decade after Foucault's remark when the sexual revolution was under attack, and as he sought to make sense of what "other, deeper levels of anxiety" might be at issue in the "phobic" responses to homosexuality so evident in the early years of the HIV/AIDS epidemic: "At some point we are surely obliged to insist that in all its variant forms, human sexuality is much of a muchness."[2] It is this doubleness of sex – its persistent inextricability from and impact on so many other realms of existence and its quality of being "much of a muchness" – that continues to make it such a vital area of ongoing investigation for historians of ideas, culture, politics, and society.

There remains tremendous opportunity for further research. Among other things, we do not know nearly enough about developments in Europe's colonies or about Eastern Europe. There is a remarkable range of things we still do not grasp about Western Europe. We need urgently to decenter Europe, and we need to see it not only from the vantage point of the USA but also from the perspective of the rest of the globe. Both comparative studies and investigations of transnational and transregional exchanges will bring out ever more clearly what we have misunderstood about the perennial historians' puzzles of periodization, causation, agency, intent, and interpretation. And as the present and future unfold, we may learn to ask further and previously unimagined questions about the past. In 2002, for instance, when the German reproductive rights organization Pro Familia formulated a declaration of human rights to sexual and reproductive self-determination, a key point was a call for "a sexual culture . . . in which the irrationality of sexuality is acknowledged and also seen as a cultural enrichment."[3] The simple fact that this

[1] Michel Foucault, *The History of Sexuality*, vol. I: *An Introduction* (New York: Vintage, 1980), 103.
[2] Simon Watney, "Preface" in *Policing Desire: Pornography, AIDS and the Media*, 2nd edn (Minneapolis: University of Minnesota Press, 1989), xi.
[3] "Pro Familia: Für selbstbestimmte Sexualität . . . Für Pro Familia ist Sexualität eine kulturelle Bereicherung," www.profamilia.de/article/show/1010.html.

position still remains both eccentric and unusual suggests how much struggle yet lies ahead.

Further reading

"*AHR* Forum: Transnational Sexualities," *American Historical Review* 114, no. 5 (2009), 1250–1353 (essays by Margot Canaday, Marc Epprecht, Joanne Meyerowitz, Dagmar Herzog, Tamara Loos, Leslie Peirce, and Pete Sigal).

Bibliography of the History of Western Sexuality, available at http://wirtges. univie.ac.at/Sexbibl/.

Peakman, Julie (ed.), *A Cultural History of Sexuality*, 6 vols. (Oxford and New York: Berg, 2010–11).

Acknowledgments

Researching and writing this book has been a wonderful if also generally daunting experience and I am grateful to the many individuals who helped along the way. My primary debt is diffuse but enormous: It is to the scholars in the field of the history of sexuality who gathered the evidence and worked carefully through the complex interpretive issues in so many varied local contexts. I am awed by their labors and the eloquence of their insights. It is a privilege and honor to be counted a member of this tribe, and I am ever aware of the many that have gone before to make morally serious work in thinking about sexuality historically possible. Other debts are more concrete but not less significant. A grant from the Ford Foundation in 2003 made the first research forays into the intersections of religion and sexuality in postwar Europe possible; I am especially glad to be able to thank the project officers Constance Buchanan and Sarah Costa for giving me so many thought-provoking issues to ponder as I began my work. No less important has been the foresight and critical acuity of Michael Watson; he has been a fantastic editor from start to finish. I am thankful as well for the anonymous readers for Cambridge University Press, and for the close and particularly helpful readings of individual chapters provided by Jeffrey Escoffier, Jonathan Fine, Dan Healey, Will Lippincott, Regina Mühlhäuser, and Robert Sommer. I am grateful as well to my mother, Kristin Herzog, and my aunt, Ruth Karwehl, for their love and for countless indispensable conversations about ethics and history alike. And through everything, Omer Bartov, Michael Geyer, Anson Rabinbach, and Joan Scott have been extraordinarily inspirational mentors and friends. In addition, I owe a great debt to the many people who answered questions about specific themes or national histories, and who located sources, shared news items and thoughts, solved problems, brainstormed energetically about intellectual puzzles, and, in general, came to my rescue in myriad ways. The list here is long – longer than I can name – but it most definitely includes: Caroline Arni, Robert Beachy, Paul Betts, Judith Coffin, Laura Doan, Peter Drucker, Khaled El-Rouayheb, Fatima El-Tayeb, Jan

Feddersen, Alain Giami, Agnieszka Graff, Anna Hajkova, Lesley Hall, David Halperin, Gert Hekma, Andrew Lee, Jürgen Lemke, Lena Lenner-hed, Myra Marx Ferree, Gisela Notz, Massimo Perinelli, Andreas Pretzel, Istvan Rev, Edita Ruzgyte, Jens Rydström, Sybill Schulz, Todd Shepard, Na'ama Shik, Volkmar Sigusch, Kurt Starke, James Steakley, Aleksan-dar Štulhofer, Judith Surkis, Oliver Tolmein, and Anette Warring. I am also happy to thank in print and not just in person my terrific research assistants: Francesca Vassalle, Miriam Intrator, Lukasz Chelminski, Cambridge Ridley Lynch, and Tracy Robey. All brought their own remarkable perceptivity, expertise, and professionalism to bear. In gen-eral, my students at the Graduate Center of the City University of New York have been phenomenal – a constant source of joy and rigorous intel-lectual exchange. My colleagues have been a vital source of support and perspective as well. I thank especially Helena Rosenblatt, Aiobheann Sweeney, Deborah Tolman, Beth Baron, Thomas Kessner, and David Nasaw for being in the trenches with me.

There are further debts which are more difficult to put into words. A handful of precious individuals have been there to give me courage at critical junctures. I thank Detlef Siegfried, Gunter Schmidt, and Brad Prager for their calm reliability and the at once flexible and durable bonds of mutual trust and emotional connection they provide. In New York, my most important anchors are John Barnhill and William Kelly, both of whom have honed the fine art of time-efficient communication; I thank them from the bottom of my heart for the steadiness of their friendships. In Europe, Pascal Strupler and Cornelia Theler welcomed me no matter how jet-lagged I was – and made essential archival research possible. And at the last minute, Markus Borgert and Jürgen Kirchner stepped in to redeem a long-ago past in ways more amazing than I could have imagined. Closer to home, I thank Kevin Riley and all the members of the Hart-Soga, Kucich-Sadoff, and Bilsky-Rollins families for their stalwart and sustaining friendships. And above all, I thank my family: Michael Staub, Lucy Staub, and Brendan Hart. These three have taught me the most about what is important in life – and whether in embrace or in skype, their strength orients me. A quarter-century ago, Michael Staub made an off-hand remark that he was "attracted to difficulty." I am certain that he had absolutely no idea what he was getting into, but I am ever so appreciative that he did. This book is dedicated to him with ever-renewed gratitude for his brilliance, intensity, and love.

Index